Sectarian Order in Bahrain

Sectarian Order in Bahrain

The Social and Colonial Origins of Criminal Justice

Staci Strobl

LEXINGTON BOOKS
Lanham • Boulder • New York • London

Published by Lexington Books
An imprint of The Rowman & Littlefield Publishing Group, Inc.
4501 Forbes Boulevard, Suite 200, Lanham, Maryland 20706
www.rowman.com

Unit A, Whitacre Mews, 26-34 Stannary Street, London SE11 4AB

British Library Cataloguing in Publication Information Available

Library of Congress Cataloging-in-Publication Data Available

LCCN 2018949598 | ISBN 9781498541602 (hardback : alk. paper) | ISBN 9781498541619 (electronic)

∞™ The paper used in this publication meets the minimum requirements of American National Standard for Information Sciences Permanence of Paper for Printed Library Materials, ANSI/NISO Z39.48-1992.

Printed in the United States of America

Contents

Acknowledgments

This book was several years in the making, and without the support of colleagues, friends, and family, would not have come to fruition. I am thankful that it has made it to print as the ideas were rolling around in my mind for some time, and the archival research involved was nothing short of fascinating. The history of Bahrain and its criminal justice system is an entry point to a deeper understanding of the current social and political problems. My work made me appreciate even more the sacrifice of Bahraini activists as they fight for human and civil rights in a context where the state benefits from an official "forgetting" of a divisive, sectarian history and state-sponsored mass violence.

I would like to thank the many Gulf Studies scholars that I have had the great fortune of encountering, and who have helped me sort through many of my ideas and also pointed me to relevant sources. In particular, Frederic Wehrey's inclusion of me in the Sources of Sectarianism project at the Carnegie Endowment for International Peace gave me the opportunity to think deeply about sectarianism and its historical development. Intellectual encounters via the Gulf Studies Research Meeting with Dr. Dalia Abdelhady, Middle Eastern Studies Center, Lund University (Sweden), Dr. May Al Dabbagh, Gender and Public Policy Program, Dubai School of Government (UAE), Dr. Jillian Schedneck, University of Adelaide (Australia), and Dr. Richard Scofield, King's College London (United Kingdom) enriched my understanding of the field greatly. And, Dr. Nicholas Gavriledes, State University of New York (SUNY) Cortland, inspired me to consider more fully the anthropological foundations of my topic of study.

The institutional support I have received has made an incredible difference in the development of this work as well. While at John Jay College of Criminal Justice, the Office for the Advancement of Research selected me for the Bramshill Police College exchange program to spend a few months in the United Kingdom in order to utilize the archives at the University of Exeter and the British Library in London. Similar support from the University of Wisconsin-Platteville's Scholarly Improvement Activity Fund (SAIF) allowed me to return to the archives. In particular, I thank Dean Melissa Gormley for helping me to carve out space from my administrative duties as a department chair to keep my research agenda alive. Dr. Valerie Stackman's coverage of my chair duties in the summer of 2017 took this project from the back to the front burner, and I cannot thank her enough for her tireless efforts.

I also would like to thank Brian Dooley of Human Rights First, who welcomed me into the fold of those working for Bahrain social justice in Washington, D.C. I thank Dr. Nickie Phillips, St. Francis College, for reading and providing feedback on a draft of the book. And, the support of the following mentor figures in my life must also be recognized: Dr. Maki Haberfeld of John Jay College of Criminal Justice and Dr. Cheryl Banachowski-Fuller and Regina Pauly of UW-Platteville.

My husband, Matt Michaels, and my son, Jaden Avila, deserve the biggest thanks for putting up with the hours that I was tucked away in our home study researching and writing rather than enjoying their company. They understood and accepted my need to disappear back to London for a few days to check the archives again and rearranged countless schedules to accommodate my project. A special appreciation is in order for Matt who read drafts of the book and aided in the incorporation of the important theoretical work of key historical sociologists. And, of course, I must thank my beagle, Jonty Strobl, who sat by my feet during the writing of this book and patiently listened to analysis and arguments about an island she has never visited in a world bigger than she probably imagines.

Introduction

From Sea to Sand

Bahrain is a beautiful desert archipelago in the Arabian Gulf with date palms, sand beaches, warm shallow waters, and panoramas of blues and browns that soften to a pleasant glow at dusk. The country has stood as a seafaring outpost for the intermingling of a variety of economic and political regional powerhouses over the centuries. Today, Bahrain remains a global crossroads. Expatriates from around the world rub elbows with locals in the constitutional monarchy with a post-oil economy that, though not the most robust in the region, holds its own. Despite being small in area (294 square miles) and no match to the glamour and glitz of nearby Dubai, there is much about Bahrain that is pleasant and friendly for the business traveler or tourist who is well taken care of in an array of five-star hotels and gourmet restaurants. Underneath that facade, however, Bahrain has an outsized problem with social and political injustice, something that became very apparent to me while working on ethnographic research in the country from 2004 to 2006. Carefully documenting the work of the Women's Police Directorate in Bahrain,[1] I could not help but become acutely aware of perhaps an even more interesting criminal justice story, that of Sunni discrimination against Shi`a who form a majority of the nation's 1.4 million inhabitants. Watching the services that police officers provided the public, I immediately noticed that sectarian identity was correlated with the quality of service, and that Sunni complaints were taken more seriously. Well before the events of the Arab Spring, which would highlight Shi`a criticism of a Sunni-dominated government, and in a more socially peaceful time, sectarianism was part of everyday life. People, from police captains to hotel and restaurant owners to unemployed laborers, spoke openly in a manner belying sectarian discriminatory biases, whether operating in police processing, hiring practices, or just present in café banter over a game of dominoes.

One day in the spring of 2006, I was observing the women's section of a local police station in a heavily Shi`a area of Bahrain. A young man, probably in his twenties, came in to bring a noise problem to police attention.[2] I remember how obviously he was set aside and told his problem did not matter, and though I felt like he was not being taken seriously, my role as an ethnographer was not to intervene, especially since, though unfair, it did not seem like a life or death situation either way. The conversation turned to an argument as the man became increasingly dissatisfied with the policewomen to which he was speaking. After about a half hour of this, he abruptly exited the station. The female police officer turned to me and said "What a rude man. And did you hear his Arabic?" I had, and although my listening of Bahraini Arabic had become quite robust, my ability to speak was still broken. "He was confusing his gender pronouns. Can you believe it?" she complained. Of course I could, since it happened to me all the time. I began to feel like it was uncomfortably ironic that she would complain to me—she had already spent the day listening to my sorry speech patterns and appeared to like me all the same. Then she said, "He's Shi`a. He's lived here his whole life and he can't even speak proper Arabic. That's the way they are." She said this to me in a very informative way, as if I needed to jot down in my notebook the very words, the basic fact that "that's the way they are."

Wanting to better understand the context I was in, and required by my dissertation to have a handle on relevant literature, I looked for academic accounts of the Bahraini criminal justice system operating in a sect-discriminatory manner. Sadly, at this time, very little in the field of criminal justice even mentioned Bahrain, let alone sectarian discrimination.[3] Security studies on the Gulf were seemingly written from the ruling Sunni perspective even when penned by Western academics; most of what I found lacked any mention of sectarian inequality when describing national security and its challenges. Some described terror plots perpetrated by Shi`a extremist groups, particularly in the 1980s after the Iranian Revolution, but did not question dubious notions of Bahraini Shi`a plotting with Iran against Bahrain.[4] There was an obvious blind spot in the security and criminal justice literature, one that was outside the scope of my research to rectify at the time. Moving into related fields such as political science and history helped to fill in some gaps, but since then I have been paying close attention to the rise of a more critical, sect-conscious literature in a variety of academic disciplines.[5] It has been through revisionist historical accounts of the Gulf region that I have been able to mine the most insight into how sect and criminal justice have interacted and continue to interact in ways that make matters complicated, and sometimes violent, for Bahraini society.

The main focus of this book is to describe connections between the rise of colonial criminal justice in Bahrain and other historical developments. It will look at sectarianism, making detailed use of an archival cache of colonial criminal court cases in the British Library, reading "against the grain"[6] and offering a critical analysis. The book extensively uses primary and secondary historical documents, including ethnographic and anthropological accounts. I link major themes in critical and cultural criminology, Southern criminology, historical sociology, post-colonialism, and Gulf studies which have not been adequately examined together. In doing so, I do not aim to advance any of these distinct disciplines, but rather use the perspectives to survey the criminal justice history of the country, drill down on an important group of surviving criminal court case files, and show how they can describe the problem of and inform solutions to sectarian discrimination in Bahrain.

Scholarship in criminal justice and criminology remain Western-dominated with empirical studies in the Arabian Gulf countries being particularly scant. Post-colonialism, though having a theoretical home in South Asian Studies and applied to many other parts of the globe, also managed to be rarely applied to the Arabian Gulf, a field dominated by rational choice and neoliberal analyses. In comparison, the present book offers a new perspective on viewing the long-range development of criminal justice in Bahrain by making connections between the colonial state-building project in general and the more specific task of criminal adjudication. Drawing on historical sociology and postcolonial theory, theoretical points about the relationship of sectarianism and criminal justice are evaluated through colonial historical evidence, bookended by relevant pre-colonial antecedents and implications for the postcolonial present.

CRIMINOLOGY, SECTARIANISM, AND THE SOCIAL ORDER

Far from natural, the criminal justice system of a nation is a social construct, a cultural artifact of the place that produced it. Using a common definition of culture as shared, public meaning,[7] national criminal justice institutions are important carriers of the dominant cultural notions of social order. The social order here refers to both mainstream and elite cultural conceptions of who is dangerous and how society should respond to dangerous people, as embodied and contested in criminal justice institutions. Mary Douglas in *Purity and Danger*, explored the more general notion of social order when describing examples of bright line rules originating in cultural conceptions of dangerousness that are the result of societies forcing amorphous moral values and experience into logical categories.[8] In this way, cultural notions of social order are maintained in rituals that create and maintain forms of visible social expression that "enable people to know their own society,"[9] forming a type of repertoire that joins customs and norms to rule making. As an institution, criminal justice is the structured site at which the cultural rituals of maintaining public safety often abide in contemporary society; these institutions sort out danger, by defining it in law and using legitimate violence to prevent or respond to it. Throughout the book, I will be referring to this general set of criminal justice rituals as "order maintenance."[10]

Criminal justice actors perform order maintenance by patrolling streets, investigating crimes, adjudicating wrongdoing, and meting out punishment. For example, Robert Reiner explains that police spend most of their time not as crime-fighters as popular media depictions would have us believe, but rather act as keepers of the social order through the seemingly neutral tasks of patrol, community contact, and outreach.[11] More classically, Egon Bittner articulated that the police are called upon to respond to who is dangerous and what "ought not be happening about which something ought to be done [now]"[12] —a culturally construed activity at the bounds of popular notions of danger or morality.

Criminal justice actors often use discretion to maintain order, although their discretion is limited by the rule of law. When being discretionary, they draw from the larger social context, making decisions that reflect the value systems of the societies in which they are embedded. Reiner explains that as a result, the police are susceptible to reinforcing any social and political realities that reify the policies and politics of inequality. In other words, if inequality is a feature of the social order, then as maintainers of order, police will be active maintainers of social inequality.[13] How criminal justice actors conceive of, apply, and explain criminal justice decisions shines a light on the politics of inequality, particularly in less-than-democratic nations that lack transparency. Meanwhile, expressions of support and/or resistance to decision-making provide important snapshots also revealing popular notions of order and what about criminal justice in a given society is contested. Official and popular variants of social order interact with each other forming an operant discursive frame, or in other words, a culturally embedded way of speaking, thinking, talking, and acting in the realm of criminal justice that seems natural to those within the milieu. These frames often exhibit particular social anxieties and unsettled questions.

Understanding crime and criminal justice systems as categories in which cultural notions of identity have social meaning and are contested has been one major theme in critical criminology for many years.[14] Importantly, then, this book builds thick cultural description, from among various sources related to criminal cases, as an empirical base for which to apply critical considerations. Cultural analyses must be careful not to paint a caricature or devolve into stereotypes, while at the same time acknowledging that peoples of the world derive social meaning in ways that are bound by the cultures in which they are immersed. It is a delicate line to walk, but an important one if the critical project at hand is to succeed. Critical criminology employs Marxist, feminist, and other radical theories to inform empirical studies of crime and criminal justice. It takes a stand against positivist criminologists who would reduce criminology to individualistic causation models and whose subtext is to control maladjusted people.[15] In analyzing social relations more deeply, critical criminology provides a space for analyses, which are qualitative in nature and sensitive to cultural dynamics and social meaning. That being said, the dominant mode of critical criminology also developed with a structuralist mindset, whereby "the [w]estern capitalist order was the root problem," so there was "little room for everyday local politics" and its cultural specificities, with the exception perhaps being studies of the social and cultural construction of race.

In the United States, for example, most critical scholars today recognize the role of racial identity in the administration of justice. Racial discrimination is a historically embedded phenomenon in the United States with its foundations in slavery, Jim Crow laws, and trends in mass incarceration, often analytically intertwined with class.[16] Events like the police shooting of Michael Brown in Ferguson, Missouri, which sparked demonstrations and later uncovered systematic, race-based enforcement of traffic violations, show that despite a robust rule of law, criminal justice actors often maintain cultural practices (whether of a local subculture, the police subculture, or a symptom of more mainstream American racism and punishment of the poor) that undermine the rule of law. Likewise, in Bahrain, sectarian discrimination, rather than racial discrimination, is the culturally and historically relevant differential identity that both affects and is affected by criminal justice processing. Despite non-discriminatory rules of law developed in the twentieth century,[17] long-standing cultural practices of anti-Shi`a discrimination continued within Bahraini institutions. And, in the current post-Arab Spring political reality, these practices have been more overtly reinforced with new laws, such as those allowing citizenship revocation, primarily used against Shi`a political activists.[18]

Sectarianism, like racism, is a transnational phenomenon because sect identity, like racial identity, crosses national boundaries. On the other hand, what race or sect means or how it affects people varies by more specific social contexts, and so the global and local interact and inform each other. Previous scholarship on sectarianism has focused on international causes and effects to the detriment of understanding more local phenomenon.[19] More recently, however, scholars are approaching particular national contexts to understand how policies and practices therein contribute to sectarian strife, much as it is important to understand the American social constructions of race as distinct from that of other countries where racial identity may also significantly matter. Frederic Wehrey's *Sectarian Politics in the Gulf* lasers in on the domestic context, arguing that by solving social and political problems within nations, the use of sectarian politics, as a strategic tactic by power-players will no longer be as salient.[20] In Bahrain, the contemporary fact of social, economic, and political subordination of Shi`a by a Sunni ruling government at the national level has been well documented.[21] The ruling government and aligned Sunni groups paint Shi`a as a dangerous class and the Bahraini criminal justice system has been routinely criticized for differential and sometimes brutal treatment of Shi`a,[22] a form of state violence. The criminalization of anti-government political speech[23] exemplifies the tenor of order maintenance as discriminatory, making an internal enemy out of Shi`a despite the fact that they make up a significant majority of the population in Bahrain.

The notion that domestic problems play into the rise of sectarian-based politics is sensible, especially when taking a longer historical view. However, the use of sectarian-based political strategies and the development of sectarian institutions is not merely the product of elite political actors choosing a strategy that best maintains their power (though it may be an effective strategy). Rather, it reflects a deeper interplay of more socially and culturally embedded notions of sectarian identity that developed historically, and then were appropriated, modified, and institutionalized during the colonial experience. George Steinmetz's study of German colonial domination takes this perspective. He describes the German colonial experience as one in which sovereignty was a clear priority over all others, existing "not just as an apparatus but an 'idea'; it inscribed its existence on the landscape, minds, and bodies; it broadcasts its presence through legal texts and political rituals" that "define, express, and reinforce a cultural difference and fundamental inferiority of the territorial natives."[24] Likewise, the problem with sectarianism in Bahrain, as formerly a part of the British Empire, is not borne out of the cold calculation of rational choice, but exists in a more phenomenological place related to the human cultural experience around sovereign power (who has it), the meaning of identity, and its ramifications for the social order. Criminal justice in Bahrain is infused with the cultural language and practice of a sectarianism even as rulers often officially couch their decision-making in other terms; further, seeing the world through a sectarian lens (even if one is tolerant of other sects) is part of the operant cultural language and practice, the very fabric of how Bahraini people have historically made sense of their world and organized their criminal justice institutions, for better or worse. We see this starkly with the popular social justice phrase, *la Shi`a wa la sunni bus Bahraini* (not Shi`a and not Sunni, just Bahraini), which although made famous during the events of the Arab Spring, had been popularized many years before. The catchphrase shows that the way to verbally signal tolerance in the Bahraini context is to accept sect differences. It also implies that this is the biggest social and political obstacle to national unity in the popular imagination, as opposed to, hypothetically, a slogan about gender, ethnicity, age, or some other identifier.

The idea that culture influences and shapes criminal justice systems is not a new idea and has been explored within criminology under the banner of cultural criminology. In this approach the social, cultural, and political meaning of crime and criminal justice is taken seriously.[25] Cultural criminologists view criminal justice from a phenomenological perspective and, like critical criminologists, favor qualitative methodologies such as discourse, textual, and visual analyses. They aim to understand how individuals find meaning in their world through cultural representations of crime and justice, focusing on "constant discovery and constant comparison of relevant situations, settings, styles, images, meanings, and nuances."[26] Although primarily used to critique the lack of social and political context that plagues many positivistic studies of criminal justice in the West, the theory can hypothetically be used to frame criminal justice–related concerns in non-Western and historical contexts as well if the focus is placed on the cultural meaning of crime and criminal justice.

The problem is that cultural criminology, and critical criminology as well, are rarely engaged in the empirical study of the intersection of cultural and criminal justice in non-Western places, essentially lacking true global engagement.[27] Theorists, more recently articulating what is being called Southern criminology, fill this void using the term "Southern" to refer to the "Global South" which is a metaphor for any non-Western social space. The "Global North," is the Western world, or alternatively a more specific metaphor referring to the "metropole" or the urban, imperial centers of the Global North. In essence, Southern criminology endeavors to more deliberately consider the crime and criminal justice experiences of non-Western and/or rural societies in order to build more globally relevant theory or theories that show either potential for global universality or flexibility in light of social and cultural relativism. Southern criminologists believe that the theoretical paradigms that might explain crime and criminal justice in the North do not translate well to the South because they were developed based on distinctly different patterns of social and political development, focusing on patterns of industrialization, capitalism, and democratic development that are North-specific. As Kerry Carrington, Russell Hogg, and Máximo Sozzo explain:

> Much research in criminology takes for granted a high level of internal peace within what is assumed to be a stable nation state system. This has led to the obfuscation of the historical role of state violence in nation-building, the expansion of colonialism across the Global South and the neglect of contemporary violent phenomena, like armed conflict, drug wars and ethnic cleansing, that are more common in the Global South.[28]

One major step forward is focusing on the historical experience of colonial subjugation or colonial settlement as often the most significant divergence from the Global North. Borrowing from postcolonial theory, and its long-standing critique of Western biases, allows for better description of the Global South (something I have been doing throughout my work on criminal justice in the Arabian Gulf region[29]).

Taking Bahrain to be a part of the Global South makes sense given it is a non-Western country, but also points to the reductionist binary that may be operating in a South versus North dynamic, when in fact, the reality may be more along the lines of Global Souths, plural, and perhaps Global Norths, too. Bahrain has experienced colonial subjugation but has not suffered the same economic effects of the recent neoliberal global order[30] due to the relative wealth provided by the now-diminishing oil industry. As an archipelago of primarily urban dwellers with a robust social safety net for Bahraini citizens, including socialized health care, the experience of Bahrain probably also diverges somewhat from a typical Global South milieu where per capita income and government resources are much slimmer. Regardless, the project of Southern criminology is very promising in providing a space within criminology and criminal justice for the criminological imagination to extend more robustly outside the Western experience. As Joseph Donnermeyer articulates about the benefit of Southern criminology: "[I]t compels scholars interested in advancing criminology beyond its Western, urban biases to avoid the development of categories of knowledge that create new forms of hegemonic thinking" within academic discourse.[31] Overall, this avenue of criminological thought provides new theoretical insight about how crime and criminal justice matters on the planet and over time: making the project more culturally specific and historically-minded.

A HISTORY OF ORDER MAINTENANCE DISRUPTION: BRINGING IN THE POSTCOLONIAL

Until criminology theoretically catches up by building its Southern sensibility, historical sociology and postcolonial theory provide the best foundation for the current project. Starting with history, understanding sectarian order maintenance in Bahrain requires a *longue dureé* approach in which social features appear to slowly evolve[32] but actually are layered, changing in fits and starts which never fully erase the past, leaving behind a sedimentary residue.[33] By taking a long historical view of the development of sectarianism in cultural and political discourse in the region, the current anti-Shia tendencies of Bahraini national criminal justice institutions emerge as the product of a particular pathway of historical events that shaped contemporary institutions into discriminatory entities.

Recent historical scholarship brings Arabian Gulf history into clearer focus in order to better contextualize the criminal justice historical developments I will describe, specifically the production of the order maintenance function within criminal justice agencies as a product of the British colonial influence in the early twentieth century. Many sources understate the role that the British played in the national development of Bahrain by characterizing it as a protectorate[34] or part of the "informal empire"[35] and not extensively colonized. However, James Onley's comparison of a fully colonized Indian princely state to the administration of Bahrain in the early twentieth century reveals striking similarities in the scope of operation and level of control by the British.[36] This is further underscored by historian Kristopher Radford's review of the annual "Table of Salutes Fired in India" published by the India Office. From 1904, Gulf Rulers are being saluted with more gun salutes than British protectorates routinely were, and were included on the same salute list as the Indian principalities, mainstays of the Empire.[37] Gulf shaikhdoms had ceased being considered foreign to India.[38]

Although nineteenth century treaties limited the British to external protection and considered the Emir as a sovereign, the drafting and eventual implementation of the Order-in-Council (OiC) laws, a series of colonial reforms, represent a deep internal takeover that was colonization in Bahrain in practice if not in name. An OiC law is a regulation agreed upon by the British Government, on the advice of the Privy Council (government ministers), and articulates a trucial relationship with a territory, most often centering on matters of the judiciary or military. Previous to the OiC reforms, "native agents," or locals who reported on the territory to the Raj and London, primarily collected taxes and passed along intelligence. The importance of Bahrain and other Gulf shaikhdoms rested in their economic and military support of British control of India; the Gulf was a "frontier" possession and was in essence a "British Lake."[39] Viceroy Lord Curzon (1899–1905) re-envisioned Indian territoriality under the banner of "forward policy" hoping to ward off competing European interests in the Gulf by assuming greater administrative control of it.[40] Demonstrating this expansion, the Viceroy took a naval tour of the Gulf in late 1903, much like viceroys did around the subcontinent. Upon his visit to Bahrain, he appointed the first full-time British political agent there, Francis Prideaux.

In Bahrain, the OiC laws granted administrative powers to non-native British political agents, like Prideaux. In a pathway similar to that at play in India, a political agent was assigned to each principality to serve as colonial administrator and ambassador.[41] The political agent working in the colonial political agency (*bayt al-dawlah*) reported to the political resident in Bushehr, who reported to the Viceroy's office in New Delhi. Implementing OiC reforms, the political agents posted in Bahrain in the first half of the twentieth century reorganized customs administration, and created a state treasury, land registry, civil, and criminal courts police, among other governmental institutions.[42]

Using this colonial moment as a key analytic frame, the sectarianism embedded in the very creation of the modern state and its criminal justice system is palpable. Historian Lawrence G. Potter asserts that by taking law and education out of religious institutions, colonial administrators showed their commitment to secularization in Gulf countries.[43] I argue that secularization was a smoke screen for more complicated and often sectarian institutional developments, particularly in the space of an emerging criminal justice system. Creating a nation-state, as the OiC laws essentially do, entails controlling a territory and centralizing the chief concentrated means of violence.[44] According to this perspective, the nation-state must gain control over internal groups who had previous authority to use legitimate violence. Subordinating local, tribal, or clan-based violence is a necessary ingredient for colonial administrators forming a modern criminal justice system. Local communities must respect the new government's security apparatus as privileged over that of their traditional patrons. In Bahraini history, this concentration of the means of violence in a modern governmental structure is a path-dependent phenomenon that embroils local actors in a culturally contested moment that sets the stage for future sectarian conflicts. Essentially, the shift of legitimate violence from multiple tribal entities and other groups in competition with each other, to a single government controlled by a specific clan (the Al Khalifah), institutionalizes that clan's long-standing sectarian *modus operandi* within the context of inter- and intra-sect competition.

Control of inhabitants' movement within a territory has also been theorized to be a major pillar of the development of the nation-state. Firming up the boundaries of the state involves "exclusion, surveillance, and containment of 'undesirable elements'" and requires an expanded state bureaucracy to organize it.[45] Colonial administrators set up the police as the agency responsible for questions of citizenship, the development of a Bahraini passport system, and the identification of deportable people. As the book will detail, Shi`a Bahrainis were disproportionately subjected to deportation, despite being indigenous to the island, as part of the larger sectarian discrimination. In fact, we will see that the police and courts were the frontlines in defining and enforcing who was Bahraini in a new nation-state that placed a high priority on shoring up Sunni privilege. In the 1920s, the Emir, British political agents, and the Emir's British advisor established a modern policing and court system, institutionalizing a sectarian framework in order to maintain power. The delegitimizing of previous tribal, religious, or clan-based authorities represents a major historical disruption that continues to resonate today.

For William Sewell in *Logics of History*,[46] major historical disruptions, are important theoretical categories in themselves. They are transformative of the social structure when they have significant cultural or symbolic significance; the interpretation of the event becomes as important as the event itself. Disruptive moments involve contested notions, when numerous results are possible, and the outcome cements subsequent authority, legitimacy, and security. Sewell defines the disruptive event as one that is the product of a fundamental upheaval that cannot be contained in the previous social order. Culturally significant modes of activity are connected in new ways, evidenced by narrative accounts of the event. As such, structure-changing moments are more fundamentally cultural transformations, shaped by particular local conditions and characterized by heightened emotion and collective creativity in wrestling with fundamental social anxieties. The new world that the event births has an "authoritative order" that sets the stage until the next major upheaval. An individual or group capacity to deploy symbols during the transformative event both establishes power relations and a repertoire of operant symbols and practices.

Sectarianism in the Gulf context can be understood as a set of operant symbols and practices often exhibited in criminal justice discourse and practice; they have utility precisely because they are part of a deeper cultural repertoire. Although the years of greatest British colonial influences in the early twentieth century are perhaps too extended a timeframe to constitute an event under Sewell's theory, we can approximate the existence of a singular state-building "event" based on the discursive ripples evident from the OiC reforms, which I examine in particular with the criminal adjudications in that time period. The cases I focus on establish a new criminal justice system based on the colonial reforms, locking in Sunni hegemony and Shi`a subordination. How this happens, from a theoretical perspective, is also again informed by Steinmetz's work exploring the German overseas colonies at the turn of the twentieth century. For Steinmetz, colonial territories are semi-autonomous fields with their own unique forms of symbolic capital grounded in imperial representatives' ability to understand and manipulate local knowledge and customs, or "ethnographic sagacity."[47] In this way, local power relations are just as, if not more important, than directives from the imperial homeland, bringing to the fore local actors—both native and from the imperial seat—and accounting for the kinds of complex political contests that allowed for variation in territories within the same empire. Similarly, Kwami Kwarteng characterized the British Empire as directed by individual political agents and administrative officers who "wielded immense power" in determining local policies leading to inconsistent colonial administration across both time and place.[48] Despite this, Kwarteng finds that the enduring thread in British imperialism is a performance of a particular class system learned in elite British public schools and universities, which is then transposed and negotiated by the individual imperial representative embedded in local power struggles, similar to the tack taken by Paul Rich who views the

Arabian Gulf in this era as heavily influenced by the pomp and circumstance of colonial actors' education in English public schools and participation in Masonic lodges.[49]

Considering the role of the imperial actor in the colonial space, Sir Charles Belgrave emerges as a major influence on Bahrain during the relevant historical disruption, representing a state builder whose role was "far more prominent than that suggested by his title" as an advisor to Emir Hamad bin Isa al-Khalifa and then Emir Salman bin Isa al-Khalifa.[50] He almost single-handedly founded the state's criminal justice system, making him the chief architect of the historical disruption detailed here. He can also be credited with a wide array of additional national development projects, including running a yearly horse race, implementing a transparent national budget, designing a prominent government building which is a symbol of the country (*Bab al-Bahrain*), designing a public awareness campaign which led to the eradication of malaria in the territory, implementing a loan scheme for government employees to buy houses, and starting a number of schools.[51] Although the British colonial nature of these innovations are clear, he also made a number of overtures to local culture and preferences in developing these institutions, such as creating a camel corps as part of the modern police force and developing schools for Shi`a to instruct pupils commensurate to their sect-based religious traditions. As such, the Bahraini colonial space reflects a Steinmetzian semi-autonomous sphere where the imperial individual is embedded in the local and improvises therein. However, the problem remains that local culture and practice being described through the filter of a colonial agent cannot be wholly recast as history, but merely a feature of the historical record as primarily penned by the powerful. To work with this bias, postcolonial theory provides a navigational strategy.

BAHRAINI CRIMINAL JUSTICE AND POSTCOLONIALITY

Masquerading as "disinterested history,"[52] historical narratives often fail to grasp the tragic meaning of colonial history as inherently disruptive. Gayatri Chakravorty Spivak describes colonial disruptions as the "tearing of time"[53] as precolonial and postcolonial "continuity [is] ruptured by the imperfect imposition of an Enlightenment episteme"[54] in the administration of seemingly secular criminal law where once cultural or religious ritual had been. Scholarship that confronts the colonial disruption head on uses "the contestatory force of an interpretive method whose material is the disparate, but intertwined and interdependent, and above all overlapping streams of historical experience."[55] Such a critical reading is crucial because many of the primary sources about disruptive colonial events were written by colonial elites in their languages. Does this render interpretive work about colonial narrative worthless? This unsettling rift, between what is being observed as local culture and how it is interpreted by a colonial agent, is what Homi Bhabha describes as a "performance of a certain uncertain writing," a situation in which reading it "repeats the incompletion of translation"[56] and leads to a type of splitting in which the reality and the scholarship are contradictory but not acknowledged as such. This acts as a defense against the possibility of not knowing, couched in the psychological terms of Freudian theorists as a unconscious anxiety about the ego splitting from reality; the result is that both the reading and the writing creates and recreates "colonial nonsense and imperial aporia."[57] The Western demand for rational narrative renders the indigenous cultural practices as subordinate, chaotic, and sometimes even less than human—and does so from a position of authority. For Spivak, "[w]e can docket it, but we cannot grasp [it] at all,"[58] in reference to subaltern women subjected to a colonial prohibition on ritual self-immolation, which had local cultural importance to them, and yet their voices about it are largely absent. In the same way, we may docket, but not always grasp the defendants, victims, and witnesses represented in the Bahraini criminal court files still relying on traditional codes of conduct in the wake of the new rational-legal regime. Therefore, in being an interpreter of this fraught space, I am taking a risk and am forcing something uncontained into a container. The risk only offset by the gained knowledge and experience of over a dozen years of ethnographic, survey, interview, archival, social, activist, and academic work on this topic at an interdisciplinary crossroads of my own making. At the very least, care must be taken to take seriously points of contestation, problems of cultural translation, and the ever-present possibility of voices that are very faint or even absent.

The present account also builds on the work begun by scholars like David Anderson, David Killingray, Georgina Sinclair, Chris Lewis, and C. J. Jeffries who pieced together colonial criminal justice history;[59] however, a more critical eye on the topic is found here. Jeffries, for example, states that the British "have taken many useful things with them when they have gone out to colonise [sic] or administer other parts of the work . . . they took nothing which was to have a more profound and lasting influence than their own particular conception of police,"[60] an attitude that took the exportation of British-style policing as a natural good. Place-based histories in postcolonial studies must be sensitive to the "cycles of progress and regression," meaning that notions of "progress" and "modernization" are often used to signal moves toward Western-style innovations,[61] like policing or criminal law, that have a complicated relationship to more indigenous practices of order maintenance.

Postcolonial places consist of individuals and institutions that are between forms, between languages, between symbols, and ultimately exhibit creolity.[62] Or put another way, it is the hybridization of imperial and local forms, forming a major analytic category in post-colonial theory; phenomena in a particular postcolonial society must be disaggregated in order to understand the nuances of meaning.[63] By focusing on words, symbols, and other cultural expressions, the tensions inherent in a particular milieu can be deconstructed: in this case as the seemingly contradictory ideas of national unity and sectarian pride coexist and compete within Bahrain. Nowhere are these signs and symbols more relevant than in the discourse around criminal justice in Bahrain, so far as what the criminal justice system represents and how it should be deployed. Cloaked in the symbols of nation-states and public protection, the system exhibits Sunni hegemonic intentions and practices routine sectarian discrimination, a tack taken since its institutional inception.[64]

The advent of secular law itself in Bahrain usurped the old reliance on tribal and sectarian law, as well as specific commercial and customary laws indigenous to the Indian Ocean culture of trade of which the Arabian Gulf was also a part. Much could be said about the intersection of indigenous and foreign law, or the interplay of religious and secular law, or sectarian differences in Muslim law. This book will describe relevant schools of law as well as specific laws as the historical narrative unfolds, yet a full theoretical treatment of the relationship of law and society is beyond the scope of the book. In general, I work from the conflict perspective within classical anthropology of law. The colonial state maintained a monopoly on violence; in the case of the British Empire this was accomplished through the use of naval power.[65] Once the monopoly was in place, the colonial state acted as the chief mediator of the contours of legal plurality,[66] placing colonial law on top and then stacking underneath it customary and religious systems.[67] The hegemony of the state-centered law creates conflicts as interest groups within the state struggle for control of the order maintenance system.[68] On a fundamental level, colonial systems encode asymmetrical power relations and attempt to provide for the colonial state's legal legitimacy, often in the face of significant social and political challenges to that legitimacy. In this way, new and conflicting forms of social control potentially become overlaid into the rules operant in individuals' everyday behavior. As an example of such governmentality, domestic conflicts are pulled into state control and have dialectic ramifications; culture and law influence and shape each other.[69]

Taking the *longue dureé* approach, what is absorbed and suppressed by colonists is never erased, but remains in the wings. The contrasting pluralistic notion of social order is the idea that the colonial project acted as a mere arbiter of legal pluralism and created multi-centric legal authorities, wherein the state was one of many.[70] This perspective suggests more indigenous agency in shaping legal cultures, but is problematic because it also underestimates the devastation of the colonial order. It appears that all who touch the new rational-legal order gets pulled into what Spivak has described as "the long road to hegemony,"[71] as if the very ethnocentrism, and economic and cultural domination of the Western rational-legal order cannot be tamed, is inherently world-conquering. At the same time, the dominant legal order surface modes of resistance (ultimately quashed or compromised through absorption) are discursively important as cultural artifacts. They point to "[t]he architecture of the . . . legal order" becoming "the object of continual struggle over definitions and markers of cultural difference."[72] Individuals subjected to the law make their way between and among the political confines of society, but also often have some agency to challenge, change, and subvert.[73]

Partha Chatterjee explains that enlightenment-era legal rationality arrives in many far-flung places by way of the colonial encounter, becomes institutionalized, and is used to eclipse local, traditional rationalities that threatened the continuance of the colonial state.[74] The courts, in essence, uphold an epistemic privilege in European rationality, "divid[ing] up the history of Western society into pre-scientific and scientific, and cast[ing] every other culture of the world into the darkness of unscientific traditionalism."[75] Eventually the distinction moves from ethnic privilege to a moral privilege and when challenged by counter-colonial movements, becomes a privilege that both "sanctions the assertion of cultural supremacy while assiduously denying at the same time that it has anything to do with cultural evaluations."[76] In fact, far from being innocuous, legal rationality and the colonial project ushered in a change in human conduct and sentiment in the direction of rationalization, what Norbert Elias described as the civilizing process.[77] Again, this is not construed in teleological terms as a move toward progress, but one of many aspects of human social modes of being that begins to take precedence when a monopoly on taxation and physical control over large territories occurs in the development of the nation-state. Intricate webs of social interaction usher in an age of "self-control" in which small-scale regulation of behavior through acts of violence based on kinship or other small group affiliation is replaced by a social pacifism (through the rule of law). Those who can conform to the new order of self-controlled behavior have social advantage in the shifting of power.

Elias explains that by virtue of class position and social upbringing, certain people within the transitioning society will be better able to conform. Advantaged social actors can emerge from clan feuds and honor systems and instead gravitate toward the acquisition of money or prestige in the new social order. "Elimination struggles" ensure in which groups solidifying power under the new order tamp down those of the older order.[78] The differently position groups vis a vis the new power exercise "reciprocal supervision . . . on one another, by the severe stigmatization and penalties they impose upon those members who breach the common distinguishing code."[79] In the process, some commingling or hybridization of forms occurs; however, the pacification or self-control in the everyday, internal workings of the society are a "smo[u]ldering fire"[80] which seldom breaks out, but when it does, can be quite devastating.

Although the current study as a discourse analysis does not directly test whether the social forms in the civilizing process existed *per se*, it instead evaluates whether the criminal court files show a representation of such in the legal record. Elias recognized the importance of discourse in signaling the shifting of power. "If the sword no longer plays so great a role as the means of decision, it is replaced by intrigue, conflicts in which careers and social success are contested with words."[81] As words recording criminal court processing, tribal and other social competitions are quashed as the state engages in "elimination struggles" in establishing its central authority: the criminal case files suggest this in the way they evidence the criminalization of traditional conflicts, and the criminalization of Shi`a identity; facets that were once part and parcel of the social milieu are now crimes and are punishable. These small-scale and even private disputes between individuals provide insight into the political, cultural, and structural stresses existing in the society from which they emerged.[82]

A "MIRACULOUS" AND MYSTERIOUS CACHE OF CRIMINAL COURT FILES

This book centers on a textual analysis of preserved criminal cases dated 1924–1940[83] found in the India Office Records of the British Library; access to these records are primarily provided by the Public Records Act of 1967 in the United Kingdom, although some files have additional rules and exceptions. The India Office Records consist of the archives of the East India Company, the precursor to British colonialism chartered in 1600; the files for the Commissioners for the Affairs of India, which date from 1784; and the files of the India Office from 1858 until Indian Independence in 1947.[84] Overall, British officials who produced the records were responsible for "the representation of British and British Indian interests and the maintenance of peaceful relations with and between local rulers. The main bulk of their reporting, therefore, was obviously concerned with diplomatic and political relations and with related questions of administration."[85] In practice, the subjects covered were quite wide and various, including political affairs and intelligence, linguistics, culture, geographic information, archaeology, and economics. As a treaty-protected state and through its colonial experience, Bahrain was an adjunct state to the bureaucracy of the Indian Government and its colonial officials reported on the Bahrain-specific aspects of these broad topics to their superiors in Bushehr at the Political Residency and in Delhi and Simla, India; ultimately from India, important information flowed to the imperial seat in London.

The criminal cases examined are relics of the political agent's (PA) court in Bahrain, which as an imperial court, tried British and foreign citizens arrested for crimes in Bahrain under the authority of the Foreign Jurisdictions Act. Meanwhile, the Emir and his British advisor operated the Bahrain Court (BC), designed to try Bahraini citizens. Although on the surface this appears to be an example of a dual legal system,[86] a closer examination sees that duality slipping away, at least when it comes to criminal law. In reality, the two courts were intertwined, both using the Indian Penal Code of 1860, and often trying the same cases if defendants were of mixed citizenship, or trading cases as citizenship determinations changed; further, judges in one court often appeared as prosecutors or investigators in the other. This book compares, corroborates, and contextualizes these cases using relevant primary sources, including Sir Charles Belgrave's diaries and other historical documents. In the time period of interest (1924–40), there are thirty case files retained in the India Office Records of the British Library (detailed in Appendix A) from among the 6,248 noted to have been adjudicated by the PA Court (Appendix B), according to annual reports. Ten of them can be considered "serious" criminal cases (rape, attempted rape, murder, and attempted murder).

These criminal case files are part of the "R/15" series of files which are a grouping broadly consisting of records from the Persian Gulf Residency in Bushehr and the subordinate local agencies at Bahrain, Kuwait, Muscat, and the Trucial Coast. To point to the massive volume of the India Office Records as a whole, there are 11,586 court files related to the Bahrain PA Court alone, and another 2,022 that relate to the Political Agency; however, the great majority reflect civil cases.[87] For additional contextual clues about how to read the criminal cases, I also reviewed some files from the "L/PS" series involving Political and Secret Records when the topics of these files related to crime or criminal justice.

The records do not indicate why the thirty particular criminal case files during the time period of 1924–1940 were shipped to London and retained over other cases.[88] Inquiries with the archival staff of the British Library did not turn up any additional explanation beyond the library's research guides. Starting in 1941, the amount of surviving cases doubles and triples per year; however, the focus on this book is on the approximately fifteen-year transition from indigenous modes of criminal justice to colonial ones. Therefore, as a small sample of cases, they are arbitrary, occurring during the time period of interest and the only case files known to have survived.[89] As one of the original India Office Records archivists explains, very little systematic preservation was done by those who retained the files in the Gulf Residency and Political Agency and ultimately sent them on to London at the end of the colonial period.

> [A] number of routine files have survived which would perhaps nowadays be subjects for destruction. The gaps which exist in the records are more likely to be the result of indiscriminate destruction, loss and haphazard record-keeping arrangements. Climatic conditions in the Gulf were certainly not conducive to the proper preservation of archives, and given the acute staff shortages and the extremely heavy workload from which most of the Agencies suffered . . . it seems miraculous that so much detailed reporting has survived.[90]

Meanwhile, it is not known if the several thousand other case files, the universe from which the preserved cache was drawn, have been retained in Bahrain or destroyed. For purposes of this book, the cases can be treated as representative of the whole despite their small number and unknown preservation status because any systematic, organizational strategy, curation, or cultivation of these documents cannot be detected; this acts as a form of *de facto* randomization in the absence of any sampling bias that would appear to affect the research outcomes.

Crime in Bahrain According To the Colonial Record

Throughout the early twentieth century, a common theme in describing Bahrain was that it was a peaceful place, yet this glosses over much violence and threat of violence, often along sectarian lines and against Shi`a people, or involving honor killings of female relatives, that paint the true picture of the archipelago. In other words, the country was safe for Sunni Arab men and expatriates, less so for Shi`a and women:

> Frequent attacks were made on Shia villages and men, women and children were murdered and robbed by armed gunmen. In the country few people dared to venture out at night, unless they were armed, and for years there was a general fear that the Dawasir [tribal] Arabs would make a descent on Bahrain.[91]

And:

> Between [Muslim years] 1350 and 1353, there were four murder cases . . . the murder by their male relations of women who brought disgrace on their families was still regarded by many Arabs as justifiable, in fact commendable . . .[92]

In an accounting of overall crime "from the time that detailed records of criminal cases have been kept," in approximately 1924 to 1936, an average of 190 foreigners and 270 Bahrainis were convicted each year. In the PA Court alone, from 1924 to 1940, as aforementioned, approximately 6,240 cases were adjudicated (see Appendix B).

In 1926, albeit a particularly violent year according to the colonial record, murder and attempted murder does not appear so rare. That we know of, there were eight murders[93] and five attempted murders, plus a rash of home invasion robberies. For a population of approximately 90,000,[94] this is high; the murder rate was at least 8.8 per 100,000 that year. The annual report for 1945–1946 recounts that between Muslim year 1350 and 1353 (May 1931 to April 1935), there were four murders. And, for the previous twenty years, the police reportedly investigated eleven murders in which six were committed by foreigners.[95] According to my accounting, however, compiling murders mentioned in the colonial files or other sources, approximately thirty murders took place between 1922 and 1936. All of these numbers, however, should be treated with caution as no reliable single tally of Bahraini murders in the1920s and 1930s exists.

There were many types of crime besides murder recorded in the time period of interest. Liquor-related offense and fraud-related offenses are notably numerous. There was opium use in the country and occasionally opium raids and confiscations[96] (but this paled in comparison to the number of alcohol-related cases processed by the police and courts). As an example, in one opium case, the sellers were sentenced to three months imprisonment, a 50 rupee fine, and deportation.[97] Meanwhile, colonial authorities worried about fraud in the pearling industry given its centrality to the Bahraini economy before the oil industry arrived. For example, on September 12, 1933, the state police received a tip that cultured pearls were being offered for sale in the Manama *suq*. A sales representative of the defendant, Khalil Ibrahim Al-Baker, a Qatari, was questioned by police, and he admitted to offering fourteen such pearls to a person named Sa'ad for 90 rupees. Approximately two weeks before, he had sold a string of cultured pearls to Muhammad Aquil for 90 rupees, who later provided them to the police as evidence. Political Agent Everald Gastrell sentenced Al-Baker to six months imprisonment and 1,000 rupees or two months imprisonment on cheating and importation convictions. Al-Baker received three months, and 1,000 rupees or two months on two sales and possession convictions.

Far from merely describing the operation of criminal courts and the implementation of colonial law, these early criminal cases show the larger state-building colonial project. As a site for performing formal social control, the criminal courts reveal the shifting power as they operate in the lives of people subject to the court as defendants. The analysis uses an ethnographic content analysis form of textual analysis. Rather than being a product of a static understanding of the criminal cases and the world from which they emerged, the process of researching for this book involved a reconceptualization of themes and meanings throughout the process.[98] The goal is to provide a nuanced and fluid understanding of the significance of the new twentieth century criminal adjudication in Bahrain: when the criminal case files are taken together, they represent an overall case study, in methodological terms, of colonial criminal justice in Bahrain—and its legacy. Because of the purposive use of additional primary and secondary sources to further illuminate the meaning and political and social consequences of the cases, the method is more aptly referred to as the "extended case study" method.[99]

Seeing the Sectarianism in the Historical Development of Bahraini Criminal Justice

Through the lens of a new interpretation of criminal justice history in Bahrain, and a cache of colonial criminal cases, the book outlines two major shifts in notions of the social order and order maintenance that characterize the twentieth century, highlighting a sectarianism modus operandi within the criminal justice system. The shifts are: 1) the criminalization of inter-tribal competition and honor-based modes of behavior in order to prevent intra-Sunni contestation and to unite Sunnis under Al-Khalifah and colonial authority; and 2) the invention of indigenous Shi`a and Persian Bahrainis as a criminal class as an extension of the sectarianism long practiced by the Al Khalifah (and other Sunni tribes). Together these two shifts birth a modern criminal justice system that institutionalizes Sunni chauvinism and Shi`a discrimination, problems evident in the Bahraini criminal justice system today. It is also through this close look at criminal justice institutions that the larger, political meaning of sectarianism in Bahrain takes on a more concrete and grounded meaning as key to establishing the sovereignty and control of Bahrain by the Al Khalifah clan.

In chapter 1, I provide a new approach to Bahrain's history, which corrects Sunni-dominated historical accounts in favor of a more balanced view, and takes into consideration the Shi`a majoritarian underclass. Two major historical disruptions are relevant: the pushing of Sunni tribes from the interior into the Gulf Coast in the eighteenth century and the British colonial project in the twentieth century; the latter is the main focus of this book. Both of these political regimes had particular notions of how to achieve social and political order and who should have the control of the legitimate means of violence; however, these notions were not inevitable or intrinsic to the region, but rather the result of power-struggles and cultural contestations that ushered in new, hybrid eras. Together, the results of the two disruptions form the basis of today's Bahrain and its sectarian-based criminal justice system. In essence, the first disruption becomes institutionalized, in part, into the second, and so broadly speaking, the problem can be defined as one of postcoloniality. The nation-state and its institutions act as a forced overlay in a milieu that—although often claimed by external and imperial powers over the centuries—was never forced into the rational-bureaucratic fold of nationness until the early twentieth century. The chapter details the British imperial modernizing mission, which ignored the legal limitations of nineteenth century security treaties and proceeded to profoundly restructure internal state criminal justice institutions. Overall the system changes from an indigenous system of Muslim *qadi*s (judges) and royal, tribal-based courts, to a colonial system of secular law and courts, state police, forensic investigations, and a state prison system that reinforced the differences between Sunni and Shi`a and maintained Sunni hegemony.

Chapter 2 explores the new criminal adjudication as it confronts contestations among Sunni tribes for power and authority in Bahrain. The new criminal adjudication shifts rivalry from a political and military problem to that of a criminal event subject to the court system, shifting order maintenance functions from tribal elites to colonists. Focusing on the assassination attempt on Sheikh Hamad in 1926 and related crimes, we can see this shift occurring in the space of approximately two decades. Though the nature of violence had not changed in the region, its meaning has altered with the rise of the colonial state. Further, this period also shows how intra-Sunni contestations for power were tamped down in Bahrain through the use of the criminal justice system to prosecute rivals, leaving the Al Khalifah as the relatively uncontested Sunni hegemons in partnership with the British imperial order.

Chapter 3 describes the criminalization of traditional honor codes. This occurred in the time period of interest—performing certain honor-based behaviors, such as using violence to avenge insults against one's relations, became an aggravating circumstance. Often, judges and court personnel characterized those operating under traditional tribal honor codes as being without sense or reason. As a result, the new, colonial secular courts failed to grasp the social meaning behind such crimes and the role they may have made in the past as a form of informal social control. There are many examples across the cases examined in which defendants, who adhered to more traditional social relations around protection and maintenance of honor, were misunderstood by court personnel and judges, and as a result may have been treated more harshly. Eventually, the criminalization of honor-based behavior will reflect a shifting social norm, as many Bahrainis are able to conform to new laws, while tribal traditionalists will increasingly be marginalized.

Chapter 4 shows how the new criminal adjudication, including the criminalization of tribal rivalry, solidified the institutional sectarianism that remains today. The colonial-era criminal justice system did this in at least three ways. First, the colonial state aided and abetted external allies and internal elites who raided Shi`a villages and perpetrated mass violence; these events were not separate from the events that also served to pacify Sunni tribal contestations discussed in chapter 2. Second, the colonial state did not protect Shi`a victims from violence in the same way it did other victims of violence, and in at least a few instances, state actors perpetrated these crimes. Third, the colonial period exhibits a peculiar form of restorative justice that in practice extended only to Sunni perpetrators and represents the absorption of tribal notions of forgiveness into the bureaucratic fold of colonial justice. What is officially forgiven in large part is violence against Shi`a.

Chapter 5 covers the new criminal justice adjudication and the invention of Shi`a as a criminal class subject to being over-policed and criminalized for behavior previously not defined as such. This stands in sharp contrast to the patterns of forgiveness extended to Sunni perpetrators. The Court found reasons to deport or deny Shi`a Bahrainis caught up in the criminal justice system at a high rate relative to other groups. Because the notion of Bahraini citizenship was only newly being constructed, the two courts often pursued prosecutions for the same events even when co-defendants were not of mixed background, and retried cases in the other courts if the original court placed a defendant in the wrong jurisdiction. King's Regulation No. 2 of 1937 ultimately defined citizenship as birth in Bahrain or one's father having been born in Bahrain, but this was often considered suspect when claims were made by defendants identified as Persian, Iranian, or Shi`a. A double-standard of citizenship proof is evident in the readiness to deport or deny citizenship to Persian, Iranian, or Shi`a—an observation corroborated by secret political memorandum of the day which reveals an official policy of trying to relieve Bahrain of "an undesirable element" who might support Persian claims on the island. From discourse around criminal and citizenship cases, the treatment of Shi`a and Iranians as a criminal class is clearly evident.

In the concluding section, I return to the contemporary Sunni-dominated sectarian state to connect past Shi`a suppression to current trends. The struggle for human and civil rights in the constitutional monarchy is a nearly one-hundred-year-old endeavor to make justice attainable for those of all identities represented in the country. Transitional justice processes and criminal justice reform are ways to kick-start a new commitment to human rights in the archipelago, but must confront the complicated culturally embedded history of a Sunni regime that consistently justifies to itself the need to subjugate Shi`a. To reform, the current regime must turn away from sectarian-based prosecutions and a public relations machine that seeks to cloak these prosecutions as seemingly legitimate, often dressing up anti-Shi`a crackdowns as part of a global effort against terrorism.

NOTES

1. Staci Strobl, "Women and Policing in Bahrain" (PhD diss., City University of New York: 2007); Staci Strobl, "The Women's Police Directorate in Bahrain: An Ethnographic Exploration of Gender Segregation and the Likelihood of Future Integration." *International Criminal Justice Review* 18 (2008): 39–58; Strobl, Staci, and Hung-En Sung, "Attitudes about Gender Integration among Bahraini Policewomen." *Policing & Society* 19 (2009): 425–441.
2. Although female police primarily work on cases related to juveniles or women as victims, perpetrators or witnesses, they also work on public nuisance complaints when stations are short-staffed, as was the case in this situation.

3. Exceedingly helpful at this time was the following source, which directly confronted sectarianism in Bahrain though not necessarily with a focus on criminal justice: International Crisis Group, "Bahrain's Sectarian Challenge," *Middle East Report* 40 (2005): 1–20.

4. e.g. Emile Nakhleh, *Bahrain: Political Development in a Modernizing Society* (Lexington Books: 2011). Nakhleh mentions the problems of anti-Shi`a policies in Bahrain, but does not provide much detail, nor uses it as a major analytic category to describe the political and social development of the country. The bare mention of sectarian discrimination and the focus on Shi`a extremism as a problem of terrorism, taken out of its local, social, and historical context, also characterizes the work of Anthony Cordesman. His work parrots the official stance of the Bahraini government without critical engagement. See Anthony H. Cordesman, *Bahrain, Oman, Qatar, and the United Arab Emirates: Challenges of Security* (Westview Press: 1997).

5. See Shehabi, Ala'a and Marc Owen Jones (editors), *Bahrain's Uprising: Resistance and Repression in the Gulf*, (London, Zed Books, 2015); Toby Mattheisen, *Sectarian Gulf: Bahrain, Saudi Arabia, and the Arab Spring that Wasn't* (Stanford Briefs/Stanford University Press, 2013); and Frederic M. Wehrey, *Sectarian Politics in the Gulf: From the Iraq War to the Arab Uprisings* (New York: Columbia University Press, 2014).

6. Homi Bhabha, *The Location of Culture*. (Routledge: 1994): 250.

7. Clifford Geertz, *The Interpretation of Cultures: Selected Essays*. New York: Basic Books, 1973.

8. Mary Douglas, *Purity and Danger: An Analysis of Concept of Pollution and Taboo* (London: Routledge, 1966).

9. Douglas 1966: 159

10. This definition is a reversion back to that coined by James Q. Wilson in which order maintenance in criminal justice is a police function of reacting to or preventing "...that [which] disturbs or threatens to disturb the public peace or that involves face-to-face conflict among two or more persons" [James Q. Wilson, "Dilemmas of Police Administration." *Public Administration Review* 28 (1968): 407]. I do not refer here to the more modern, criminal justice conception of "order maintenance" as a style of policing associated with crackdowns on public nuisance offenses as a bulwark against greater criminality, alternatively called zero tolerance policing [David Thacher. "Order maintenance policing." in *The Oxford Handbook of Police and Policing*, ed. Michael D. Reisig and Robert J. Kane (Oxford University Press: 2014): 122–124].

11. Robert Reiner, *The Politics of the Police* (Brighton: Wheatsheaf, 1985).

12. Egon Bittner, *The Functions of the Police in Modern Society* (Oelgeschlager, Gunn & Hain: 1970/1979): 30.

13. Jean-Paul Brodeur, *The Policing Web* (Oxford University Press, 2010).

14. William J. Chambliss, *Power, Politics and Crime* (Westview Press, 2001); James Messerschmidt, *Crime as Structured Action: Gender, Race, Class, and Crime in the Making* (Sage Publications: 1997); Jock Young, "Radical Criminology in Britain: The Emergence of a Competing Paradigm." *British Journal of Criminology* 28 (1988): 159; Thorsten Sellin, "Culture Conflict and Crime," *American Journal of Sociology* 44 (1938): 97–103.

15. Young 2002.

16. e.g., Michelle Alexander. *The New Jim Crow: Mass Incarceration in the Age of Colorblindness* (The New Press, 2012); Ian Lopez, *White by Law: The Legal Construction of Race*. New York: New York University Press: 2006); Loïc Wacquant, "The New 'Peculiar Institution': On the Prison as Surrogate Ghetto." *Theoretical Criminology* 4 (2000): 377–389.

17. Article 18 of the *Constitution of the Kingdom of Bahrain* (2002).

18. The Arab Spring-related events in Bahrain are also known as the "Bahrain Spring," which." They occurred throughout 2011, starting on the social-media orchestrated "day of rage" of February 14, and consisting of demonstrations throughout February and March by Bahraini Shi`a, human rights advocates and others standing in opposition to the government. Crackdowns by the government led to violence killing 30 civilians and 5 policemen. Three thousand people were arrested. Since March 2011, 45 people have been killed related to this conflict (British Broadcasting Corporation [BBC]), "Arab Uprising—Country by Country: Bahrain," December 2013, http://www.bbc.com/news/world-12482295). New laws have been

passed in order to revoke the citizenship of anti-government activists, criminalizing anti-government speeches, and serving as punishment for the unrest. Kareem Fahim, "In crackdown, Bahrain revokes the citizenship of 31 people." *The New York Times*, November 7, 2012; Bahrain Center for Human Rights, "Bahrain Revokes Citizenship of 71 People," February 2, 2015, http://www.bahrainrights.org/en/node/7264http://www.genocidewatch.org/images/Bahrain_12_11_07_in_crackdown_bahrain_revokes_the_citizenship_of_31_people.pdf; Zahr Albarazi, and Jason E. Tucker. "Citizenship as Political Tool: The Recent Turmoil in the MENA and the Creation and Resolution of Statelessness." (Tilburg University Law School: 2014).

19. Imad Salamey and Zanoubia Othman. "Shia revival and *welayat al-faqih* in the Making of Iranian Foreign Policy," *Politics, Religion, and Ideology*, 12 (2011): 197–212; Magdalena Karolak, "Religion in a Political Context: The Case of the Kingdom of Bahrain." *Asia Journal of Global Studies* 4 (2010): 4–20; Laurence Louër, *Transnational Shia Politics: Religious and Political Networks in the Gulf* (London: Hurst, 2008); Roschanack Shaery-Eisenlohr, "Imagining Shi'ite Iran: Transnationalism and Religious Authenticity in the Muslim World." *Iranian Studies* 40 (2007): 17–35; Vali Nasr, *The Shia Revival: How Conflicts Within Islam Will Shape the Future* (W.W. Norton & Co., 2006).

20. Wehrey 2014.

21. Ibrahim Sharif, "A trial of thoughts and ideas," In *Bahrain's Uprising: Resistance and Repression in the Gulf*, edited by Ala'a Shehabi and Marc Owen Jones (London, Zed Books, 2015): 43–60; Frederic M. Wehrey, *Sectarian Politics in the Gulf: From the Iraq War to the Arab Uprisings* (New York: Columbia University Press, 2014); Toby Mattheisen, *Sectarian Gulf: Bahrain, Saudi Arabia, and the Arab Spring that Wasn't* (Stanford Briefs/Stanford University Press, 2013); Staci Strobl, "From Colonial Policing to Community Policing in Bahrain: The Historical Persistence of Sectarianism," *International Journal of Comparative and Applied Criminal Justice* 35 (2011):19–37; Vali Nasr, *The Shia Revival: How Conflicts Within Islam Will Shape the Future* (New York: W.W. Norton & Co., 2006).

22. Marc Owen Jones, "Rotten Apples or Rotten Orchards: Police Deviance, Brutality and Unaccountability in Bahrain" In *Bahrain's Uprising: Resistance and Repression in the Gulf*, ed. Ala'a Shehabi and Marc Owen Jones (London, Zed Books, 2015): 207–238; Bahrain Independent Commission of Inquiry, *Report of the Bahrain Independent Commission of Inquiry*, November 23, 2011: http://www.bici.org.bh/BICIreportEN.pdf; Brian Dooley (with Staci Strobl), "Four Years On, U.S Should Push Bahrain to Reform Security Forces," *Huffington Post*, February 13, 2015, http://www.huffingtonpost.com/brian-dooley/four-years-on-us-should-p_b_6680326.html.

23. Zainab Al-Khawaja, "Bahrain, a Brutal Ally," *The New York Times*, December 25, 2012, https://www.questia.com/newspaper/1P2–36296158/bahrain-a-brutal-ally. Human Rights Watch, "Saudi Arabia: 5–Year Sentence for Rights Defender: Increasing Crackdowns on Activists," June 23, 2013, https://www.hrw.org/news/2013/06/22/saudi-arabia-5–year-sentence-rights-defender.

24. George Steinmetz, *The Devil's Handwriting: Precoloniality and the German Colonial State in Qingdao, Samoa, and Southwest Africa*. (University of Chicago Press, 2008): 40

25. Young, Jock, J. Ferrell, and Keith Hayward. *Cultural Criminology: An Invitation*. (Sage: 2008).

26. David L. Altheide, "Reflections: Ethnographic content analysis." *Qualitative Sociology* 10 (1987): 68.

27. Carrington, Kerry, and Ashleigh Larkin. "The Politics of Doing Imaginative Criminological Research." *Liquid Criminology: Doing Imaginative Criminological Research* (2016): 188.

28. Carrington, Kerry, Russell Hogg, and Máximo Sozzo. "Southern Criminology," *British Journal of Criminology*, 56 (2016): 1–20.

29. Staci Strobl, "Not so Notorious: Crimes Committed by Bahraini Women in the Kingdom of Bahrain." *Al-Raida Journal* (2006): 18–24; Strobl 2008; Staci Strobl, "Postcolonial Policing and the 'Woman' Question: A History of the Women's Police Directorate in Bahrain," *Policing and Prisons in the Middle East: Formations of Coercion* (Hurst: 2010); Strobl, Staci. "Progressive or Neo-Traditional?: Policewomen in Gulf Cooperation Council (GCC) Countries." *Feminist Formations* 22 (2010): 51–74; Strobl 2011; Staci Strobl, "'The Dream Recently Came

True': Globalization and Media Discourse about Kuwaiti Policewomen." *Nidaba* 1 (2016): 6–18.

30. Meant here as referring to the process of globalization of economic activity and capitalism that has radically altered most countries' institutions and social relations [Wacquant, Loïc, *Punishing the Poor* (Durham, NC: Duke University Press: 2009)].

31. Joseph Donnermeyer, "The Place of Rural in a Southern Criminology," *International Journal for Crime, Justice and Social Democracy* 6 (2017): 128.

32. Braudel, Fernand, and Immanuel Wallerstein, "History and the Social Sciences: The *Longue Durée*," *Review (Fernand Braudel Center)* 32 (2009): 171–203, http://www.jstor.org/stable/40647704.

33. Michel Foucault, *The Archaeology of Knowledge* (New York: Harper and Row, 1972).

34. Glen Balfour-Paul, *The End of Empire in the Middle East: Britain's Relinquishment of Power in its Last Three Arab Dependencies* (Cambridge University Press, 1991).

35. Nelida Fuccaro. *Histories of city and state in the Persian Gulf: Manama since 1800.* (Cambridge University Press, 2009): 55.

36. James Onley, *The Arabian Frontier of the British Raj: Merchants, Rulers, and the British in the Nineteenth-Century Gulf* (Oxford: Oxford University Press, 2007): 280.

37. Radford, Kristopher "Curzon's Cruise: The Pomp and Circumstance of Indian Indirect Rule of the Persian Gulf." *The International History Review* 4 (2013): 884–904; 894.

38. Radford, Kristopher "Curzon's Cruise: The Pomp and Circumstance of Indian Indirect Rule of the Persian Gulf." *The International History Review* 4 (2013): 884–904; 894.

39. Radford 2013: 891.

40. Radford 2013.

41. Radford 2013: 892.

42. Mahdi Abdalla Al-Tajir, *Bahrain 1920–1945: Britain, the Shaikh and the Administration* (London: Croom Helm, 1987).

43. Potter, Lawrence G. "Introduction" in *Sectarian Politics in the Persian Gulf*, edited by Lawrence G. Potter (Oxford: Oxford University Press, 2014): 8.

44. Charles Tilly, "War Making and State Making as Organized Crime." In *Bringing the State Back In*, ed. Evans, Peter B., Dietrich Rueschemeyer, and Theda Skocpol (Cambridge, MA: Cambridge University Press, 1985): 169–187.

45. Torpey, John. *The Invention of the Passport: Surveillance, Citizenship and the State* (Cambridge University Press: 2000): 7.

46. William Sewell, *Logics of History: Social Theory and Social Transformation* (Chicago: University of Chicago Press, 2005).

47. Steinmetz, 2008: 598.

48. Kwami Kwarteng, *Ghosts of Empire: British Legacies in the Modern World* (New York: Public Affairs: 2013): 3.

49. Paul J. Rich, *Creating the Arabian Gulf: The British Raj and the Invasions of the Gulf* (Lanham, MD: Lexington Books, 2009).

50. Fuccarro 2009: 115.

51. Charles Dalrymple Belgrave, *Personal Column* (Beirut: Librairie du Liban, 1960/1972).

52. Spivak 1999: 208

53. Spivak 1999: 208

54. Spivak 1999: 239

55. Edward Said, *Culture and Imperialism* (London: Vintage Books, 1993): 378

56. Bhabha 1994: 185

57. Bhabha 1994: 188

58. Gayatri Chakravorty Spivak, "Can the subaltern speak?" *Can the Subaltern Speak? Reflections on the History of an Idea* (1988): 21–78.

59. David M. Anderson and David Killingray. *Policing the Empire: Government, Authority, and Control, 1830–1940* (Manchester University Press: 1991); Georgina Sinclair, and Chris A. Williams., "'Home and away': The Cross-Fertilisation between 'Colonial 'and 'British' Policing, 1921–85." *Journal of Imperial and Commonwealth History* 35 (2007): 221–238; Charles Joseph Jeffries, *The Colonial Police* (M. Parrish, 1952).

60. Jeffries 1952: 17.

61. Hills, Alice, Gary N. Siperstein, Norman Anthony Wieseler, and Ronald Halton Hanson, *Policing Africa: Internal Security and the Limits of Liberalization* (Lynne Rienner Publishers, 2000): 5.
62. Gayatri Chakravorty Spivak, "World Systems and the Creole," *Narrative* 14 (2006): 102–112.
63. Said 1993; Spivak, 1999.
64. For example, in *Al-Amn* magazine, published by the Ministry of the Interior to highlight security-sector accomplishments, we see the use of Western-style inclusive and democratic language to paradoxically condemn political and ideological speech, a thinly disguised way of constructing the Shi`a as an internal enemy. An editorial in the magazine, entitled "Our Belief in Dialogue Remains Firm," blamed the country's unrest on those "claiming to call for freedom and democracy" but who have a "selfish mindset." For the sake of the "homeland" we must criminalize "the abusers of social media who sing out of tune." [Lt. Col. Muhammad bin Dana, "Our Belief in Dialogue Remains Firm," *Al-Amn* 42 (March 2013): 38.]
65. Radford 2013: 889.
66. Leopold J. Pospisil, *Anthropology of Law: A Comparative Theory* (New York: Harper Row, 1971). Like Pospisil, I also assume here a very elastic notion of what is law, including any social code or formation of rules that regulate a social group through designating punishable behavior, and not just the codified formalism of modern legal regime.
67. Roberto Mangabeira Unger, *Knowledge and Politics* (New York: Simon and Schuster: 1976).
68. Bracey, Dorothy, *Exploring Law and Culture* (Long Grove, IL: Waveland Press Inc., 2006).
69. Merry, Sally Engle, "Foreword," in Goodale, Mark, *Anthropology and Law: A Critical Introduction* (New York: New York University Press, 2017): ix-xii.
70. Lauren Benton, *Law and Colonial Culture: Legal Regimes in World History, 1400–1900*. (Cambridge University Press: 2002).
71. Spivak 1999: 310.
72. Benton 2002: 254.
73. Goodale, Mark, *Anthropology and Law: A Critical Introduction* (New York: New York University Press, 2017): 18.
74. Partha Chatterjee, *Nationalist Thought and the Colonial World: A Derivative Discourse* (London: Zed Books, 1986).
75. Chatterjee, 1986: 16
76. Chatterjee, 1986: 17
77. Norbert Elias, *The Civilizing Process* (Malden, MA: Blackwell Publishing, 1939/1982).
78. Elias, 1939: 253.
79. Elias 1939/1982: 254.
80. Chatterjee, 1986: 303.
81. Elias, 1939/1982: 271.
82. Bracey 2006: 21.
83. I intended to include all criminal cases since the beginning of the OiC reform in Bahrain in 1919. The first surviving case from this time period, however, is dated 1924.
84. Tuson, Penelope. *A Brief Guide to Sources for Middle East Studies in the India Office Records*. (London: India Office Library and Records, 1982); Tuson, Penelope. *The Records of the British Residence and Agencies in the Persian Gulf.* (London: India Office Records [IOR R/15], British Library, 1979).
85. Tuson 1979: xiv.
86. Bracey 2006: 38.
87. Tuson, Penelope. *A brief guide to sources for Middle East Studies in the India Office Records*. (London: India Office Library and Records, 1982); Tuson, Penelope. *The records of the British Residence and Agencies in the Persian Gulf.* (London: India Office Records [IOR R/15], British Library, 1979).
88. Tuson 1982; Tuson 1979.
89. Tuson 1982: 8.
90. Tuson 1979: xiii-xiv.

91. "The Police: Conditions Twenty Years Ago," Annual Report of the Bahrain Government, 1945–1946 (India Office Records, R/15/2/306).
92. "The Police: Development of the State Police," Annual Report of the Bahrain Government, 1945–1946 (India Office Records, R/15/2/306).
93. Annual Report of the Bahrain Government, 1365 (India Office Records, R/15/2/306, 1933).
94. This is the population at the 1941 census; it was estimated as lower in the late 1920s. Fahim I. Qubain, "Social Classes and Tensions in Bahrain," *Middle East Journal*, 9, 3 (Summer, 1955): 270.
95. Annual Report of the Bahrain Government, 1945–1946 (India Office Records, R/15/2/306).
96. Belgrave, personal diaries, August 12, 1935; January 7, 1936.
97. Belgrave, personal diaries, August 14, 1935.
98. Altheide 1987: 68.
99. Bracey 2006: 21.

Chapter One

Land and Sea

The Two Historical Disruptions and Sectarian Order Maintenance

In 1900, a murder occurred in the Arabian desert that may represent one of the last major external Sunni tribal skirmishes to significantly impact the sovereignty of the Al Khalifah, freeing them up to concentrate their powers on criminalizing internal tribal rivalry and subjugating Shi`a communities. In the final years before the advent of the full British administration of Bahrain, security treaties solidified the imperial relationship between the Al Khalifah and the British, the latter of whom used Gulf tribes to balance its main rivalry in the region before World War I, the Ottomans. At the turn of the century, native agents in Manama reported to New Delhi and London as to the state of affairs in Bahrain, but did little to influence or impinge upon Al Khalifah rule. After this murder of an important member of the Al Khalifah family and his entourage, the British would favor a more hands-on approach to its Bahrain protectorate.

THE MASSACRE WHILE HUNTING *HUBARA* AND THE CRIMINALIZATION OF INTRA-SUNNI COMPETITION

On November 18, 1900, Sheikh Salman bin Daij Al Khalifah, a close relative of the ruler, Sheikh Isa bin Ali Al Khalifah, traveled to the Arabian mainland south of Qatif, crossing into Ottoman territory, on a hunting expedition. Accompanying him were his sons Daij and Bishir, a nephew named Abdulrahman bin Rashid, twenty followers, and some representatives (*rufaqa*) from various regional tribes.[1] Sheikh Salman bin Daij had a *rafiq* from the

Al-Murra tribe, one from the ‘Ajman, and two from the Bani Hajr. Imagining such an expedition, the likes of which have been largely lost to history, the Sheikh probably packed tents on camels, camped in a desert spot near water, and enjoyed the pleasant winter weather hawking and hunting *hubara* (the lesser bustard). According to an ethnographic account of early twentieth century *hubara* hunting, the sport is not without its spectacle. “If the attack is successful, the spectator sees a white flutter of feather and tail, a scuffle on the ground, possibly several swoops on the part of the hawk, then all is quiet as the hawk seizes his quarry by the neck.”[2]

Unfortunately, the elaborate hunt would come to an end a couple weeks later in early December when a group of about fourteen men of the Dawasir tribe encamped near Sheikh Salman, and then were joined by a large group of Al-Murra tribesmen. One night, a little after midnight, the Dawasir and Al-Murra ambushed Sheikh Salman’s hunting party “and massacred them all except Bishir and two followers who escaped with wounds. One of the Sheikh’s negroes was said to have killed three of the attacking party before he was killed. The [Dawasir] . . . managed to escape to their boats and offered no assistance to Sheikh Salman,”[3] according to John C. Gaskin, a British political assistant assigned to investigate the matter.

The apparent cause of the violence was a two-year old blood feud between the Amamera tribe of Bahrain and the Al-Murra. The Al Khalifahs had not previously been directly involved in the feud; however, their association with the Amamera, in the eyes of the Al-Murra, legitimated the massacre as retaliation against past killings. According to traditional blood feud customs, an intentional death can be paid for with a revenge killing; however, another option is that the aggrieved party can instead extract money compensation (*fasl* or *diyah*). According to the Political Assistant, Al Khalifah outrage was so immense at the murder of Sheikh Salman and his followers that they appealed to their security alliance with the British to assist them in punishing the Al-Murra. The assistant wrote:

> [Sheikh Isa, ruler of Bahrain,] begged me to request you to move Her Majesty’s Government to make strong representations to the Turkish Government for the summary punishment of the murderers. He added that if the perpetrators of the outrage are permitted to remain unpunished the prestige and peace hitherto enjoyed by the rulers on Bahrain through the protection afforded by the British Govt will be destroyed and it will be thought that the people of Bahrain are incompetent to defend themselves and consequently they will be open to much maltreatment when met by lawless tribesmen, and under the circumstances he would be obliged to ask the British Government for permission to organize with the help of some friendly tribes, an expedition against the Almurra.

The massacre turned out to be a thorny political situation for several years. The British apparently convinced the Turkish government to punish the tribes, but ultimately no such punishment occurred. The following account of contact between the political assistant and the relevant pasha in Al-Hasa tuned up skepticism at the purpose of Sheikh Salman's hunting party:

> Mohsin Pasha stated . . . that he had given orders for the arrest and punishment of the guilty parties, not only in order to satisfy the Sheikh of Bahrein [sic], but also because the laws of Turkey required it in the ordinary course of procedure. But in the meantime he would like to know what was the real object of the murdered men's visit to the Main land [sic] at a place where they had already incurred the enmity of the inhabitants by committing a murder last year. His Excellency seemed to imply that they had gone there again with some object which would not bear investigation, and that the hunting excursion was only a blind.[4]

At the allegation of nefarious Bahraini intentions, Britain and Turkey began to argue in the weeds of Arab tribal conflict. Gaskin pointed out that the Al Khalifahs had nothing to do with the Amamera blood feud against the Al-Murra "having no connection with the Amamera except that the latter reside in their territory, [and they] are therefore not liable to answer for any murderous acts committed by the Amamera who have in this instance taken the life of the son in the place of the life of one of their tribesmen killed by the Behaih [branch of the Al-Murra]." Further, he argued that the Al-Murra could have opted for blood money to resolve the issue under tribal custom.[5] And, it was also determined that the Al Khalifah had already paid *diyah* to the Al-Murra on behalf of the Amamera tribe for the underlying conflict. They provided a mare, clothes, and 1,060 rupees in cash. Meanwhile, with the conversations between Turkey and Bahrain leading to no action, the Al Khalifah asked for permission from the British to engage in a blood feud with the Al-Murra by:

> arrang[ing] with some friendly Arabs on the mainland to attack them with a view to avenge the murder of Sheikh Salman. I informed [the Al Khalifah] that such an attempt on their part would be displeasing to the [British] Government and be harmful to the issues with the negotiation with the Turkish Government, and [they] being strictly prohibited from undertaking operations beyond [their] own territory.[6]

In the subsequent years, other solutions to the problem of Al-Murra impunity were debated, including sailing British gunboats near the Al-Hasa shore while negotiating with the Turkish government to pay compensation to Bahrain (as a creative substitute for resolving the blood feud in local style),[7] having the Qatari government punish the Al-Murra when they decamp in Qatari territory, having the Qataris act as meditators in the conflict,[8] or implementing a trade embargo against the Turkish ports of Al-Hasa. Ultimately, the issue was never resolved and Sheikh Isa, ruler of Bahrain, was forced by the British to accept a limited response of merely excluding the guilty parties from his archipelago. "Sheikh Esa [sic] should at the same time be informed that His Majesty's Government will not countenance any excessive action on his part in pursuance of this policy."[9]

Several important themes emerge around the massacre of Sheikh Salman and his entourage, and the subsequent political crisis. First, the world of Sunni Arab tribes from the interior of the Arabian peninsula contrasted greatly with the Turkish and British worlds of the contestations in the Great Game. Where the European powers were competing for control over trade routes for the resource depletion of wide swathes of land demarcated by fixed boundaries, the Arab tribes were semi-nomadic, routinely moving in mutually inhabited areas despite various inter-tribal animosities. Sheikh Salman's hunting party crossed into the mainland in a historic and customary route, but in 1900, that excursion meant leaving one major empire for another. What may on the surface appear to be a local conflict ultimately would drag in high-level imperial authorities who found themselves debating customary blood feud traditions and coming close to blows.

The Al Khalifah's lack of violent response to the massacre in 1900 broke with their customs, showing how performance of political power in the Arab Gulf was dramatically changing. In pursuit of *pax Brittanica* in the region,[10] the British used their influence to effectively criminalize tribal warfare; the result of this incident was to deter the Al Khalifah from acting as a powerful tribe in the customary way, gradually replacing that with the kind of administrative command and control of the nation-state. The might of the Al Khalifah would no longer be performed with the Arab tribal sword, but rather with the alliance of a much more powerful weapon, the backing of the British navy in the Gulf. For the Al Khalifah, the advantage of acquiescing to Britain meant they and their claim on Bahrain would not get swallowed up by the many larger powers around them, such as the Ottomans, Iran, and the Wahhabis, at various times.[11] Other Sunni tribes would be mostly kept in check by the Al Khalifah alliance with the British. Meanwhile, the maintenance of Al Khalifah social order would increasingly center on subjugating Shi`a, another source of competition for legitimacy in the archipelago, and one that continues to challenge Al Khalifah rule today, long after tribal warfare.

SECTARIANISM AND THE TWO HISTORICAL DISRUPTIONS

Two major historical disruptions in Bahraini history are central to understanding how sectarianism and order maintenance developed into the shape criminal justice takes today. These two historical disruptions, understood as structure changing events that are also cultural transformations,[12] together ushered in the contemporary Sunni hegemony and Shi`a oppression that takes stark form in the criminal justice system. The tribal murder of Sheikh Salman bin Daij occurred on the eve of the second major event. Even before that, the first historical disruption occurred: the Al-Khalifa tribe conquering Bahrain in the eighteenth century. The second major disruption is the colonial, administrative restructuring and the building of the modern nation-state of Bahrain between 1919 and 1927. In fact, the cache of colonial criminal case files examined in subsequent chapters point to the ripple effect of the second disruption as it became articulated in the official criminal, legal record, showing the quickly changing contours of Bahraini society, politics, and criminal justice.

THE "PEOPLE OF THE SEA": DIVERSITY AND TOLERANCE AROUND TRADE

To paint a picture of how the first disruption profoundly unsettled Bahraini society, it is necessary to begin many centuries back. Before the first disruption in the eighteenth century, many external entities claimed whole or parts of Bahrain, including the Persians and the Portuguese; however, these powers never invested in major social or political reform of what was then a Gulf Coast society distinct from other parts of the Middle East. Without overly reducing the importance of their influences, the Portuguese, for example, focused primarily on profiting from Gulf trading routes and allowed local mercantile communities to govern and police themselves (except in the more heavily colonized Musandam Peninsula along the Strait of Hormuz).[13] In Bahrain, the Portuguese ruled from 1507 to 1622,[14] and an indigenous tradition of order maintenance carried on as it always had been in the context of free trade and religious tolerance, existing within a larger network of communities along the Arabian Gulf littoral and into the Indian Ocean. The Gulf's people moved freely and migrated often among small port villages and cities, more connected to each other than to the interior, which was difficult to get to due to long desert stretches between oases and settlements. As a result of cross-coastal travel and exchange among the people of the Arabian and Persian shores of the Gulf, the water, not the land, was the center of things.[15] Compared to other regions of the Middle East, at this time Gulf people were less urbanized. Large groups were semi-nomadic, travelling with the trade winds and by season along the Gulf Coast and into the Indian Ocean.

The Arabian Gulf Coast experienced the waxing and waning of a variety of Muslim empires that claimed it, such as the Abbasid, Seljuk, and Safavid. Despite their strong influence in other parts of the region, these empires had little effect over the routine lives of Bahraini people except by way of military pass-throughs and requisite tax collections. Practically speaking, Gulf society before the seventeenth century can be considered a history of loose political networks which allowed the Indian Ocean culture to flourish as a maritime system of small businesses, trade by dhow, pearling and fishing endeavors, and agriculture.[16] Within this system, more affluent owners of small-scale operations did not consider their laborers as employees in a capitalist sense, but rather as their *jama'a* (followers), understood in a clan-based sense. Despite social cohesion around trade, the political structure was devoid of a center and could be characterized as a system of negotiated economic relationships between sea-faring commercial families or clans.[17] Some historians have put forth the argument that these networks should be considered bona fide political states, such as post-Safavid Gulf society based on pearl trading[18] and the political cohesion of the Qawasim tribe (sea-faring group from Sharjah and Ras al-Khaimah who converted to Wahhabism in the early nineteenth century) along the coast from approximately 1750 to 1860.[19] Constructed as "pirates" by the British in the nineteenth century, they were rivals to the British navy in the Gulf; in the early nineteenth century they attacked ships of the East India Company for failing to pay tribute for passage. In 1819, the British navy destroyed Qawasim boats and ports, effectively crippling them.[20]

The common culture of the Indian Ocean had an elastic sense of social order. Mutually beneficial trade effected unity among a wide variety of ethnic, religious, and racial clans who cooperated, intermarried, and held a common folkloric tradition with elements borrowed from the coasts of East Africa and South India (e.g., musical styles, traditional foods). Among cultural and material artifacts that signal a Gulf/Indian Ocean common identity, a syncretic spiritual tradition, *zar*, evolved from African and Muslim roots, forming a major Gulf religious orientation outside of traditional Islam. Performed in small pockets of Bahrain today is the shaman-like ritual for healing during which practitioners go into a trance in order to manage the *jinn* [evil spirits] that are possessing them and causing strife. In addition, folk wisdom and small superstitions based on *zar* also survive.[21]

Gulf people labeled themselves the "people of the dhow,"[22] the *ahl-i-hava* ("people of the wind" in Persian)[23] and the "people of the sea."[24] The cross-cultural unity of being a people despite differences in ethnic, racial, and even religious identity, may have its origins in the variety and diversity of the crews on the trade dhows. Many were virtual slaves to their masters, but cooperated on long journeys over the course of a pearl diving season. It was not uncommon for workers and captains to have relationships with women in multiple ports and multiple families across the coast, contributing to regional unity.[25]

Importantly, the Gulf Coast (as well as the Swahili Coast) was a relatively safe region for divergent religious sects to settle, particularly when Sunni imperial masters and tribes in the interior cracked down on alleged Shi`a apostasy.[26] Shi`a religious practices freely developed in Bahrain well into the eighteenth century. When claimed by the Safavid Empire, Bahrain was a particularly rich Shi`a theological and cultural space. The Safavids permitted Bahrain and other Gulf societies to police and govern themselves, relying on Shi`a and Persian ties to bolster a political patronage system. At the same time, Safavid rulers used forced conversions of Sunnis to the Shi`a sect in order to control and punish throughout their empire, and unlike the sect-tolerance of the indigenous Gulf people, the Safavids privileged Shi`a throughout their conquered lands.

Alternatively, some historians believe that in the eighteenth century the Al Madhkur tribe of Iran held Bahrain. The tribe was stationed at that time in Bushehr, and collected taxes and tribute from Bahrainis,[27] but scant evidence exists to determine how much direct control it wielded. Notably, Shi`a oral tradition avers that Shi`a jurists kept control of Bahrain at this time and it was not a part of Iran via the Al Madhkur. The oral tradition indicates that Bahrain was "three hundred villages and thirty cities and towns" organized under "a council of three, elected by an assembly of thirty-three" who together organized property rights via Islamic law.[28]

In any case, indigenous Gulf crime and justice were reflected the most important customary laws of the day, revolving around commercial pursuits. According to historians, pearl divers and other workers were not paid in wages, but shared in profits; as a result, their livelihoods were subject to Gulf market conditions. Colonial observers reported that by the late nineteenth and early twentieth century, the pearl traders charged exorbitant interest fees being charged for profit-sharing advances, practiced shady bookkeeping, and used unpaid labor that could be characterized as virtual slavery. An evolved practice of commercial arbitration developed with commercial conflicts heard and resolved at the *majlis-al-urf* (customary council)[29] or in the municipal *majlis* within port enclaves.[30]

Non-commercial matters were the purview of the *qadi*s, Muslim clerical judges who heard conflicts related to social behavior and wrongdoing and made decisions based on Muslim legal tradition and local custom. The *qadis* were trained within their sect-based religious traditions (mostly Shi`a at this time, but there were Sunni *qadis* as well).[31] They adjudicated orally and in a variety of moving venues and did not record information about their cases in any existing written format. It is important to highlight that within the Gulf sea-faring communities, the two sect-based traditions of adjudication were separate, but coexisted.

Any manifestation of institutional sectarianism could hypothetically extend back to the original conflicts within Muslim societies around the caliphate's leadership, which gave rise to the fundamental split between the Sunni and Shi`a branches in the first place. Indeed, the original upheaval is a historical antecedent to the topic at hand, but the focus here is how the social groups and identities that embody the split have symbolic power during competitions for control in Bahrain in later centuries. It is very difficult to talk about "Islam" as it has been experienced and practiced in Bahrain without considering "sect." Islam has almost never been practiced in the Gulf region outside one of these sect-based traditions, nor has any major pan-Islamic ideology ever taken hold in the Gulf; in other words, the day-to-day practice of Bahraini Islam has been within a sectarian framework and its return to Muslim piety in recent decades involves sect-adherences.

Therefore, this book avoids essentializing the split as setting up an inevitable path to sectarian conflict, nor erroneously asserting that any sectarian conflict is necessarily a theological argument. Rather, the historical importance of previous events related to sectarianism factor into the forms that social life takes locally, and the identities of social groups in competition for power and authority. Additional social identities around mercantile groups and hereditary tribal clans also form facets of social organization, but as will be shown below, eventually become secondary to the sectarian framework cemented into the modern state of Bahrain and its criminal justice system.

THE FIRST DISRUPTION: "PEOPLE OF THE SEA" OVERTAKEN BY THE "PEOPLE OF THE LAND"

Imperial neglect of indigenous Bahrain comes to an end in the eighteenth century as two major powers, with distinct notions of political and cultural order, find themselves in contest for local authority: the aforementioned proto-capitalist Arabian Gulf/Indian Ocean common seafaring society; and Sunni tribal groups encroaching from the interior, including the Al Khalifah, an off-shoot of the Bani 'Utab tribe, who arrive in the eighteenth century. Historians differ as to the cause for the migrations with some pinning down the motivation as drought and famine conditions further in the interior.[32] Others believe that the growing power of the Wahhabis in the interior forced them out. Another account points to internal strife in the Jumaila tribe, which led to new alliances.[33] Under this causation narrative, the Al-Khalifa faced the choice of either being subjugants to the Jumaila or migrating, and they chose the latter.[34] All of these motivations amount to the resulting Al Khalifah commitment to conquer Bahrain and make it their home.

In establishing their presence as the royal family of Bahrain (by way of Zubarah on the Qatari peninsula, taking the territory from Persia), they enforced a new political and social order in the region that was structurally and culturally divergent from the indigenous Gulf/Indian Ocean mercantile communities. In an important contribution to the understanding of Bahraini sectarianism, Justin Gengler describes contemporary Sunni oral history about the coming of the Al-Khalifah as a manifest narrative of conquest. The Al Khalifa leader who led his people to Bahrain is referred to as "*Al Fatih*" (the conqueror; Ahmed bin Muhammad Al Khalifah). *Fatih* comes from the root "to open" and, Gengler explains that Shi`a, as a play on words, remember themselves in the same event as the "*al-maftuh*" (the opened).[35]

In any case, interior Sunni tribes can be categorized as proto-states or small-scale societies. The tribes in and around Bahrain numbered from 5,000 to 25,000 members. Many scholars have characterized the juxtaposition of Sunni tribes and indigenous littoral peoples as a *badu-hadar* heterogeneity with the *badu* being interior Sunni tribal Arabs like the Al Khalifah, and the *hadar* being the indigenous urban, seafaring settled people[36] (though as aforementioned, many sea-farers were semi-nomadic). The tribal leadership of the *badu*, in the form of a sheikh, organized protection for the tribe's people, administered justice, and collected taxes, for which they required loyalty.[37]

The Sunni tribes brought with them customs related to honor and loyalty to a patriarchal and hereditary clan-based structure,[38] different from the exchange-based relationships of the indigenous Gulf. For example, the *dakhalah* system of protector-protégé relationships[39] in tribal culture involved interacting with other groups, including Bahrain's more indigenous people, in a hierarchical manner. The Sunni tribes extracted tolls for protection (*khuwa*) from local Bahraini populations. They also warred with each other and brought interior tribal conflicts to the coast, as shown above in the massacre of the Sheikh Salman bin Daij and his followers south of Qatif on the mainland. The Sunni tribes moved within broadly defined and relatively fluid spheres of control on land (*dirah*) that sometimes overlapped with each other. Arab tribes internally did not view the land they travelled upon as a distinct territory in the Western sense.[40] Rather, the *dirah* was an orbit or a softly defined zone by which points of contact with other tribes, often at oases, were negotiated and renegotiated. Tribes granted safe passages through each other's *dirah*, and breaches of any oral agreements could lead to conflict.[41] During proceedings of the International Court of Justice case *Bahrain v. Qatar* (1996),[42] in which the two countries were at odds over territorial boundaries, members of the Naim tribe described their *dirah* as a homeland established by negotiations and *ikrimiyyah* (payments of patronage) with the Al Khalifah tribe. A Naim member testified to the court in 1996:

> When I was young, I would spend the winter with my family towards the north of the Qatar peninsula, and move further south in the summer. We lived mainly in the area between Hulwan and Lisha (about four kilometres [sic]

> from the shoreline of the Gulf of Bahrain) and Masaicha [Masarehah] but wandered up as far north as the ruined city of Zubarah, Al Arish and Al Thagab. At other times in the year we would reach places further south such as Al Na'man, Al Judaydah, Al Maharaqa and Umm Gabrain (Umm alGhubbur). We would set up a camp wherever we could find water nearby. This was our homeland.[43]

Another explained:

> The Zubarah region included Al Na'man Lisha, Hulwan, Aim Muhammed, Zubarah and Al Furaihah. There were about 3,000 Al Naim who lived there, about 2,000 of whom were Bedouin and about 1,000 who were *hadar* (settled). My family was *hadar*. The Zubarah region was part of the Ruler of Bahrain's territory and people were free to come and go between the main island of Bahrain and Zubarah.[44]

The tribal mode of expansion was primarily land-based though tribes sometimes took to the sea in order to reach land. Warfare was common among the tribes when they competed against each other for control of *dirah* throughout the Gulf littoral.

Meanwhile, the indigenous merchant communities were drawn into these conflicts happening in and around their ports of call, forced into paying *zakat* or *khuwa* or *ikrimiyyah* to a dominating tribe. The merchants, however, possessed some bargaining power. The merchant families exhibited an impressive diversity as Arab and Persian Sunnis and as Arab and Persian Shi`a, who competed with each other commercially but shared a common Indian Ocean culture, tolerated sect differences, and were savvy managers of the tribal powers in their vicinities. Settling in the littoral, the Sunni tribes began to rely on merchant operations more heavily for food, water, and other basic needs, and their taxation and tribute-paying operations expanded. In the course of the conquest, sect tolerance in the archipelago began to wane. Although disgruntled indigenous communities could switch their allegiances or transfer their operations to another *dirah*,[45] the encroachment of the Sunni tribes would inject sectarian worldviews into local cultures throughout the Gulf even as specific alliances shifted.

Group alliances at this time were inherently unstable (when considered from a Western perspective) although there is some historical evidence that this frequent alliance switching was part of the normative way of life on the Arabian Gulf littoral. For example, the Dawasir tribe was sometimes an ally of the Al Khalifah and at other times not. The Jalahimah tribe, also competing for Bahrain at the time of conquest, retreated to the Qatar peninsula, but continued a relentless attack on the Al Khalifah's acquired trade and shipping interests for several decades afterwards.[46] In 1800 and in 1801, the sultan of Muscat captured Bahrain, both times losing it, first to Al Khalifah retaliation and the second time to an Al Khalifah-Nejdi (Saudi) alliance.[47] The Al Khalifah themselves, in turn, paid tribute to Ibn Saud in the eighteenth and nineteenth centuries.

Meanwhile, the Persians claimed Bahrain throughout this period after having lost the archipelago in the post-Safavid period. Gulf ethnographer Peter Lienhardt suggests that before the adoption of the formal nation-state system in the early twentieth century, the people of the Gulf were accustomed to wide variations in power and influence over the course of their lifespans.[48] This wide variation, however, would stabilize as a result of colonial administration around the fixed rule of the Al Khalifah, making the back and forth of Sunni tribal power and control a historical relic, sometimes present but with waning effect on the overall state of affairs. Furthermore, as we shall see in the next chapter, unrest perpetrated by non-Khalifah-aligned Sunni tribes would increasingly be defined as criminal in the new Bahraini administrative order.

For now, suffice it to say, that the customary rules within the Sunni tribes and how they administered justice diverged from the indigenous, sea-faring societies. On a fundamental level, political legitimacy stemmed from tribal conquest, and the conquest of the Al Khalifa over its Shi`a subjects figures largely in contemporary, as well as historical, imaginings of the Bahrain state.[49] Customarily, in Sunni tribes, the leader was a *sheikh* among *sheikhs*, labeled such not based on a hereditary system, but rather after being selected from among the group of leading males in the tribe, who together organize conquests and/or tributes in relation to other nearby tribes. According to ethnographic accounts, a sheikh needed to have the following characteristics in order to be a suitable ruler: the personal attributes of wisdom, eloquence, and courage; the capacity to act paternally towards his people and protect them; the capacity to be accessible to his people by holding court regularly; and the characteristic of generosity in the form of sharing his resources among his people.[50] Conflicts within tribes were managed by an all-male tribunal (*majlis*) of *sheikhs* who would hear the grievances of people wronged and order a resolution. Sanctions for wrongdoing were enforced by the *majlis* as the primary protectors of their people's safety. It was routine to engage in consultation on decision making with other adult males in the tribe; this helped to maintain the legitimacy of the *majlis* within the tribe.[51] However, unresolved conflicts among the elites often resulted in new branches of the tribe splintering off under a disgruntled sheikh.[52]

Disputes related to Muslim law (*shari'a*) were dealt with in consultation with the *qadis* (customary judges) and his circle of *ulema*, or learned elite.[53] Third-party mediators emerged to resolve disputes before they were brought to the *majlis* and *ulema*.[54] Traditional conflict resolution customs used "sensitive symbolics."[55] Quranic passages instruct Muslims to maintain the peace among themselves, advocating for *hall wasat* (solution as middle way). Because of the Arab cultural focus on honor (*sharaf*) and the interconnectedness of the individual's reputation with the larger family, clan, or tribe, face-saving techniques within the tribe are preferred to overt conflict. A crucial part of the role of a Sunni Arab mediator is coming to a solution in which all the parties have an opportunity to save face (*dakhilah*). Within the Al Khalifah tribal context, qadis emerged and lived with tribes, acting as functionaries within the tribal system and organized into a tribal controlled hierarchy. At the same time, because their authority drew on religious tradition, they could also challenge the legitimacy of tribal rule.[56] It should be noted that their Shi`a counterparts were differently embedded and had more regionally-based legitimacy, falling under the authority of a *marja'* or religious cleric usually outside the archipelago. As Fuad Khuri explains, Sunni *qadi*s understood their authority as being derived through their tribe sheikhs, whereas the Shi`a jurists understood their roles more broadly. They served as a link for the religiously less knowledgeable with the more knowledgeable and had a populist bent. This communal orientation is represented by the religious community centers known as *ma'tam*s. The centers function as both places of worship but also headquarter village social and political life.[57] Bringing Shi`a *qadi*s under the purview of Sunni tribal chiefs and then the Bahraini state represents one of the major shifts on the archipelago in the colonial age.

The Rise of Sunni Hegemony

After the coming of the Al Khalifah, Sunni hegemony became deeply embedded in the identity of the ruling elite and the state. Among Sunnis, the Arab tribal cultural systems operated among themselves, but the tribes' relationship to people in the Gulf, largely Shi`a, was one of subjugation. The Shi`a in Bahrain can be roughly categorized into two groups: the *Baharna* (Shi`a agriculturists of Arab ethnic origin) and the *Ajam* (Shi`a of Persian ethnic origin). Meanwhile, the *hawala* were another indigenous group in Bahrain. As Arabs from the Persian coast, they often spoke Persian natively, but were primarily Sunni, and of a different tradition therein.[58] They were a merchant, sea-faring group, often straddling the political and social aims of the Shi`a and the Sunni on the archipelago, depending on the issue. Categorizing the *Baharna*, *ajam*, and *hawli* as indigenous "people of the sea," recent ethnographic research suggest that they were a multiethnic people, drawing from Arab and Persian cultures, but belonging to neither hegemonic identification. Their common culture derived from their long-standing exchange relationships. Arab coastal dwellers of Hormuzgan, for example, by oral tradition claim that coastal dwellers on the other side of the Gulf "also belong to us."[59] Customs in the province are often labeled Arab without also being considered foreign. Taken all together, we see that despite being "people of the sea," there were multiple and overlapping identities operating at the same time.[60] The "people of the sea" were primarily Shi`a and if not, in the case of the Sunni *hawli*, were Shi`a tolerant.

The Al Khalifah family, in shoring up resources for themselves in Bahrain, enslaved the *Baharna* agriculturalists in a kind of feudal order, and held themselves politically privileged over other groups as well, in particular the *ajam*. This system of feudal control is referred to in Arabic as "*imara*."[61] *Baharna* and *ajam*, who previously existed within local spheres of power in cooperation with maritime trading communities such as the *hawala*, suddenly had tribal masters and became an underclass. The sheikhs, through their armed supporters, were a proto-state as:

> the "government" without offices, the "administration" without bureaucracy, the "state" without public delegation or consent, standardized law, or equity.[62]

Meanwhile the *hawala*, as primarily port merchants,[63] were eventually coerced into paying tribute and taxes to the Al Khalifah upon conquest (and relieved of that financial burden once oil was discovered).[64]

Control over Shi`a and the "people of the sea" was the main job of a proto-criminal justice system based on tribal tradition, the Al Khalifah's *fedawiyyah* or *fedawi*, tribal militias. Indigenous settlements within the Bahrain *dirah* were divided among the royal *sheikhs*. Each of them controlled their personal *fedawiyyah* and directed them in maintaining the social order of Shi`a subjugation in their designated locale. Additionally, *jama'a* (male followers) of the *sheikh* were obliged to take up arms in defense of the tribe in a crisis.[65] *Fedawiyyah* and *jama'a* reportedly extracted bribes, violently treated accused wrongdoers, and were known for their "repeated excess earn[ing] them the animosity of the people."[66]

Alongside this system, the two sect-based conflict resolution traditions continued for disputes and offenses that did not directly interest the Al Khalifah: one for the Sunni tribe and its allies and another for Shi`a. The Shi`a *qadis* followed the Jafari legal school and the Sunni adopted the Maliki school.[67] A third system continued around the existing pearling industry and its customs for the arbitration of commercial disputes. In the urban center of Manama, another proto-judicial venue at the time was the *lawhah al-aqfal* (council of chains) in Manama where *shari'a* and/or customary wrongdoers were subjected to public scrutiny by a council of municipal elites.[68] In all matters, whether brought through the rough justice of the *fedawiyyah*, the council of chains, or the Muslim tradition, the court of last resort was the royal one in Muharraq, based on Al Khalifah customs and whims, rather than *shari'a* or other written or customary law. For example, under Sheikh Isa's rule, crimes were adjudicated by him only when the qadis and/or council or chains failed to resolve the issue. Tribal councils (*majlis*) still operated, but were more concerned with resource management than individual conflict resolution.[69]

British colonial officers reported the discriminatory and violent nature of the Al Khalifah approach to justice, particularly related to issues involving Shi`a. They noted "years of oppression by the ruling family" that are "far too numerous to quote, but details are on record . . . [of] illegal seizure of property, wrongful imprisonment with cruelty, and political murders, for which no one has been brought to trial, and no [effort] made to enforce justice."[70] To aggravate matters, one of Sheikh Salman's wives administered her own trials of local peasants, meting out harsh punishments.[71] She was not the only member of the royal family to hold a personal court for criminal wrongdoing; colonial administrators marveled at the allegedly inconsistent results of a family holding separate tribunals of criminals brought to their attention through personal *fedawiyyah*, among other means. Allegedly, the system of justice before colonial reforms was engendering "bitter relations between the Sunni and the [Shi`a] . . . deliberately encouraged by the rulers for years."[72]

The unsavory details of the historical encroachment on the indigenous Bahrainis have long been suppressed in official narratives. Although the Al-Khalifa acknowledge having first arrived in Bahrain in the eighteenth century, their violent occupation, warring resource competition, and enslavement of *Baharna* goes unemphasized and mostly forgotten. After colonial independence, and with the push toward an independent national identity, government public relations programs to build a new *turath* (cultural heritage) had focused primarily on Arab Bedouin (Sunni tribal) heritage,[73] the identity of the Al Khalifah and their historical allies. This white-washing of the disruptive nature of the Sunni tribes to the way of life of the indigenous people became exacerbated later by official colonial policies around "preserving Sunni influence"[74] and "demonstrat[ing] that an Arab state can advance on Western lines under British protection and still retain its Arab character."[75]

Meanwhile, merely swinging back the pendulum to a pro-Shi`a, "golden age" narrative[76] that glorifies Bahrain's Shi`a-dominated days (in the Safavid empire, during the Qarmati movement, or as part of the Indian Ocean culture of tolerance) can become its own form of chauvinism. Laurence Louër has argued that Shi`a oral history around this golden age is one-sided and cannot be relied upon, but this is too dismissive of the importance of the narrative.[77] Taking what can be corroborated from this revisionist oral tradition of the Shi`a "golden age," which is not everything a Bahraini Shi`a purist would claim, still points us in the direction of a substantial revision to the historical understanding and calls into question large swathes of the official narrative.

We can understand the "golden age" narrative as having two goals: to remember what is not adequately recorded nor recast as official *turath*, and as a means of inspiring a continued struggle toward civil equality in the archipelago. The second goal may generate historical exaggerations in order to inspire a social movement such as the Arab Spring, but there are demonstrable kernels of truth in the overall thrust of the narrative along the lines of the first goal—kernels that are completely ignored in the official narrative, developed as it was by the Al Khalifah and colonial administrators. The events of the second disruption and beyond illustrate the problems with "forgetting" the sectarian nature of Bahraini society, itself a source of the Al Khalifah hegemony.

THE SECOND DISRUPTION: THE BRITISH REFORMS LEGITIMATE THE PEOPLE OF THE LAND

British influence in Bahrain, formalized in the nineteenth century in the treaties of 1820, 1880, and 1892,[78] acted as a buffer against the archipelago's absorption into either the Saudi state, expanding from the interior, or Persia. The British curtailed the back and forth of tribal conflicts and sea piracy that, from their perspective, challenged the development of industrialized trade in the region.[79] J. B. Kelly points out that the British began to tire of the instability and in particular, the conflicting alliances with both the Ottomans and the Persians. Bahrain played the conflicting alliances off each other and managed to "harry shipping in waters around Bahrain and to oppress British Indian traders" in the archipelago.[80] As a result, the British used military threats to coerce the Al Khalifah into a treaty relationship.

James Onley writes that in cooperating and ultimately being subjugated by the British, Gulf tribal regimes operated within their own cultural frameworks, treating the British as if they, too, were a Gulf tribe—albeit one with more military and economic strength.[81] Anthropologist Marshall Sahlins' work on cross-cultural historical encounters point to the capacity for events to be differentially understood by the parties mutually involved. Sahlins articulated that past cultural frameworks are used to make sense of new and emerging realities. Parties attribute meaning to others' behavior and intentions within the discursive framework of their own understanding of the world.[82] In this vein, the Al Khalifah understanding of the consequences—and permanence—of the written treaties establishing their protectorate status may have been different than how the British understood them at the time. There are examples within the twentieth century colonial record of the Al Khalifah pleading with the British to perform their treaty support because, from their perspective, the relationship is in a state of constant re-negotiation and is perpetually being tested. From the British point of view, however, the relationship is contractually permanent and from there follows responsibilities on both sides that are not a matter of negotiation.

Without disrupting the sectarian framework, and instead embracing it, colonial administrators and the Al Khalifah together invent the archipelago as a nation-state, creating the foundation for today's criminal justice system. British influence in the region is a major force in the development of Bahrain as a nation, as was the case with many of the Gulf trucial states. As Paul Rich describes:

> British cultural hegemony changed the Gulf through endorsement of a system of Gulf nation-states, a concept taken for granted by Western thinkers but which was antithetical to Arab and nomadic tribal structures . . . British prestige encouraged the growth of Western-style institutions and the diminishing of traditional systems, contributing to new power cent[ers] and unforeseen developments.[83]

Bahrain arrived at the institutionalization of its on-going sectarian anxieties, finding ways to build the existing Sunni hegemony and anti-Shi`a order maintenance traditions into the new national foundations, an example of post-colonial hybridization. As Benedict Anderson states, nations are not natural or organic ways for people to organize and identify themselves. Instead, they are complicated webs of ideas creating coherence among complete strangers that requires much work to create and maintain.[84] In Bahrain's case, the prior oppression of the people of the sea by the people of the land becomes absorbed into the nation-state. What emerges is a curious hybridization of colonial administration and Sunni hegemony. Further, the imposition of the Order-in-Council (OiC) colonial laws and their immediate social and political consequences represent the second upheaval that forever changed law and order.

As mentioned, colonial Bahrain had long been considered a protected state[85] (distinct from protectorates and full-fledged colonies) and part of Britain's "informal empire,"[86] and not as extensively colonized as India or Aden (Yemen). However, historian James Onley compared the dimensions (including defense, trade, transportation, communications, and control over subjects) of a fully colonized Indian princely state to the post-reform Bahrain state and found that any differences were marginal.[87] The Deputy Secretary to the Government of India wrote in 1929, "a British Financial Adviser [sic], a British Police Officer, and a British Customs Officer; that is, actually more British Administration than in an ordinary Indian state . . . "[88] The reform laws effected a deep and significant colonization of the state, shifting the state apparatus from the mere monitoring of affairs by "native agents" to the importation of British political agents specifically tasked with state-building.

The Orders-in-Council Reforms

The OiC laws gave full administrative oversight to the British political agent after a series of political intrigues that in 1923 removed the ruler, Sheikh Isa bin Ali Al Khalifah, from power in favor of his son, Sheikh Hamad bin Isa Al Khalifah[89] (while another aspirant to the throne and son of the ruler, Sheikh Abdullah bin Isa Al Khalifah, led a politically problematic opposition campaign several years thereafter[90]). Sheikh Hamad had British backing because of his willingness to support the OiC reforms—although the full extent of the laws were never presented to him in advance; meanwhile, "secret" memos circulated between the Political Agency, Political Residency, New Delhi, and London discussing how to make the comprehensive restructuring of Bahrain palatable to him and other elites. The officials settled on a gradual approach and although the OiC was written and approved in London in 1913, the laws, touching on education, criminal justice, land use, and taxation, among other realms, were introduced one at a time[91] from 1919 to 1927. Through their unveiling, the reforms caused considerable tension between the political agent, Sheikh Hamad, and the opposition sheikhs.[92] To reassure Sheikh Hamad, the British convinced him to hire a British special advisor who would be his employee and tasked with working with the political agents to implement the modern state, a role first suggested by political agent Major Clive Daly and then subsequently undertaken by Sir Charles Belgrave.[93]

The reforms tempered some of the worst abuses the Al Khalifah ruling family inflicted on the indigenous people, such as forced labor (*sakhra*) of the Baharna. It is important to note that *sakhra* was not merely an Al Khalifah peculiarity, but that forced labor of indigenous Gulf and Indian Ocean people (of the sea) by Sunni tribal people (of the land) occurred throughout the Gulf. For example, the Dawasir tribe engaged in the practice in the late nineteenth and early twentieth century. Advisor Charles Belgrave documented that in April of 1935 a slave freed by the British was kidnapped back into slavery by members of the tribe.[94] The British vehemently opposed *sakhra* as part of their century-old, empire-wide crusade against slavery. Yet, other anti-Shi`a policies and institutions were cemented into Bahrain's reform administration state, particularly in the new criminal justice system.

For example, the British maintained the separation of the Sunni and Shi`a courts, but transformed the *qadi*s into salaried, governmental employees. The reforms rendered them subject to contractual obligations with defined job descriptions and relegated them to personal status cases (divorce, custody, etc.), a far cry from their former status as emerging organically from within the community of learned Muslim scholars and informally financed by their communities or tribes.[95] The reforms took criminal matters out of their purview, and many civil ones as well. Candidates for *qadi* positions were subject to rigorous interviews by Belgrave, reportedly to overcome the many complaints from the two sect-constituencies over the corruption of the existing *qadis*. In addition, an appointed council was developed to oversee the administration of justice by the new *qadis*;[96] it was particularly scrutinizing of Shi`a *qadis*. The council, for example, uncovered alleged bribery by a Shi`a *qadi*, "Sheikh Khalaf," and administered a very sectarian punishment: "He was ultimately told by the Government of Bahrain to go to the [h]oly places in Iraq and he went away in May 1927. His existence in Bahrain was deemed undesirable."[97] The Bahrain government later received a letter confirming Khalaf's good behavior from Iraq's King Faisal; the Iraqi security sector was monitoring him on behalf of the Bahrain authorities.[98]

Absent from the colonial record is any mention of de-sectarianizing the Muslim adjudicators. Although many memorandums and letters indicate an overarching concern with breaking *qadi* corruption within both sect-communities, it appeared unimaginable in this cultural context that the two groups could ever merge their legal traditions, or choose one over the other, even during a period of massive social and political change. Sectarianism was deeply engrained in the social and political order operating across the society and the colonial administrators, using their "ethnographic acuity,"[99] to manage Bahrain, found that they could better gain the trust of the Al Khalifah, and achieve their aims of pacifying the region for trade, by at least tolerating the sectarian biases and sometimes stoking them.

In particular, the reform of order maintenance hypothetically could have ushered in a breaking away from the sectarian discursive framework while policies and procedures were in flux and being rewritten. However, many options which could have addressed sectarian power inequalities were selected *against* the colonial administrators and the Al Khalifah rulers. The OiC reforms did little to address the sectarian divisiveness exacerbated by the royal family, instead favoring a balancing act between the disempowered *Bahrana*, and other indigenous subjects, and the Al Khalifah monarchy,[100] that only perpetuated inequalities.

The New Courts

The OiC reforms removed criminal matters from the tribal, commercial, or religious courts and *majlis*es. The diving court, a major cultural container of tradition for the Arabian Gulf littoral proto-capitalist past, was abolished; pearling cases were handed over to the *majlis al-tijara* (commercial court), and cases of criminal fraud in the pearl industry would eventually be tried in the new secular criminal courts.[101] On the surface, it may seem that a secular-based criminal court system could be designed to break the extant sectarian framework, but its apparent that sect-neutrality in title was compromised by its application in practice, as will be more fully detailed in subsequent chapters. The political resident in Bushehr established The Political Agent's

Court (PA Court). The political agent presided over the court as a district magistrate,[102] with the court's main purpose being the trying of criminal (and civil) cases consisting of non-Bahraini citizens as defendants. Prior to this administrative development, British subjects who had a legal dispute relied on the political resident in Bushehr to intervene, which was rare.[103] Practically speaking, the category of non-Bahraini subjects was composed of British citizens, citizens of British colonies and protectorates, and individuals from other countries not in the British Empire. The Indian Penal Code and Criminal Procedure Code of 1860/1861 was the source of law. Appeals to the PA Court's decisions were decided by the political resident in Bushehr. A final appeal was possible in the Full Court for the Persian Gulf, also in Bushehr, but it was presided over by two or three additionally appointed judges, often brought in from colonial courts in Kenya or Cyprus, or from Britain.[104] There was also the Joint Court, established in 1919, which was a combined court ruled over by the Al Khalifah ruler and political agent for significant cases that intersected both authorities.

For Bahrainis (Sunni and Shi`a), the Bahrain Court (BC) handled criminal and civil cases not in the jurisdiction of *qadi* courts, or the PA Court. Essentially, the BC was the invention of Belgrave as part of his mission to bring the Bahraini court system into the rational-legal fold; it was the highest local court. The source of law for the Bahrain Court was a patchwork of English laws in translation, the Indian Penal Code and Criminal Procedure Code of 1860/1861[105] and "common sense alone."[106] Belgrave put himself on the bench, despite having only minimal legal training in a previous post in the Colonial Service. Initially, two members of the Sunni royal family served as judges, at Belgrave's appointment with the ruler's approval. One was Sheikh Salman, ruler of Bahrain from 1942 to 1961, who sat on the court prior to his ascension for a period of eight years. His biographer credits the judgeship as the legal and bureaucratic training that helped him to lead the country in the late colonial era.[107] With the implementation of this court, criminal matters were successfully transferred to British and Sunni adjudicators.

The New Law Enforcement Apparatus

Policing also underwent significant reforms during this time. Previously, Indian sepoys protected imperial interests as part of the Levy Corps. In 1926, the Levies had 200 Baluchi officers.[108] However, with the reforms, a Bahraini police force (still with many Indian officers) was created as an arm of the municipal administration of Manama, with the intent to replace the tribal *fedawiyyah* system and leaving only a few *fidawi* for the emir himself. According to Belgrave, Sheikh Hamad's *fidawi* were opposed to the new police force and courts. They did not want their "squeezing" of local people criminalized.[109] In actuality, the new police, known as the State Police, were not envisioned as so divergent from the *fedawiyyah* system in terms of its main task. The State Police were "to support [Sheikh Hamad's] prestige [and] enable him to exert some authority"[110] over forces that opposed his emir-ship in the forced abdication of his father in 1923, as well as over subjugated Shi`a populations. Sir Charles Belgrave instituted the professionalization of the police, introducing salaried positions, uniforms, training, and written policies and procedures. Although at first some Shi`a were included as officers in the State Police, this soon was reversed after complaints from the royal family and its allies. Thus, the first colonial-style police were directed toward preservation of the Sunni monarchy and were largely composed of foreigner officers, something that characterizes the Bahraini police today.

As OiC reforms moved ahead, the new law enforcement regime attempted to manage sectarian flashpoints evolving from the unresolved absorption of anti-Shi`a discrimination into Bahraini state operations. In late 1921 or early 1922, one of the Emir's *fidawi* badly beat a *Baharna* man during an arrest. In response, Baharna individuals attacked a *fidawi*. By February of 1922, Baharna "demonstrations"[111] erupted in the Manama *suq* after the Baharna initiated a strike, ceasing work at their agricultural and shop-keeping jobs and uniting in protest, challenging Al Khalifah authority. The Baharna, accompanied by a few Sunni notables, met with Sheikh Hamad (deputy ruler at the time) and made their demands: reform of the courts, an end to the havoc being wrecked by the sheikh's wandering camels, an end to *sakhra*, and land reform. The deputy ruler capitulated to the demands, but in reality failed to make good on any of them. He reportedly revealed to the political agent in a debriefing, however, that the difficulty with the Shi`a stemmed from "past misrule."[112]

The dearth of concrete action to meet Shi`a demands may have been justified by the continued Persian claims to the Bahraini territory. In 1922, Persia was finalizing their League of Nations case arguing that Bahrain belonged to it. Making it known that the Shi`a were experiencing Sunni subjugation may have given Persia a sympathetic case on the world stage. The state either did not punish or reluctantly punished defendants in cases involving Shi`a victims; it was an order maintenance regime that did not protect Shi`a communities from internal or external violence. The state itself participated in this violence insofar as members of the royal family have at times been directly implicated or, at other times, have given tacit approval of violence against Shi`a communities. The British were aware of the sectarian framework they were exacerbating, but did so for the larger political cause of stabilizing the region for trade by solidifying the boundaries of a nation-state system. Explaining the effects of this policy, Political Resident Cyril Barrett stated:

> [The policy] means administering the islands for sake of the Chief of the tribes, exploiting the people for the rulers, and treating the Shi`ah [sic] as people of an unprivileged class . . . The family—the Al Khalifah [are] uneducated savages with the veneer of town manners.[113]

Overall, the rule of law in the form of the OiC reforms of the 1920s was insufficient to contain sectarian anxieties; such unrest was almost always interpreted from the perspective of a royal family whose persistent preference is to see the granting of Shi`a rights as a challenge to its very legitimacy.

The newly-invented criminal justice system and early criminal cases discussed in the following chapters represent the way in which OiC reforms were enacted on the ground. As shown here, the context for these cases is a highly charged sectarian environment in which the ruling family was militarily and administratively backed by the British, but whose legitimacy in the eyes of many ordinary Bahrainis was circumspect. There were two major threats to Al Khalifah legitimacy: opposition from Sunni tribes supporting the deposed Sheikh Isa and the Persian-Shi`a opposition to continued Sunni hegemony. As we shall see in the next chapters, the Al Khalifah and the British together built the Bahrain nation-state by pacifying other Sunni groups and simultaneously maintaining Sunni alliances, and then effectively casting the Shi`a as the most dire threat to sovereignty, employing the new criminal adjudication to their advantage.

NOTES

1. *Rufaqa* traditionally acted as protection from within one tribe against other tribes.
2. H.R.P. Dickson, *The Arab of the Desert: A Glimpse into Badawin Life in Kuwait and Saudi Arabia.* London: George Allen & Unwin Ltd., 1949: 371.
3. Political Agent Report no. 219 by Major Clive Daly to the Political Residency [India Office Records, British Library, R/15/2/28, December 1900].
4. Letter from Charles Kemball, Political Resident to John C. Gaskin, Political Assistant [India Office Records, British Library, R/15/2/28, January 2, 1901].
5. Letter no. 9 from John C. Gaskin, Political Assistant to Charles Kemball, Political Resident [India Office Records, British Library, R/15/2/28, January 27, 1901].
6. Letter no. 105 from John C. Gaskin, Political Assistant, to Political Resident [India Office Records, British Library, R/15/2/28, June 30, 1901].
7. Letter no. 1346 from Political Resident Charles Kemball to a senior naval officer, Persian Gulf division [India Office Records, British Library, R/15/2/28, December 27, 1901].
8. Letter no. 178 from John C. Gaskin, Political Assistant, to Charles Kemball, Political Resident [India Office Records, British Library, R/15/2/28, August 24, 1902].
9. Secret letter no. 10, letter from the India Office to the Governor General of India in Council [India Office Records, British Library, R/15/2/28, March 16, 1906].
10. As summarized by Political Resident Percy Cox in 1910, *pax Brittanica* in the Gulf meant "enhancing our good name and influence among the trading classes of the Gulf and enabling the latter to obtain a measure of even-handed justice which otherwise they could hardly hope to get." [Letter no. 3134 of 1910 from Political Agent Percy Cox to J.B. Wood, Esq., Secretary to the Government of India in the Foreign Department, Calcutta (India Office

Records, ior.neg.5956, November 27, 1910).] Andrew Wheatcroft explains that specifically in the time period of 1900–1918 the British also hoped to secure an alternative route for communications between British India and Britain, following the lines of telegraphic communication, that did not rely on the increasingly vulnerable Suez Canal. [Andrew Wheatcroft, *The Life and Times of Shaikh Salman bin Hamad Al-Khalifah, Ruler of Bahrain 1941–1961* (London: Kegan Paul International: 1995).

11. Wheatcroft, 1995.
12. Sewell 2005.
13. Jaou Teles e Cunha, "The Portugese Presence in the Persian Gulf." In *The Persian Gulf in History*, edited by Lawrence G. Potter (London: Palgrave Macmillan, 2009): 207–234.
14. Philip K. Hitti, *The Near East in History*. (Princeton, NJ: D. Van Nostrand Company, Inc., 1967).
15. M. Rheda Bhaker, "The Cultural Unity of the Gulf and the Indian Ocean: A *Longue Durée* Historical Perspective," In *The Persian Gulf in History*, edited by Lawrence G. Potter (London: Palgrave Macmillan, 2009): 163–172.
16. Lawrence G. Potter, "Introduction," In *The Persian Gulf in History*, edited by Lawrence G. Potter (Palgrave Macmillan, 2009): 1–26.
17. Peter Lienhardt, *Shaikhdoms of Eastern Arabia* (New York: Palgrave, 1950).
18. Louise Sweet, "Pirates or Polities? Arab Societies of the Persian or Arabian Gulf," *Ethnohistory*, 11, 1964. pp. 262–280.
19. Onley, James and Sulayman Khalaf, "Shaikhly Authority in the Pre-Oil Gulf: An Historical-Anthropological Study," *History and Anthropology* 17 (2006): 189–208.
20. Fuad I. Khuri, *Tribe and State in Bahrain: The Transformation of Social and Political Authority in an Arab State*. (Chicago: The University of Chicago Press, 1980): 20.
21. William O. Beeman, "An Anthropological View of the *Khalijis*—Their Evolution and Way of Life," In *The Persian Gulf in History*, edited by Lawrence G. Potter (New York: Palgrave Macmillan, 2009): 149.
22. Dionysius Agius, *Seafaring in the Arabian Gulf and Oman: People of the Dhow* (London: Routledge, 2005).
23. William O. Beeman "The Zar in the Persian Gulf: Performative Dimensions," *Anthropology of the Contemporary Middle East and Central Eurasia* 3, no.1 (2015): 1–12.
24. Agius 2005.
25. Abdul Sheriff, "The Persian Gulf and the Swahili Coast: A History of Acculturation over the *Longue Durée*." In Lawrence G. Potter's (editor), *The Persian Gulf in History* (Palgrave Macmillan, 2009): 173–188.
26. Sheriff, 2009.
27. Khuri 1980: 28.
28. Khuri 1980: 28.
29. Nelida Fuccaro, *Histories of City and State in the Persian Gulf, Manama since 1800* (Cambridge: Cambridge University Press, 2009).
30. Later, this court's authority derived from the ruler who appointed judges, but British interests were monitored by native agents, followed by the political agents, who had influence over the court. In this way, the British, though at this time not fully established in internal judicial affairs, could practice a degree of control. *Na'turs* (port watchmen) were the enforcers of customary and commercial law in the ports and markets. *Na'turs* belonged either to private merchant fleets or port municipalities, and later, with the advent of industrialized colonial trading operations, were hired and absorbed into corporations, such as the Mesopotamian-Persian Trading Corporation (MESPERS). Sir Charles Belgrave, the British advisor to the ruler of Bahrain from 1926 to 1957, became fascinated with these customs. As the pearling industry was collapsing in the 1930s due to the introduction of cultured pearls from Japan, Belgrave claimed to have written down the traditional pearl diving laws—a completely oral tradition. Unfortunately, his record of this oral legal tradition was not found in his preserved papers at the University of Exeter. [Onley 2007:124; Onley 2007: 221; Reider Visser, "Britain in Basra: Past Experiences and Currents Challenges," July 11, 2006 (http://hisotriae.org/cosmpolitanism.asp)].
31. Gengler 2015: 39.

32. Potter 2009; Agius 2005.

33. Mohammed Ghanim Al-Rumaihi, "Social and Political Change in Bahrain Since the First World War" Ph. D. diss. (University of Durham, March 1973).

34. Abdulaziz Mohamed Hasan Ali Al Khalifa, "Relentless Warrior and Shrewd Tactician: Shaikh Abdullah bin Ahmad of Bahrain 1795–1849 A Case Study of Shaikhly Statecraft in the Nineteenth Century Gulf" Ph.D. diss (University of Exeter, April 2013): 30.

35. Interestingly, the Al Khalifah may also be referencing the 7th century Islamic notion of "fath al-islam" referring to the forced conversion of non-Muslim peoples by Muslim armies, assigning to the indigenous Bahrainis the status of not being real Muslims (Gengler 2015: 39).

36. Khuri 1980: 35.

37. James Onley and Sulyman Khalaf, "Shaikhly Authority in the Pre-oil Gulf: An Historical-Anthropological Study," *History and Anthropology* 17: 191.

38. Lienhardt 2001.

39. Potter 2009; James Onley, *The Arabian Frontier of the British Raj* (Oxford: Oxford University Press, 2007).

40. This is shown in the aforementioned complicated aftermath of Sheikh Salman's murder. Sheikh Salman was a member of the Bahraini ruling family who was protected by British treaty, but killed in Ottoman territory, leading to ambiguity as to how the British should respond in both fulfilling its treaty obligation with Bahrain, but also not inflaming already tense relations with Turkey.

41. Dickson 1949.

42. Kingdom of Bahrain, *Memorial submitted by the state of Bahrain (Merits) Volume 1, Qatar v. Bahrain*. (International Court of Justice, The Hague: 1996).

43. Kingdom of Bahrain 1996: 35–36.

44. Kingdom of Bahrain 1996: 36.

45. Frederick Anscombe, "The Ottoman Role in the Gulf" in *The Persian Gulf in History*, edited by Lawrence G. Potter (New York: Palgrave Macmillan, 2009): 277–294.

46. J.R.B. Kelly. *Arabia, the Gulf and the West* (London: Basic Books, 1980): 179.

47. Kelly 1980:179.

48. Peter Lienhardt, *Shaikhdoms of Eastern Arabia* (New York: Palgrave, 2001).

49. Diwan 2014: 148.

50. Onley and Khalaf 2006: 199

51. Fuad Khuri, *Tribe and State in Bahrain* (Chicago: Chicago University Press, 1980).

52. Interestingly, in Bahrain there persists among the ruling family and other Sunni conservatives an enduring preference for consultative councils (*shura*) and other *majlis*-like governance bodies. The Al Khalifah and other Sunni elites routinely make overtures and exhibit intellectual agreement with the parliamentary democracy at the national level of government (when not suspended). Yet, the use of appointed elites in closed-door sessions remains a mainstay of Bahraini politics and can be argued to be a more comfortable governance style in the eyes of contemporary tribal traditionalists.

53. Onley and Khalaf 2007.

54. Lienhardt 2001.

55. Nahla Yassine, "Arab Political Dispute Resolution." (Diss., Wayne State University: 1999): 7.

56. Khuri 1980: 9.

57. Khuri 1980: 70.

58. The *hawala* adhere to the Shafi'i legal tradition. Khuri 1980: 3–4.

59. Shahnaz Razieh Nadjmabadi, "The Arab Presence on the Iranian Coast of the Persian Gulf," In Lawrence G. Potter's (editor), *The Persian Gulf in History* (Palgrave Macmillan, 2009): 130.

60. Lawrence G. Potter, "Introduction," *Sectarian Politics in the Persian Gulf*, Lawrence G. Potter (ed.): 7 [1–29]; Najmabadi 2009: 140.

61. Wehrey 2014; Fuccaro 2009: 114; Gengler 2015: 41; Khuri 1980.

62. Khuri 1980: 50.

63. Fuccaro 2009: 69.

64. Gengler 2014: 42.

65. Lienhardt 2001.

66. Mahdi Abdall Al-Tajir, *Bahrain 1920–1945: Britain, the Shaikh and the Administration* (London: Croom Helm, 1987): 2.

67. The distinctions between these two schools of Islamic Law are complicated and beyond the scope of the present analysis. However, the two, descending from eighth century jurisprudence, are sometimes characterized as divergent as to *ijtihad* or interpretation. The Maliki school places a strong emphasis on *hadith* (sayings of the Prophet) and the lives of the Prophet's companions, including his wives. Maliki allows for clerics to use personal opinon (*ray*) and analogies (*qiyas*) to make judgments. Meanwhile, the Jafari focuses on the connection between human reasoning and revelation, seeing a concordance between the two, and encouraging clerics to use a variety of sources for Islamic law (including the Quran, the sayings of the Prophet, and the life of the prophet) in order to infer categories and thereby make judgments.[John L. Esposito (Editor), *The Oxford Dictionary of Islam*, Oxford: Oxford University Press, 2004: 190, 276.]

68. Fuccaro 2009: 20–24.

69. Khuri 1980: 35–36.

70. Major Clive Daly, "Note on the Political Situation in Bahrain," Report to Political Residency [India Office Records, British Library, 15/2/131, 1921]

71. Despatch no. 90, C.A. Gault to Selwyn Lloyd [Papers of Charles Dalrymple Belgrave, 1926–1947, University of Exeter, United Kingdom, 148/2/1, 1956].

72. Confidential Report no. 28/c by Major Clive Daly to the Political Residency [India Office Records, British Library, 15/2/131, February 11, 1923]

73. Lawrence G. Potter, "Introduction," *Sectarian Politics in the Persian Gulf*, Lawrence G. Potter (ed.): 7 [1–29].

74. Letter, June 15, 1923, Political Resident Stuart Knox to King Abdul Aziz Ibn Saud, explaining British policy in the Gulf. [Papers of Charles Dalrymple Belgrave, 1926–1947, University of Exeter, United Kingdom, 148/2/2.]

75. Sir Denys Bray, Foreign Secretary to the Government of India, "Notes on Reforms in Bahrain" [India Office Records, British Library, 15/2/131,November 6, 1927].

76. Potter 2014:13.

77. Louer 2014: 118–121. Louer prefers to point to economic competition and control as the root causes of cleavages in Bahrain.

78. Sayed Hassan Amin, Middle East Legal Systems (Royston Publishers: 1985).

79. Fuccaro 2009.

80. Kelly 1980: 179.

81. Onley 2007: 3.

82. Marshall Sahlins, *Mythical Realities and Historical Metaphors*. (Ann Arbor, MI: University of Michigan Press, 1981).

83. Paul Rich, *Creating the Arabian Gulf: The British Raj and the Invention of the Gulf* (Lanham, MD: Lexington Books, 2009): 73.

84. Benedict Anderson, *Imagined Communities* (New York: Verso, 2006).

85. Hitti, 1967; Glen Balfour-Paul, *The End of Empire in the Middle East: Britain's Relinquishment of Power in its Last Three Arab Dependencies* (Cambridge: Cambridge University Press, 1991).

86. Fuccaro 2009.

87. Onley 2007: 280, Appendix D.

88. Letter from J.G. Acheson, The Deputy Secretary to the Government of India, to the Political Resident [India Office Records, British Library, R/15/2/112, May 28, 1929].

89. Letter, Political Agent Hugh Weightman to Political Resident Col. Trenchard Fowle no. C/720–1.b/5 [India Office Records, British Library, R/15/1/343, November 26, 1938].

90. File r/15/2/100 [India Office Records, British Library].

91. Letter from Major T.H. Keyes to the Political Resident [India Office Records, British Library, r/15/1/299, May 20, 1915].

92. Al-Tajir 1987.

93. Although we do not know exactly why hiring a British Advisor to the Bahrain Government was met with approval, one could speculate that the tribal parallel is the *rafiq*, or an

internally-controlled representative from an important exterior tribe. The purpose of the *rafiq* is to stave off external challenges from the *rafiq*'s tribe and to consult with the Sheikh in managing exterior threats from that tribe.

94. Belgrave, personal diary, April 25, 1935.

95. Government of Bahrain Notice no. 26/1357, "Shia Kadis" [India Office Records, British Library, r/15/1/343, October 27, 1938]; Letter no. 404/25 from Adviser Charles Belgrave to Shaikh Ali bin Jafar bin Muhammad [India Office Records, British Library].

96. Belgrave, 1960: 28.

97. Undated note in "Sheikh Khalaf" file [India Office Records, British Library, r/15/2/112].

98. Letter from King Faisal to Sheikh Hamad, July 24, 1928 [India Office Records, British Library, r/15/2/112].

99. Steinmetz 2007: 48

100. Zoe Holman, "On the Side of Decency and Democracy: The History of British-Bahraini Relations and Transnational Contestation" In *Bahrain's Uprising: Resistance and Repression in the Gulf*, edited by Ala'a Shehabi and Marc Owen Jones (London, Zed Books, 2015): 175–206.

101. Criminal case no. 398 of 1933 (India Office Records, R/15/3/7012); Memorandum no. 1822/9A from Advisor Sir Charles Belgrave to Political Agent (India Office Records, R/15/1/343, December 9, 1938).

102. Article 14(1) of the Bahrain Orders-in-Council.

103. Onley 2007: 119–120.

104. S.A. Amin, *Middle East Legal Systems* (Glasgow: Royston Publishers, 1985).

105. Amin, 1985.

106. Belgrave, 1960: 28.

107. Wheatcroft 1995: 32, 68.

108. Belgrave, Memoirs.

109. Al, Tajir, 1987: 69.

110. Confidential Report no. 209/8/1 by Major Clive Daly to the Political Residency [India Office Records, British Library, 15/2/131, August 31, 1924].

111. Letter no. c/84 from Captain C. G. Prior, Political Agent to the Political Resident [India Office Records, British Library, r/15/2/307, June 29, 1929].

112. Al-Tajir 1987: 37.

113. Letter from Political Resident Cyril Barrett to the Foreign Secretary to the Government of India [India Office Records, British Library, R/15/1/307, August 23, 1929].

Chapter Two

Shooting at the Sheikh

The Criminalization of Tribal Rivalry

In 1869, the Ruler of Bahrain, Sheikh Ali bin Khalifah Al Khalifah was murdered in battle by his cousin during a tribal crisis of succession.[1] The year before, the British had installed him after the deposing of the previous ruler, Sheikh Muhammad bin Khalifah Al Khalifah. Not going away quietly, Sheikh Muhammad hoped to regain the chiefdom[2] and aligned with the exiled Al Abdullah branch of the Al Khalifah sheikhdom. Together they gathered a tribal force of Bani Hajr from Hasa to attempt a coup. Meanwhile, Sheikh Ali, hearing of the plot against him, appealed to the political resident for help but got none. When Sheikh Muhammad's force landed in Bahrain, a battle ensued and Sheikh Ali lost his life. Sheikh Muhammad reinstalled himself as ruler, allowing the Bani Hajr to plunder Manama as a reward for their assistance. But the Bani Hajr proved to be less than loyal. In a few days they turned against Sheikh Muhammad and named their own leader from among their ranks, Sheikh Muhammad bin Abdullah. This Sheikh Muhammad did nothing to rein in the Bani Hajr and they continued to terrorize Manama. Facing political instability and violence in an important trucial state, the British political resident intervened, using the British Navy to capture both Sheikh Muhammads, installing Sheikh Isa bin Ali Al Khalifah instead.[3] (Sheikh Isa would go on to rule Bahrain until his forced abdication in 1923.) International powers, such as Turkey and Iran, cried foul, fearing the rise of British supremacy—during the same year of Sheikh Isa's installation, the Suez Canal had also opened under British control.[4]

The intrigues of tribal succession represent a political problem made more complicated by the involvement of the British Empire. Crises of tribal succession in the region were often settled by tribal rivalry and violence, but the British found these flashpoints of political dynamism to be a sign of political weakness and instability. More important, violence threatened the *pax Brittanica* policies and was considered a danger to stability for British and British-protected merchants, such as those from India; violence threatening the *cordon sanitaire* that the British desired in and around British India.[5] By the early twentieth century, as the British began to reorganize the administrative affairs of the Bahrain state, ushering in a new regime of order maintenance, inter-tribal and intra-tribal rivalry became criminalized as treason and murder.

Adjudicating customary tribal behavior in a new criminal justice system is a major structural shift that ushered in a cultural one as well. The Al Khalifah, in aligning with the British, lost the supremacy of tribal customs in determining their leaders, thereby diminishing their sovereignty. As Fuad Khuri explains, for tribal chiefs and others invested in tribal systems of governance, the colonial order was a direct encroachment on their power and control.[6]

The colonial record also shows colonial agents using their "ethnographic acuity" in a new way: to criminally investigate and prosecute threats to Al Khalifah hegemony as an alternative to tribal customs, and to control the nature of the Al Khalifah response to threats to their authority. The new order maintenance regime characterized tribal competition as no longer legitimate, but criminal, and the goals of power and control involved in tribal rivalries of the Al Khalifah are absorbed into the colonial state. However, vestiges of tribal justice survived at points of discretion. Despite colonial prosecutions, the rulers often forgave and/or pardoned criminalized behavior related to tribal politics and sought to restore Sunni tribal criminals' standing in society (discussed in chapter 4). To better understand the cultural shift brought on by the implementation of rational-legal justice in this tribal milieu, we must first understand how customary tribal authority worked before British involvement, particularly in terms of the succession of rulers, the underlying issue in some of the criminal cases in the sample.

SUCCESSION AND TRIBAL AUTHORITY

Tribal rulers, or chiefs, emerged, as described in the previous chapter, from among the sheikhs, or adult males in the tribes, as a matter of internal political consultation. At the same time, rulers could also fall under the authority of external tribal rulers through payments of subsidies and tributes. Tribal rulers that consolidated multiple tribes under their control can be considered to control a grouping of tribes, or a sheikhdom. Tribes in tribute to the same ruler were disallowed from attacking each other.[7] Rulers of sheikhdoms maintained armed retainers from among their tribal ranks and maintained their legitimacy through both the consent of their people, but also through their ability to garner the resources necessary for these armed retainers.[8] Rulers of sheikhdoms often maintained alliances with other nearby sheikhdoms, necessitating seasonal trips through the region in order to maintain ties and exchange information with other tribes and sheikhdoms. Thus, the Sunni tribes of the Gulf could be characterized as a complex network of political alliances and loyalty. Taking the region, and the way of life as a whole, we see that power among the tribes was diffuse, but strongly interconnected.

The succession of rulers often posed problems for sheikhdoms. Ideally, upon the death of a ruler, a successor was already waiting in the wings. Adult males of the ruling tribe consulted in *majlis* well ahead of the ruler's death, agreeing upon a successor from among hereditary males of the family (not necessarily the first-born son of the previous ruler). Although this system relies on family loyalty, it has the potential problem of sibling- and cousin-based rivalry, as hereditary male candidates are numerous.[9] For example, in the case of the abdication of Sheikh Isa in 1923, Sheikh Hamad (installed) and his half-brother Sheikh Abdullah (the two did not share a mother) competed for power and control well after the contest had been put to rest from the British perspective. Onley and Khalaf note that between 1793 and 1965, among Gulf Shaikhdoms there were thirty-five coups and four territorial secessions.[10]

Ideally though, if all goes smoothly with tribal succession, the new ruler maintains the existing tributary tribes and alliances, though this often necessitated sending tribal emissaries out to travel to the networks of patronage for the renewal or renegotiation of support. Customarily, however, in situations when the *majlis* were not in agreement over a successor, and the ruler perished, there surfaced a crisis of authority. One of three things happened when looking at historical struggles for successions. As a solution of first resort, the problem was mediated by someone who could resolve the conflict to the satisfaction of all parties. Failing this, the second option was for the sheikhdom to split, with followers dividing their loyalties among the two or more candidates for Sheikh, thus inventing new branches of the tribe, which then must renegotiate their relationship to each other. The other outcome was for the two or more groups to war over the claim to the single rulership.

In ethnographic accounts, the rules for war have their own nuances. Sheikhly leaders discussed plans with the leaders of their allies at least a week ahead of time, allowing conversation as to the pros and cons of the operation. If going forward, a *ghazzu* (tribal force) is compiled from among all the forces available (*qaum*). The leader must send a warning (*niga*) to the opposition, although the exact nature and timing of the subsequent attack is kept as a surprise. Surrender is possible at any time and the code of war says that if a combatant surrenders, orally stating that he puts himself under the protection of his foe, he is not to be killed. In successionary battles, as opposed to other kinds of warfare, surrender appears less frequent historically, and the death of a leader himself, as was the case with Sheikh Ali bin Khalifah Al Khalifah in 1869, sometimes occurred. Far from being a sign of weakness or instability, as long as the customs of war were followed, such violence among potential candidates to the rulership was culturally acceptable, and although perhaps unpleasant, a part of the way of life for the tribes.

As aforementioned, the British colonial regime had less of a stomach for these violent controversies, finding trade, treaties with rulers, and regional peace difficult to maintain in the wake of these ever-shifting struggles for power. The British Empire embroiled itself in the world of the tribal sheikh, first lightly in the nineteenth century, and then more systematically and forcefully in the twentieth century, complicating the tribal dynamic and putting into place successionary outcomes that did not necessarily have legitimacy in the eyes of tribal people themselves, let alone other Bahrainis. Sheikh Isa bin Ali was effectively installed by the British in 1869, though hypothetically, and the Sheikh Muhammads, from the Al Khalifah and the Bani Hajr tribes, had political legitimacy as well, perhaps more so. Sheikh Muhammad bin Khalifah Al Khalifah certainly played out his successionary claim within the bounds of tribal customary practices (although on the other hand, he seemed to lack the normative qualities of a good leader since he did not protect the people of Manama under his care[11]). His lack of success had much to do with British involvement. Sheikh Muhammad bin Abdulla, meanwhile, had a more dubious claim to the sheikhdom, depending on whether his taking of the sheikhdom had legitimacy within the Al Khalifah and Bani Hajr tribes as allies, and whether the tribes were adequately consulted and warfare customs followed. Regardless, this claim also was ultimately unsuccessful, not due to a tribal process, but the external meddling and threat of gunboat intervention by the British.

THE STRUGGLE FOR SHEIKH ISA'S SUCCESSOR

Though reigning for a long time, ultimately Sheikh Isa was forcibly removed by the British in 1923. The resulting conflict was not solved by tribal customary warfare. This time, in the much more developed colonial administration of the early twentieth century, it was not framed as merely a military problem to be managed by threat of British military intervention. Rather, the problems of succession ended up in the criminal justice system as outlawed behavior in several prosecutions in the late 1920s.

First, it is important to explore why Sheikh Isa was removed. According to colonial documents, the British felt that he was not cooperating in the reformation of Bahrain's government. Sheikh Isa resisted the reduction of his powers as a result of the colonial Order-in-Council (OiC) reforms enacted in

1919. Although he had ceded judicial authority over tribal subjects in Bahrain, such as the Hasawis, to the colonial administration, he later infringed on that agreement, much to the chagrin of colonial agents.[12] He also apparently felt that the British did not treat him with the same privilege and respect as other trucial sheiks, for which Deputy Political Resident Arthur Trevor wrote him that his government was "singularly inefficient and weak. Its tendency to exploit the Islands and their inhabitants for the benefit of the Alkhalifah [sic] and one or two leading Arab families."[13] In the early 1920s, Shi`a claims of subjugation briefly had the ear of the British, and they cited this subjugation as one of the reasons to remove Sheikh Isa (however, as history will show, this concern for the Shi`a population will ultimately take a back seat to other goals in the region).

Sheikh Isa further angered the British by changing the composition of the *Majlis al-'urf* (commercial council) without consulting the political agency. Importantly, Sheikh Isa attempted to place on the council a number of Sunni Arabs hailing from mainland tribes while the political agent, Harold Dickson, preferred a slate of mostly Shi`a notables,[14] again revealing a political agency that briefly takes up the call for Shi`a social justice. Likewise, the agency condemned the perpetuation of *sakhra*, or slavery of the *Baharna* by Sheikh Isa, for which, according to the colonial record, he was reprimanded by the political resident sometime in 1921.[15]

Within the Al Khalifah family and the larger Bahraini society, some people remained supportive of Sheikh Isa and wanted to see him reinstated. In addition, some foreign, but allied, Sunni tribes also remained loyal to Sheikh Isa over the newly installed Sheikh Hamad. The possibility of foreign intrigue in a successionary issue was presaged by colonial administrators who understood the basic contours of tribal and sheikhly power. While drafting the OiC reforms, an administrator noted that an early draft of the OiC was silent on the issue of "the subjects of Arab Chiefs with whom [Sheikh Isa] had private 'treaties,'" and whether those agreements should be examined, "[to] find if they are acknowledged by the parties, and then if suitable, formally recognize them."[16] Ultimately, the OiC laws gave the political agent jurisdiction over all foreigners, taking out of Sheikh Isa's hands the capacity to independently retain his own foreign alliances. But these alliances were exactly who the Sheikh turned to when he sought to contest his removal.

Meanwhile, Sheikh Abdullah bin Isa Al Khalifah also had designs on taking power. In the 1920s, colonial administrators noted that intrigue and unrest characterized the dissent over succession: "Abdulla will never cease intrigues to regain power and by fair means or foul to secure for himself the succession of his father."[17] In fact, before the forced abdication of Sheikh Isa, the British attempted to persuade Sheikh Isa to deport Sheikh Abdulla, in order to protect their heir designate, Sheikh Hamad.[18]

Belgrave, shortly after his arrival in the country to serve as Sheikh Hamad's advisor, observed that Abdulla was "frightfully jealous" of Hamad and that he had his hand in "a lot of mischief and [is] said to have done quite a number of murders,"[19] although which murders was not specified, if known. We do know that people in Muharraq complained that Abdullah abused his power regularly. Stories circulated that a pattern of missing young girls in Muharraq had been kidnapped for his pleasures.[20] His pimps would "bring him . . . any woman he wants. People are much too afraid to complain" and if they do so "face ill treatment by Abdulla[h]'s fidawis."[21] Another record reveals: "Secret murders by [Abdullah's] followers were becoming quite common and kidnapping girls in the streets of Muharraq after which they were not seen again was becoming one of Abdullah's pastimes."[22]

Abdullah's accomplice in agitating against the state was Jasim Chirawi who was blacklisted and deported by Political Agent Clive Daly.[23] On May 2, 1923, Chirawi contested his deportation order of April 17, 1922. In a telegram from India, he asked that his deportation be revoked on the grounds that if he is a Bahrain subject, he cannot be deported.[24] Interestingly, here we see the tribal allies of Abdullah, and their customary loyalty to him as being effectively criminalized and punished. Though there is no existing criminal case file on Chirawi, many files mention his intrigues, including a political file which indicates that he admitted his poor conduct and engaged in a negotiation with the political agency, promising to refrain in the future. In one telegram from the political agent to the political resident he was known to:

> . . . intimidate people and spread about that he could remove Hamad and the Political Agent and has thus discouraged movement which could have helped consolidate Hamad's position and restore lost Agency influence. Hamad is perturbed and asks for definite assurance of our support against Abdulla[h].[25]

Chirawi was ultimately found guilty of the crime of sedition, "conducting himself to be dangerous to peace and good order, or . . . excit[ing] . . . enmity between the people of Bahrein [sic] and His Majesty, or is intriguing within the limits of this Order against His Majesty's power and authority," section 21(11) under the Orders-in-Council, and banished for two years.[26]

The contestations over the rightful heir caused political ripples felt throughout the Sunni tribes, affecting relations even into the interior. A letter from King Hussein of Jordan on February 8, 1924, complained to the British that the deposing of Sheikh Isa was causing unrest and rivalry among the Arab tribes in his territory. The King asked the British to reexamine the case,[27] but a letter from Downing Street declined the request.[28]

The forced abdication happened in a way contrary to tribal law. The British had been warning Sheikh Isa that his government must submit to

British demands or face repercussions as early as March 7, 1922, during a personal visit from Political Resident Arthur Prescott Trevor.[29] This appears to have been a warning demanded by the Raj in order to provide due diligence before a virtual dethronement.

> Government of India telegrams that they are not prepared to consider drastic action regarding Bahrain misrule until they are satisfied that all local resources bringing pressure to bear are exhausted and that such intervention is imperative to secure the protection of foreigners and our interests. They therefore instruct [the political resident] to proceed to Bahrain at the earliest opportunity to warn [Sheikh Isa] and make it clear to him that in the event of any uprising Government will find it difficult to give him any support whatsoever . . .

However, uprisings followed. After the disturbances between Persians and Nejdis in 1923 (described in chapter 4), the new political resident Captain Stuart Knox, travelled to Bahrain with two warships, meeting with Sheikh Isa and Abdulla and demanding that Isa abdicate.[30] Isa refused, saying consultation with the tribes was necessary, probably attempting to reframe the question within customary tribal politics. Instead Knox called a meeting of the major sheikhs of the Al Khalifah on May 26, 1923, himself, and announced Sheikh Isa's abdication in favor of Sheikh Hamad without any open consultation or debate. Abdullah was thereafter deported for some time.[31]

Secret memos between the Viceroy and the Secretary of State from India in London appear to be aware of the consequences of such a blatant move on the part of colonial administrators. In a memorandum the month before, the Viceroy indicated that he believed that Sheikh Isa should be cajoled into abdicating voluntarily, but that if he would not, the British should be prepared to enforce reforms themselves through supporting Sheikh Hamad as the ruler. They knew that drawing the ire of the people against the colonial administration in Bahrain was a likely result, not to mention a negative reaction from the Saudis, a powerful neighbor and ally to Shiekh Isa.[32] After the events, Political Agent Arthur Trevor writes of the abdication as a "coup" pulled off by the political resident, suggesting that the British knew that their actions usurped the indigenous powers, but that was "absolutely necessary" in light of the obstinance of Sheikh Isa, as well as the dubious behavior of Sheikh Abdulla, likely Sheikh Isa's pick for his successor.

ASSASSINATION ATTEMPT ON SHEIKH HAMAD

Like Sheikh Muhammad in 1869, Sheikh Isa did not take his forced abdication in stride, but rather sought to regain his position in the following years. Sheikh Abdullah also maintained his claims as the rightful heir. Rumors of

Sheikh Abdullah's unsavory character continued to proliferate. This political imbroglio ultimately led to the assassination attempt of Sheikh Hamad in 1926, the subject of a criminal case in the newly created criminal courtroom of the PA Court. What before was a matter of loyalty in the context of tribal politics, was now a matter of the colonial state's newly-formed criminal justice system.

The assassination attempt on Sheikh Hamad was charged as attempted murder. Of the small sample of cases focused on in this study, four out of the thirty total involved attempted murder, seven involved murder (although one file is a continuation of another file in the sample and refers to the same murder), and one related to death by negligence (a fatal car accident). The criminal case files on this assassination attempt, and related criminal behavior, spanned several files in the Indian Office Records at the British Library (R/15/3/7001; 7002; 7003; 7004; 7005); they are relatively thin accounts for events that arguably were of significant political importance. This suggests that due to the sensitive nature of the matter, the case was sparingly recorded by administrators in a way pertaining only to the criminal case proceedings that resulted; the other interpretation is that documents failed to be retained or were removed. Interestingly, there is also a large gap in Charles Belgrave's diaries in late 1926, around the time of the assassination attempt. Although this cannot be verified, it appears that diary entries related to this event and during the same time period were removed from his archive. Belgrave consistently wrote in his diary almost daily, during his entire career, from when it began in North Africa during World War I and through his time in Bahrain from 1926 to 1957. Yet, a gap occurred from October 24, 1926 to January 4, 1927; Belgrave is silent when the assassination attempt on November 13, 1926 happened and for almost two months thereafter. His diaries and memoir make no mention of any personal upheavals or other reasons that explain that he could not or did not write; indeed when he first arrived in Bahrain that year he was writing profusely.

Regardless, the facts as recorded in the case file are as follows. On November 13, 1926, four or five shots, depending on witness statements, were fired at Sheikh Hamad's car while it traveled near a garden known as Bajaweiyah. The attempt at murder was a violation of section 307 of the Indian Penal Code[33] suitable for a defendant who "does any act with such intention, or knowledge, and under such circumstances that if he by that act caused death he would be guilty of murder . . . "[34] The code goes on to indicate that the punishment for the crime is imprisonment up to ten years and a fine. If hurt is caused, the crime is punishable by transportation for life. Further, if a person is already under the sentence of transportation for life and commits the crime, it is punishable by death.

Three Saudi subjects from Al-Hasa, Mohammad bin Isa (Mulla), Mohamed bin Muhasin, and Khamis bin Ali, were the accused in the case, but were not brought to justice until 1929. A fourth attacker, noted as only "Ghuwaili" was not tried because he was never apprehended. Connecting the dots across colonial records, these defendants were members of the Dawasir tribe,[35] pearling fleet owners and allies of the Al Khalifah, but feared by the inhabitants of Bahrain, particularly Shi`a. In a statement to police, Musaid said he was hired for 800 rupees to shoot Sheikh Hamad at the request of Sheikh Hamad (through an unnamed intermediary), alleging a strange twist of affairs in which the victim ordered his own assassination.[36] However, many believed that the culprit was Sheikh Abdullah who Sheikh Isa believed was aligned with him, but was also angling for his own enthronement, either immediately or following a reinstatement of Sheikh Isa.

Although details are murky, the case went un-prosecuted in 1926 due to a lack of political will within the Al Khalifah family to bring to justice a branch of their own family; however, when new evidence surfaced in 1929, colonial authorities felt compelled to criminally try the Saudi defendants in the PA Court. The evidence produced was a written communication by Sheikh Ibrahim bin Khalid bin Ali Al Khalifa (a nephew of Bahrain's former ruler Isa, and a member of the Khalid branch of the Al Khalifah family), through an intermediary, providing instructions and ten rounds of ammunition for use in the assassination plot.[37] Sheikh Ibrahim was prosecuted in the Bahrain Court; by this time Sheikh Hamad was willing to bring his relation to justice. Sheikh Salman, Sheikh Abdullah, Belgrave, and four assessors (two Sunnis and two Shi`a) judged the case.[38] Although Sheikh Ibrahim was found guilty in the case, Sheikh Hamad opted to take no action against his relation, and no sentence for the crime was issued.[39]

Meanwhile, in the PA Court, co-conspirators Mulla and Muhasin were sentenced to transportation for life (or twenty-five years).[40] Co-conspirator Khamis bin Ali was sentenced to ten years imprisonment. Further drama ensued when Khamis bin Ali attempted to escape from the Bahrain jail a few weeks after sentencing. According to the case file, Khamis bin Ali broke from his stocks and then through his cell door and the outer door. Upon discovery of this escape, jail guards shot bin Ali as he ran away, and he died in the hospital on May 22, 1929.[41]

The culpability of Sheikh Ibrahim was later corroborated through defendants Mulla and Muhasin (although some find Sheikh Abdullah to be behind events[42]; alternatively Sheikhs Abdulla, Ibrahim, and perhaps even the deposed Isa, could have been working together to murder Hamad to effect his ouster). On November 25, 1935, the Karachi District Prison Superintendent took a statement from prisoners Mulla and Muhasin in which they said that they were ordered to murder Sheikh Hamad by Sheikh Isa through Sheikh Ibrahim. As the subjects of Sheikh Isa, Mulla and Muhasin explained that they were "in the service of [Isa] bin Ali [and] had to obey the order whether willing or un-willing under great force. We had otherwise no enmity with

[Sheikh Hamad]. We never meant to secure the throne for ourselves."[43] The statement further requested a reduction of their sentences in light of this information, but the political agent responded that the conviction and sentence must be upheld as it had already gone through the appeals process.[44]

Overall, the interconnection of tribal contestations, Dawasir crimes, and sectarian strife are key to understanding the overall meaning of the attempted assassination. Chapter 4 further connects this event to the sectarian violence associated with Sheikh Ibrahim and his Al Khalid branch of the Al Khalifah family. For now, we examine the related cases for examples of the criminalization of tribal violence.

Tubli, Farsiya, Garyah, and Senabis Home Invasions: Dawasir Tribal Raids Become Crime

Four other existing criminal case files in the sample (R/15/3/7001; 7002; 7003; 7004) document tribal raids related to the controversy over Sheikh Hamad's accession and involve many of the same defendants: Sheikh Ibrahim, two of his relations, and Dawasir tribesmen. These events also occurred earlier in the 1920s and were originally the subject of trials *in absentia* by Major Clive Daly in 1925 (the perpetrators had absconded to the mainland or were serving sentences of banishment for other crimes). Like in the assassination attempt, these crimes were prosecuted in 1929.

In the Tubli case, the file indicates that in the winter of 1923, Mulla and Muhasin were part of a group who attacked the house of Hajji Hassan Al-Arabi, murdering him by shooting, and injuring his son, wife and daughter, in violation of section 460 of the Indian Penal Code, conspiracy to commit dacoity with murder.[45] The motive for the attack was reportedly a conflict about land boundaries and water rights. Al-Arabi was a tenant of Sheikh Humud bin Sabah's, a co-conspirator and close friend of the Al Khalifah family.[46]

In the Farsiya case, Mulla and Muhasin, along with Mubarak (first name unknown), were convicted after an armed attack on a household in the village of Farsiya. Mulla and Mubarak were found guilty of sections 396 (dacoity with murder) and 460 (conspiracy to commit dacoity with murder) of the Indian Penal Code. Muhasin, as the look-out in the conspiracy, was guilty of only section 460. According to the description of events, in the spring of 1924, three men armed with rifles, pistols, and revolvers broke into a house. An accomplice, Hamad bin Ghattam, tried in the Bahrain Court, killed two victims, Mohamed bin Qambar and Abdulla bin Hassan. Maryam bin Ali was violently dragged out of the house by the perpetrators.[47] The victims were bin Ghattam's *Baharna* tenants who refused to pay taxes to the Al Khalifah, a sectarian pattern in this slew of violence which will be taken up in chapter 4.[48] Although the case was subject to criminal prosecution in

1929, the file notes that the incident had already been subject to the customary responses. Ghattam attempted to pay blood money to Maryam bin Ali and the relatives of the deceased.

In the Garyah case, in the winter of 1924, Mulla and Muhasin, one of them armed with a rifle, entered a house in Garyah village where a man and his wife were sleeping. Either Mulla or Muhasin said to them, "State and deliver what you have or we will kill you." The man gave them 4,000 rupees, some additional cash, two pistols, gold bangles, a carpet, gold nose-pieces, coffee and tobacco. Muhasin reportedly choked the man by the throat and beat his wife. The punishment for this violation of section 457 of the Indian Penal code was not recorded in the file.[49]

In the so-called Senabis case, we see that much of the contents of the criminal case file pertain to a different attack on a Shi`a community on Sitra island, at the village of Wadyan (also known as the "Second Sitra Outrage," discussed again in chapter 4). It is not clear as to why the file labels do not match all the file contents. What we know from other sources is that there was an attack at Senabis in 1926 during which half a dozen people were killed. It probably is the subject of the recorded charge in the file, that the Dawasir defendants Mulla, Muhasin, and Musaid (first name unknown) were convicted of dacoity in violation of section 460 of the Indian Penal Code. But the narrative portion of the file details a more brutal attack than the charges implied. They indicate that the defendants attacked the household of Abdul Hassan in Wadyan and that Hassan was murdered by co-defendants tried in the Bahraini court, along with Hajji Radhi. Other Shi`a villagers were subsequently shot in the street. Implicated in the crime was Sheikh Ibrahim bin Khalid Al Khalifah. The Khalid branch of the royal Al Khalifah family, led the attack, reportedly on behalf of Sheikh Isa.[50] For the attack at Wadyan, the Dawasir defendants received transportation for life. Many requests for appeal of the sentence were noted as denied. In April 1930, the political resident dismissed an appeal because Wadyan was "a particularly brutal offense." Another notation indicates that Mulla was not released early because he was part of the related assassination attempt on Sheikh Hamad.[51]

TRIBAL JUSTICE AS COLONIAL CRIME

Contextualizing the above criminals case begins with how they represent the criminalization of tribal rivalry. Belgrave's diary refers to a conversation with Sheikh Hamad in 1927 during which Sheikh Hamad implied concern that the Dawasir tribe was going to maintain a feud with his branch of the family because the Ghattam murder victims' relatives were unwilling to substitute further violence with blood money, per tribal custom, after the events in Farsiya in 1924. As such, the crime at Ghattam exemplifies the tribal succession problem; the Dawasir were aligned with Sheikh Isa, and further, the Dawasir and Shaikh Isa had managed to gain the support of the Saudis in actively working against Sheikh Hamad. As was customary, Shiekh Isa had reached out to the Saudis and his other external, as well as internal, tribal allies in his bid to regain control of Bahrain. One could speculate that Sheikh Hamad did not want to pursue the formal criminal prosecution of Ghattam for fear of exacerbating the tribal rivalry, which could undermine his hold on the rulership. Regardless of Sheikh Hamad's fears, however, the prosecution went forward. As Belgrave notes in his diary on July 31, 1929:

> Started the case against Hamed bin Abdulla al Ghattam. Took the evidence of the relations of two Bahrainis who were murdered. To my mind, there was absolutely no doubt that Hamed was with the people who attacked the house. He is a nasty little creature. The Court consists of [Salman] and I and Abdulla. [Salman] is very obviously prejudiced in favour of the accused. It is natural as they are relations. The brother of the man asked if he could appear instead of him as he was more accustomed to courts. [It's] altogether a most awkward business.[52]

Although the files indicate the home invasion cases are related to the royal assassination attempt, the files do not say precisely what the relationship is; the only explicit relationship is the involvement of Mulla and/or Muhasin in all the events. Exactly who Mulla and Muhasin are and how they came to involve themselves as regular characters in the home invasions, and central to the plot to kill Sheikh Hamad, again, is implied, but not explicit in the criminal case files. The problem rests in the style of discourse in criminal cases in the Western tradition: because of a narrow focus on charges and conduct that relates to those specific charges, they read like individually-motivated street crimes. That they actually have their root in the tribal succession problem is inferred, given historical evidence around the events, but never stated directly. Reading narrowly, Mulla and Muhasin are merely hired hands in the crimes and under this assumption, have committed violence purely for pecuniary gain. However, some other options present themselves when the behavior is taken in context. Mulla and Muhasin could have established themselves as highly effective violent raiders and plunderers for their own gain in the various home invasions, and so Sheikh Ibrahim and/or whoever the underlying Al Khalifah culprit was, decided they would make great royal assassins and offered them the job. Or, if we take their later disclosure from the Karachi Prison to be true, the assassination was not merely a monetary transaction, but one based on their tribal loyalty to the oppositional branch of the Al Khalifah led by Sheikh Isa, who was actively waging a campaign against Sheikh Hamad's government. Taking the political context even more to heart, the criminal events are related to the larger political problem of the tribal succession from Sheikh Isa to Sheikh Hamad in a very particular way, which speaks to the transition from tribal to colonial law and justice. Mulla, Muhasin, and company can be read as a type of neo-tribal *ghazzu* (tribal force and/or armed retainers), representing how an old-school oppositional sheikh mobilized against the emergent colonial order.

Regardless of the exact nature of Mulla and Muhasin's participation in events, they were entangled in a web that drew various actors into violence. As Al-Tajir sums up the general situation in the early 1920s: "Both the tribes and the disaffected members of the Ruling Family were now involved in a campaign against the [political agent] whose interference in the internal affairs of the country was, they believe, in excess of the powers invested in him." Although many protestations were peaceful and involved petitions and negotiations, this was not the case with the assassination attempt. Importantly, with the new criminal adjudication, enemies of the colonially-backed ruler in the contest, whether diplomatic or violent about it, do not win the day through tribal alliances and warfare like in the days of yore. Instead regime enemies are treated as criminals by the state and prosecuted, often banished from Bahrain for a period of time.

BLOOD MONEY AND COLONIAL HYBRIDITY

Some aspects of tribal justice, however, found a place in the criminal justice system. The Bahrain Court, the criminal court for Bahraini citizens, became entwined in the administration of customary blood money in the late 1920s. The government kept track, or was willing to act as an administrative intermediary, in the paying of customary blood money, a curious absorption of tribal law into the formal state and a prime example of colonial hybridity. In records produced by Belgrave for the Farsiya home invasion file, Hamid bin Ghattam paid blood money, received by the government to pass along, but the deceased's relatives refused to accept the money. Belgrave wrote that the money may have gone to Bombay or to Customs or back to Ghattam; there was no record of its final destination after not being accepted.[53] Similar comingling of the customary and colonial justice system is inferred by a diary entry in 1927 in which Belgrave reports that when he asked the Sheikh about the Tubli home invasion case "of course he said 'let them settle it by compromise' that being the most simple way out of it."[54] This shows that incidents that came to the attention of the State Police, which Belgrave headed, were sometimes diverted to customary justice systems.

Seen another way, the Al Khalifah used the customary tribal system to ally themselves with a regional power that ushered in the colonial mode of order maintenance, thus forever changing how the tribal system would operate, subjugating that system. Under customary understandings, the Al Khalifah were "casting the British in the culturally acceptable role of 'protector' (*mujawwir*) within the regional system of Arabia,"[55] but at the expense of the traditional functioning of that system. For the British notion of protection (*pax Brittanica*), enmeshed in the imperial modes of economic expansion and political pacification,[56] was entirely different from the tribal one, and given British military superiority and eventual colonial restructuring of Bahrain, the British notion of protection and order maintenance would be privileged over all others.

Colonial administrators hoped to phase out tribal justice with the administrative reforms,[57] but many also thought the colonial state would be more legitimate if it could manage to incorporate some tribal law, as well as Muslim law, into the new state. This would, of course, occur selectively, based on colonial preference (and indeed, the structure of the new state allows for Muslim law for family and personal status cases). For in the eyes of the British, tribal justice in general leads to violence, particularly in the way that it could be mobilized to threaten the colonial state, as Sheik Isa had attempted. As the administration took shape under Belgrave's advisorship, blood money was somewhat absorbed into the colonial state function as an alternative method to criminal prosecution. Whether absorbing or suppressing other forms of justice and other notions of the social order, the main thrust was the stabilizing of native conflict resolution so that it would fit into the colonial order.

THE SEDITION OF SHEMLAN AND CHIRAWI

In a later court prosecution, occurring in the Bahrain Court in 1939 and 1940, we see the maturation, after several years, of the capacity of the legal process to quash Sunni criticisms of Sheikh Hamad's government. The case of Sa'ad bin Shemlan and Ahmad Chirawi, although not an overtly tribal-based criticism of the state, reflects a vestigial tribal concern over whether Sheikh Hamad is a suitable ruler for Bahrain.

Tucked away in a file of paintings and other art within the archive of the personal papers of Sir Charles Belgrave at the University of Exeter was a rough draft, in Belgrave's hand and in pencil, of the Bahrain Court's judgment in the Shemlan and Chirawi case. The pair were two ardent supporters of Sheikh Isa, who were tried for the crime of sedition.[58] According to the judgment, the two defendants visited various Sunni notables in Muharraq and Hidd and spoke against the government under Sheikh Hamad, specifically labeling the government *muthalim*, meaning that the government was defiled of honor and of ill repute, and specifically citing the institutions of the courts and municipal councils. According to the draft of the judgment, they also belonged to a group known as the "young nationalists of Bahrain" along with Ali bin Khalifah and Ibrahim bin Kamal. In the more mature, yet still relatively new colonial regime, opposition forces framed themselves as national movements and formed alliances more broadly with other social sectors, including newly influential Shi`a merchants. They "spoke to [the people they visited in Muharraq and [Hidd] in such a way as to excite disaffection to the Government."[59] They described the oppressed Arabs [Belgrave's word] as "*mutathayera*" or revolutionaries who were "rising to obtain their general rights."[60] Ibrahim bin Kamal turned state's evidence in the matter.

Although Belgrave recognized that it was not a crime under colonial law to air grievances, it was a crime "to force a government to change by causing public disturbances."[61] He wrote, "The question which the court has to decide is not whether the alleged words were spoken, because this is not denied, but whether the words would cause disaffection to the Government and whether the accused were aware of this."[62] Although Belgrave does not cite a specific law in the draft judgment, he does say the crime of sedition is punishable by four years hard labor and a fine. This does not seem to correspond directly to any of the punishments in chapter 6 of the Indian Penal Code (Offences Against the State), but similar offenses in that code are punishable by a fine and up to three or up to seven years imprisonment (but without specific mention of hard labor).[63]

Belgrave further indicated that the speech of the accused caused bloodshed in the country, but does not cite specific instances. Ostensibly the bloodshed related to the disturbances of 1938, in which a feeling of resentment against the colonial administration was palpable, related to "falling school standards, inefficient Courts, the rising cost of living, high unemployment and cases of bankruptcy brought about by the decline of the pearl trade and the shift in the financial base in favour of the Ruling Family."[64] Further, Sheik Hamad's failing health was fomenting concerns about succession with two main competing preferences, the succession of Sheikh Hamad's son, Sheikh Salman, and the other possibility being Shaikh Abdullah.[65] In July 1938, the day after the arrest of Shemlan and Chirawi, Bahrain Petroleum Company's (BAPCO) workers went on strike, almost paralyzing operations. Demonstrations also rose up in the *suq*.[66] The colonial state refused to tolerate this kind of unrest and insecurity, even more so given that by the late 1930s oil was the new impetus for British control of the region. Much ink was spilled by administrators trying to strategize ways to best suppress the dissent and restore colonial order.

THE PRIVILEGING OF COLONIAL VIOLENCE OVER TRIBAL VIOLENCE

The British eschewed the dynamic, flexible, and violent order maintenance of the Al Khalifah and the Sunni tribes when left to their own customs and criminalized the vestiges of tribal rivalries. The pacification of clan-based violence echoes Norbert Elias' notion of the "civilizing process" as the taking of power from a diffuse and dynamic warrior culture and subsuming it under the self-restraining regime of the Western nation-state.[67] Yet, the colonial state's use of violence is rarely questioned. Assumed under the colonial project is the notion that the British Navy, as is the case with many contemporaneous imperial modes, is a necessary threat on the waters of the Gulf in order to usher in the regional stability for the development of trade in general, and increasingly, oil in particular. Randall Collins, writing about twentieth century violence, takes this double standard further by articulating that interpersonal violence "comes to be succeeded by other forms of violence, new forms of bureaucratic domination and of asceticism. Passionless, impersonal callousness, in which more persons than ever before in history are now killed or mutilated" by the state instead of each other.[68]

When the external security mission crept into the internal one, as was the case with Bahrain in the early twentieth century, the criminal code now asked Bahrainis, particularly Sunni tribal leaders, to pacify their behavior in order to conform to the Indian Penal Code. Reading against the grain, we see that what appears as several criminal cases that are the result of marauding Hasawi tribespeople of ill-repute (primarily the Dawasir), are actually, or in addition, representative of the Al Khalifah internal-external tribal resistance to the colonially-installed ruler. The suppression of this behavior as criminal is an elimination struggle under Elias' definition—complete with formal stigmatization and penalties. And, the absorption of the blood money tradition into the practical workings of the Bahrain Court is also an example of hybridity between the old and new forms of order maintenance. For Elias, the old ways never fully extinguish in the move from a warrior culture of diffuse legitimacy to a regime that centralizes legitimate violence. Instead, the new social order requires a more complex set of individual expectations for everyday people to show restraint in violence,[69] even when state power and militaries are unrestrained. The next chapter details some of the more ordinary crimes that exhibit this civilizing process. Prosecutions of these crimes, however, serve the purpose of tamping down Sunni tribal customs in general and shoring up colonial and Al Khalifah power and control in everyday life.

NOTES

1. Despatch no. 90, Foreign Officer to Bahrain, Charles A. Gault, to Foreign Secretary Selwyn Lloyd [Papers of Charles Dalrymple Belgrave, 1926–1947, University of Exeter, United Kingdom, 148/2/1, 1956].
2. Khuri 1980: 33.
3. Onley 2007: 157–159; Khuri 1980: 22.
4. Khuri 1980: 33.

5. James Onley, "Britain's Informal Empire," *Protection and Politics in Bahrain, 1869–1915*. ed. Farah, Talal Toufic (Syracuse University Press, 1985): 42.
6. Khuri 1980: 93.
7. Onley and Khalaf 2006: 199.
8. Khuri 1980.
9. Khuri 1980: 45; Onley and Khalaf 2006:194.
10. Onley and Khalaf 2006:194.
11. Onley and Khalaf 2006.
12. Al-Tajir 1987: 23–24; Clive K. Daly, "Annual Report on the Operation of the 'Bahrain Order in Council' for the year 1921" (India Office Records, R/15/1/305, no date).
13. Letter no. 246–s from Arthur Trevor, Deputy Political Resident to Acting CC Baghdad (India Office Records, R/15/1/319, December 28, 1919).
14. Al-Tajir 1987: 26
15. Despatch no. 90, C.A. Gault to Selwyn Lloyd [Papers of Charles Dalrymple Belgrave, 1926–1947, University of Exeter, United Kingdom, 148/2/1, 1956].
16. Letter from David Lorimer Political Agent to Percy Cox Political Resident (India Office Records, R/15/1/299, April 20, 1912).
17. Telegram no. 56/c from Political Agent to Political Resident (India Office Records, R/15/2/100, no date, circa 1925).
18. Confidential memorandum from Political Agent to Political Resident (India Office Records, R/15/2/100, May 20, 1923); Secret memorandum from India Office Whitehall to Secretary of the Government of India, Foreign and Political Affairs Department (India Office Records, R/15/2/1394, May 4, 1922).
19. Belgrave, personal diary, July 28, 1926.
20. Major Clive Daly to the Political Resident [India Office Records, British Library, r/15/2/100, June 18, 1921].
21. Handwritten note of complaint (India Office Records, R/15/2/100, no date, circa 1925).
22. Confidential letter from Arthur Trevor, Political Agent, to Percy Cox, Political Resident, (India Office Records, R/15/2/8, May 13, 1923).
23. Confidential memorandum from Political Agent Clive Daly to Political Resident (India Office Records, R/15/2/100, May 20, 1923).
24. Telegram from Foreign Office in Simla to Political Resident in Bushehr (India Office Records, R/15/2/104, May 2, 1923).
25. Telegram no. 56/C, Political Agent to Political Resident (India Office Records, R/15/2/1394, undated, probably summer of 1921.)
26. *Orders-in-Council*, London, August 12, 1913 (India Office Records, R/15/2/7): 6.
27. Letter from King Hussein of Jordan to Government House Jerusalem (India Office Records TJ/221, February 8, 1924).
28. Letter from J.B. Thomas for the High Commissioner to King Hussein of Jordan (India Office Records TJ/221, March 26, 1924).
29. Radhi 2003: 40.
30. Radhi 2003: 41
31. Al-Tajir 1987: 45–46.
32. Memorandum No. 475–s from the Viceroy to the Secretary of State for India (India Office Records, R/15/2/100, April 17, 1923).
33. Criminal case file no. 66/400 of 1929 (India Office Records, R/15/3/7005).
34. *The Indian Penal Code, Act XLV of 1860* (Srinivasa, Varadachari & Co., 1893).
35. Al-Tajir 1987: 67.
36. Criminal case file no. 66/400 of 1929 (India Office Records, R/15/3/7005).
37. Al Tajir 1987: 77.
38. Al Tajir 1987: 77.
39. Al-Tajir 1987: 77; Letter no. 355 from Charles Belgrave to Political Resident (India Office Records, R/15/2/88, August 19, 1929.
40. Criminal case file no. 66/400 of 1929 (India Office Records, R/15/3/7005).
41. Criminal case file no. 66/400 of 1929 (India Office Records, R/15/3/7005).

42. Marc Owen Jones, "Who Really Tried to Assassinate Sheikh Hamad?" *marcowen-jones.wordpress.com* (blog), April 1, 2013, https://marcowenjones.wordpress.com/tag/shaikh-hamad/.
43. Criminal case file no. 66/400 of 1929 (India Office Records, R/15/3/7005).
44. Memorandum no. 367/VC from George Cole Officiating Political Agent to the Superintendent of the Karachi Prison (India Office Records, R/15/3/7005, December 11, 1935).
45. Case no. 62/396 of 1929 (Indian Office Records, R/15/3/7001)
46. Al-Tajir 1987: 77.
47. Case no. 65 of 1929 (India Office Records, R/15/3/7004).
48. Al-Tajir 1987: 77.
49. Case no. 63/397 of 1929 (India Office Records, R/15/3/7002).
50. Handwritten notes of the Indian Assistant about interrogations in case no. 34/398 of 1929 (India Office Records, R/15/3/7003).
51. Case no. 34/398 of 1929 (India Office Records, R/15/3/7003).
52. Charles Belgrave, personal diary, July 31, 1929.
53. Case no. 65 of 1929 (India Office Records, R/15/3/7004).
54. Charles Belgrave, personal diary, December 10, 1927.
55. Onley 2007: 223.
56. Steinmetz 2007:2–3.
57. Gengler 2015: 3.
58. Charles Belgrave, personal diaries (University of Exeter, 148/1, January 8, 12, 14, 26, 29, 1940).
59. Charles Belgrave, draft of judgment (Papers of Charles Dalrymple Belgrave, University of Exeter, 148/2/4, circa 1940): 1 (my numbers of unnumbered pages).
60. Charles Belgrave, draft of judgment (Papers of Charles Dalrymple Belgrave, University of Exeter, 148/2/4, circa 1940): 2 (my numbers of unnumbered pages).
61. Charles Belgrave, draft of judgment (Papers of Charles Dalrymple Belgrave, University of Exeter, 148/2/4, circa 1940): 4 (my numbers of unnumbered pages).
62. Charles Belgrave, draft of judgment (Papers of Charles Dalrymple Belgrave, University of Exeter, 148/2/4, circa 1940): 3 (my numbers of unnumbered pages).
63. *The Indian Penal Code, Act XLV of 1860* (Srinivasa, Varadachari & Co., 1893).
64. Al-Tajir 1987: 238.
65. Al-Tajir 1987: 239
66. Al-Tajir 1987: 241–242.
67. Elias 1938/1982.
68. Randall Collins, "Three Faces of Cruelty: Towards a Comparative Sociology of Violence," *Theory and Society* 1, 1974): 418.
69. Elias 1938/1982.

Chapter Three

"You Brother of a Prostitute"

Honor, Insults, and Crime

In 1925, Syed Muhammad Ahmad Juma'a Al-Lail, a Yemeni, was convicted in the PA Court for the crime of criminal intimidation by anonymous communication, in violation of sections 506 and 507 of the Indian Penal Code. According to the criminal case file,[1] the victim was Ali Yateem, who received letters in what appeared to have a "marked resemblance" to the defendant's handwriting (though he tried to disguise it), threatening death and grievous harm. The letters indicated that a secret society had formed to kill him. In a search of the defendant's house, a revolver and a sword were confiscated by police at which time Al-Lail's son-in-law was arrested. Charles Belgrave, normally acting as a judge in the Bahrain Court, prosecuted this case at the Political Agency. At trial, the defendant said he was falsely accused and framed by someone who routinely takes bribes, thus intimating that the case was drummed up by an interpersonal enemy who paid the complainant. Further, Al-Lail sought mitigation in the case for having previously helped Major Clive Daly, a former political agent, in a matter related to unspecified "Bahrain disturbances," (most likely those between1922 to 1923; see chapters 2 and 4). In being framed, Al-Lail alleged that the main witness against him was a member of Hezbul Moaredh, a political party aligned with the deposed Sheikh Isa. He further intimated that this person was against him because he encouraged a local sheikh not to sign an unspecified petition circulated by the Hezbul Moaredh.[2]

The contemporary political agent sentenced Al-Lail to nine years transportation. On appeal, the political resident reduced the sentence to three years. Although this case did not end up in a violent episode, the police, in searching and documenting weapons, likely felt there was violent potential.

The use of threatening letters and the interpersonal drama that the case represents, though only barely described, shows how words and conflicting versions of what words mean and why they are being unleashed by a speaker or writer, are a recurring theme across the cases we focus on here. Whereas this particular case is relatively minor, many of the other cases documented below show how personal and family honor, previously fought about within tribal and merchant communities and settled by tribal sheikhs or religious *qadi*s, now entered the newly formed, colonial criminal courts. The previous chapter explained how the ruling sheikhs suffered attacks on their honor in the form of succession crises and how the new state criminalized much of the tribal behavior of sheikhs in order to control the territory. This chapter explores the criminalization of the honor-based behavior of everyday inhabitants of Bahrain who fought for their families' reputations in the wake of insults.

The criminalization of certain honor-based behaviors, in particular using violence to avenge insults against one's relations, becomes an aggravating circumstance. Often, judges and court personnel characterized those operating under traditional tribal honor codes as being without sense or reason. The news failed to grasp the social meaning behind such behavior even as they documented it, sometimes in great detail. Instead, colonial administrators were culturally blinded by their own notions of proper behavior and committed to tamping down violence that would make Bahrain unsafe for trade and later oil exploration. There are many examples across the cases examined in which defendants who adhered to more traditional social relations around protection and maintenance of honor, a key part of Arab social order, were misunderstood by court personnel and judges and even treated more harshly than others. Eventually, the criminalization of honor-based behavior will reflect a shifting social norm, as some inhabitants of Bahrain conformed to the new social order codified in the Indian Penal Code. The code marginalized traditionalists and neo-traditionalists, or those uneducated in the ways of colonial civility, through new types of authority, processes, and punishments.

In the criminal cases examined in this study, including some involving women as victims, traditional behaviors and modes of being were in conflict with the new social order, and through the courts, those exhibiting these newly discouraged ways of being are formally punished, as part of any overall process of assimilation by the prevailing power in the form of the colonial state. The transitioning social order, then, makes conduct "an acute problem. . . . Much is open to scrutiny in conduct that previous generations took for granted."[3] Norbert Elias theorized about this social problem in the context of a transitioning Europe after the honor-based modalities of the Middle Ages in *The Civilizing Process*. He asserted that the newly centralized, bureaucratic state of affairs permitted the government "to rule people through themselves" and in this Freud-influenced conception, "through the moulding

[sic] of their super-egos."[4] In other words, the law would be enforced in such a way as to ensnare the purveyors of the old social order in processes and punishments on an individual level, changing the behavior of people over time as they seek to avoid those fates.

CULTURAL NOTIONS OF PERSONAL AND CLAN-BASED HONOR

Before the imposition of the colonial regime, the Al Khalifah ruled based on honor (*sharaf*) related to traditional social norms and the realization of social ideals in their tribal society. Pierre Bourdieu characterized honor in Arab culture as self-image that is then enacted in front of other people. When it is central to a culture, a person will defend it at all costs.[5] The place of honor is high in Arab culture and provides a differential basis for conflict resolution when compared to Western legal models. Honor in Arab culture can trump other needs.[6] It increases with moral conduct considered laudable in the eyes of the Arab tribal society and decreases by bad moral conduct. Traditional Arab honor is also a gendered affair. For men, masculine honor is derived from achieving success in a warrior culture and by showing hospitality and protecting surrendered enemies and women. In the Gulf, honor is sometimes referred to as *shaff*[7] or *shima*.[8]

For women, a separate social construct is evident around what is labeled *'ird*, translated as purity or chastity. Gulf tribal women hold the good name of their male relatives, and at the center of this is modesty and keeping the prohibition against friendships, or other relations, with unrelated men. The latter particularly falls on unmarried females. As Dickson explains: "The most dreadful thing that can happen to them is to be talked about," for gossip easily leads to a soiled reputation.[9] Gulf ethnographer Peter Lienhardt found that family honor depends more heavily on the behavior of women, and that if a woman strays from moral conduct it is a socially-approved response for a male of the family to kill her,[10] what in the West has been called honor-killings. Dickson further elucidates that girls are traditionally seen to belong to the father's brother's son (first cousin) and that she must marry him unless he refuses. If he refuses, she may not marry another without the first cousin's approval. If a first cousin desires to marry the girl and she refuses, she can be slain.[11] Although these customs may not have been followed in detail in Bahrain in the early twentieth century, the general cultural concern with *'ird* and pockets of tolerance for customarily-legitimate honor killings existed in the country (though overall such crimes were not frequent).

Under these social constructions of honor, words can hurt. At the center of an honorable reputation is that public opinion is in one's favor. Negative gossip, or personal or family insults, can lead to an individual and his family to lose face (*wedj*), and shame can attach.[12] As such, public accusations can lead to violence if the offended party becomes socially strained, or is afraid of the consequences, enough to seek a violent correction to the matter. Or perhaps the violence is expressive, a passionate reaction to what is experienced as a fundamentally horrible accusation, something that could lead to social death.

"I HAVE BEEN KILLED!": PERSONAL INSULTS ARE WORSE THAN GOVERNMENTAL POWER

A 1933 murder case provides much insight into the devaluation of traditional honor codes by the court even as they are directly adjudicating honor-based conflict. In *Crown v. Ali Mohamed Eddorsi*, a Nejdi (Saudi) shepherd (Ali Mohamed Eddorsi) was tried for the murder of a *mullah* of western Manama, Ibrahim bin Yusuf bin Kalban, in violation of section 302 of the Indian Penal Code, which refers to an intentionally caused homicide, and is punishable by death or transportation for life.[13] According to witness interviews, Eddorsi rented a portion of a shop from bin Kalban. Living there for only four days, Eddorsi became dissatisfied with the accommodations because the roof leaked water when it rained; one of the walls was severely water-damaged and Eddorsi began to fear the overall structural safety of the edifice. He decided not to live there; however, he left some of his things behind. A detailed list of his possessions included a coffeepot, matting, water pots, nails, baskets of date-stones, dates, and a cushion. When the defendant attempted to reclaim his items, the victim asked for a rent payment. Eddorsi was unwilling to pay more than four days' rent given that he had only lived there that long and the shop was in his eyes not fit for human habitation. According to two witnesses, on January 10, 1933, an argument ensued between Eddorsi and bin Kalban in the vicinity of a nearby mosque, and two witnesses heard a scream of "*Aqatalu*!" (I have been killed). The witnesses reportedly saw a dagger in Eddorsi's hand, and he was crouching over the stabbed victim. The two witnesses, and another who came to the scene upon hearing the commotion, together apprehended the defendant, tying him up with rope for responding *naturs* (who then summoned the police to come and arrest him). The police recovered the dagger and noted that it had stains of blood and mud on it. They brought bin Kalban to the hospital for medical treatment. In addition, the police noted that Eddorsi had a wound on his side, not consistent with the murder weapon, and was also taken to the hospital.

When cross-examined by the Indian Assistant (IA) to the PA, the defendant said "I made up my mind to stab [the victim] because [he] had seized my kit and thus shown insult to me more than the power of *hakumat* (government)." In another statement Eddorsi added that he asked the bin Kalban if he represented the *hakuma* and if not, he was only "after mischief." Eddorsi also stated that he feared bin Kalban was going to beat him, and that his intention in the stabbing was only to injure. These details were taken into consideration as potential mitigating factors. But, in a report to the file, the IA revealed that Eddorsi's explanation made no sense to him, suggesting that there was a gulf between the purveyors of the old customs and administrators of the new criminal justice apparatus. The IA, an educated product of the imperial order, embodies the legalistic logic of the penal code he is applying in Bahrain. Meanwhile, the uneducated Nejdi shepherd exists in a milieu of traditional honor codes in which verbal insults are taken seriously, grievously so. If indeed the defendant believed that his honor was injured in the exchange with bin Kalban, then lesser charges may have been called for than those applied. In essence, the crime was victim precipitated to a larger extent the court may have realized, perhaps placing it akin to a crime of passion in the Western legal tradition. In addition, Eddorsi himself indicates that his intent was only to injure, thus suggesting that the necessary *mens rea* for deliberate murder may not have been met. But because the IA either does not, or refuses to, "see" the gravity of the insult, and chalks it up to Eddorsi "foolishly taking the law in his own hands," the criminal case file fails to capture the meaning of the violence for those involved. It glosses over the fact that colonial reforms which ushered in the current legal regime had only in the last few years been instituted officially in Bahrain, and the new regime diverged from the honor-based tribal codes to which Nejdi shepherds were most likely accustomed. The IA charged the defendant and referred his case to trial. The sessions case file picks up the story and indicates that the trial court convicted him and that death was considered as a possible sentence.[14] The ultimate result in the case, however, is not recorded. In correspondence dated Feb. 5, 1933, the Political Agency reported to the political resident: "The Adviser [Belgrave] tells me that he does not think there is any likelihood of trouble being caused by such a sentence, so far as the Shaikh is concerned . . . "[15] This likely refers to any tribal opposition that may follow a state execution.

At trial, interestingly Sa'ad bin Shemlan, who was later convicted of sedition (see previous chapter) acted as the *wakil*, or representative of the defendant. *Wakil*s were legal proxies used in the new courts. They were not lawyers (*muhamin*) as they did not have legal training. Instead, they stood in for adjudicants who lacked or were perceived to lack the capacity to successfully represent themselves,[16] and were often used for uneducated agriculturalists, like Eddorsi, women, and children. In this case, Shemlan questioned Eddorsi in order to help him represent himself, confessing to the court that he felt that his client was "ignorant and unintelligent." Shemlan reportedly highlighted many inconsistencies in the facts alleged by the prosecution. He presented this statement:

> His intention was to frighten [Ibrahim], so that he would return his things. But Ibrahim pushed himself forward, so that when the (accused) had the dagger raised in his hand Ibrahim attacked him . . . the force of the rush on Ibrahim made him give the blow. Also, the evidence of the witnesses show that none of them saw with his own eyes, the accused strike him nor could anyone in the quarter say on what spot the accused struck Ibrahim. There are many wounds which, inflicted on any part of the body of a person, cause death: the accused struck the deceased as other people strike, and he had the misfortune to kill him.[17]

The defendant also reportedly told the PA Court: "I was provoked to do this since [the victim] was saying that he was Government. Since he was saying he was [the] Ruler and his head was high, I was forced to do this act." This statement contextualizes the defendant's comparison of the personal insult as compared to governmental power, for he believed that the mulla was an agent of the colonial government. It is possible that Eddorsi confused the fact that the mulla was probably registered with the government as a result of the colonial reforms, and may have even been on the governmental payroll for his role as a Sunni religious leader. This would have been another recent arrangement as a result of the OiC reforms, something that Eddorsi may not have understood as a matter of administering the colonial state.

I WOULD NOT MIND A SENTENCE OF DEATH FROM THE GOVERNMENT

Another criminal case also involved a matter of honor that seemingly goes misunderstood. On December 18, 1936, the police responded to information that the defendant, Mahmud bin Abdulla, an Iraqi, had stabbed Ahmed bin Abbas, an Iranian, with a knife on a Manama pier.[18] The police immediately arrested bin Abdullah and brought bin Abbas to the hospital. Bin Abbas told police when interviewed that the accused asked to be taken aboard his steamer as a hired coolie, but bin Abbas did not have any need for his services. He told the defendant that the "up mail" steamer (going toward Basra) the following day may have need for him. The defendant then began to argue with bin Abbas about not being hired and reportedly called bin Abbas a "son of [a] bastard" before taking out a knife and stabbing him. Bin Abdullah was charged with attempted murder in violation of section 307 of the Indian Penal Code.

Meanwhile, the accused stated that there were two encounters related to the incident in question. Earlier in the day before the stabbing, the victim said he would not hire the accused on account of his reputation of being "rude." The accused then went home, changed his clothes, bought a knife, and returned to the pier to confront bin Abbas again. When the interviewing judicial assistant asked the accused why he responded in such a way, the defendant stated that bin Abbas had verbally abused his sister "without any reason and without knowing her." Couple this with not getting a job at a time when he was quite strapped for money, the defendant "felt angry and said to myself that I shall kill this man and if, afterwards, the Government pass[es a] sentence of death against me I would not mind it. But I would not like begging nor ask[ing] [anybody] for one pie."

When he returned to the pier, bin Abbas reportedly called the defendant "you brother of a prostitute." Bin Abdullah explained, "A man dies for his religion, for his family, and for his property . . . It is a great disgrace for a man to be called [a] brother of a prostitute." During the trial, Political Agent Percy Loch questioned the defendant's motives, indicating in the file that the sister lived in Khandaq and had never been to Bahrain, nor met the victim therefore. Thus, Loch believed the disgrace alleged could not possibly have been all that great. He wrote to the file on January 19, 1937, "I explained that if he had a sister here and the man Ahmed [bin Abbas] had murdered her, this was one thing—but if Ahmed had just used a general term of whore, that was another." In the judgment he explained:

> The crime is a serious one, but I consider that the accused is a man so lacking in mental power that it is preferable, having regard to local circumstances, to return him to his country rather than he should be kept in prison in Bahrain.

He was sentenced to banishment from Bahrain for a period of two years under OiC provisions, section 21(1).

However, Loch was likely mistaken as to the gravity of bin Abdullah's insult to bin Abbas. Under customary notions of honor and reputation in the Sunni tribes, the insult itself is enough to disgrace. As the aforementioned ethnographic accounts of tribal customs show, insults, gossip, and words that would sully reputations are serious matters, especially when a female relation's honor is a stake. The thought of his sister being slighted by a powerful merchant like bin Abbas may have created such an emotion in the defendant because of its social and cultural import, as to put him on the attack. Loch cannot sufficiently understand the violence using his own (Western) judgment of what is a disgrace. He fails to understand or accept it even when the defendant explains that the words were a devastating blow, and even when the defendant also says that the insult put him in such a rage that he did not mind if colonial justice should come down on him and sentence him to death. Instead, the lack of sense being attached to the defendant contributes to a further judgment that he also lacks mental capacity. In the files, a common theme emerged: That which was not an acceptable motive in a Western sense inevitably led to judgments of madness and/or mental incapacitation. Such judgments did not always lead to mitigation in sentencing as one might expect.

"HALF MAD AND HAS NO COMMON SENSE"

The murder of Shaika bint Zayid is another case in which colonials see only senselessness. On July 10, 1939, the defendant Shari bin Sa'ad Al-Hajiri visited a *barasti* (indigenous palm-branch dwelling) of ill-repute and was seen running away. Inside was a strangled woman, bint Zayid. Al-Hajiri was charged with intentional murder in violation of section 302 of the Indian Penal Code.[19] During questioning, the defendant alleged he was not guilty of the crime because he did not intend to kill bint Zayid. Rather, he was defending himself against attacks she made in trying to strangle him and steal his money. He also implied that bint Zayid had drugged him, telling the Indian Assistant on July 22, 1939, that he "wanted nothing from her but a glass of water . . . drank the water and felt [my] head going round and also felt pain . . . when he told bint Zayid she caught hold of his throat and he could not relieve himself." Not believed by the Court, he was ultimately sentenced to death, losing on appeal. The political resident who reviewed the case indicated that self-defense was not supported by the evidence since the defendant was able to easily evade a hostile mob as he was fleeing the *barasti*, and before that, had supplied consistent and sustained pressure on the woman's throat, noting a medical examination of the body by Dr. J. Jow. Further, he sought sanctuary in a variety of sheikhs' homes, a practice that is part of the social construct of honor in tribal society. A proper tribesmen will give a stranger a minimum of three days of protection from any harm.[20] It is not clear from the record whether protection was offered. Questioning of the defendant is not noted in the file until July 22, but the defendant was seen in custody by Belgrave earlier, on July 18, 1939.[21]

Al-Hajiri was executed by shooting on November 1, 1939. He received the ultimate punishment, after a one-day trial.[22] Being related to the Al Khalifa family and receiving a letter of support from one of them did not seem to mitigate the sentence (as usually occurs in the cases examined here). Abdullah bin Abdur Rahman Al Khalifah wrote a letter of support for Al-Hajiri putting forth that Al-Hajiri was of diminished capacity and had engaged in mutual combat.

> He is half mad and has no common sense. He had not been to the woman with the purpose to kill her but for love play when he was going to leave her house, she caught hold of his neck, and asked him to pay money in return he too caught hold of her neck and thus both were pulling each other and thus the woman expired.[23]

The document indicates that several character letters were enclosed although none could be found in the file. Enclosed was also an English translation of an Arabic newspaper clipping on the case from *Bahrain* no. 21, dated July 27, 1939, in which the defendant "is known as being of unsound mind."[24] The Al Khalifah supporter seemed to feel that being mad and lacking common sense was a partial defense of diminished capacity and served to offer an explanation of how the defendant over-reacted or erred in the situation without particular malice.

Meanwhile, Belgrave felt differently, referring to the defendant as a Bedouin with no discernible reasons for his conduct and therefore underserving of mitigation. In his diary he notes: "The man, who I saw, is a wretched little creature, a rat, can't find any motive for having strangled the woman."[25] Using the label "Bedouin" in this context appears to be in tacit contrast to civilized Bahrainis, a distinction of *civilized-uncivilized* that resonates with Elias' notion of the emergence of self-control as a centralized feature of the transition to a state-centric bureaucratized regime of the civilized. Only those who can self-regulate their own behavior in the eyes of the state are law-abiding, reflecting a "whole reorganization of human relationships" around violence.[26] He writes:

> this [new] external control is founded on the assumption that every individual is himself or herself regulating his or her own behaviour with the utmost exactitude in accordance with the necessities of this [new social and legal] network. The chief danger that people here represent for others results from someone in the bustle losing their self-control . . . forms of non-physical violence that always existed, but hitherto had always been mingled or fused with physical force, are now separated from the latter . . . [27]

Where once the tribal men in small communities backed their social regulation of honor-based speech with the possibility of interpersonal violence, the colonial regime demands a splitting of verbal provocation from physical violence. Although it is not clear from the evidence what actually occurred in the *barasti*, we see that an uneducated, Arab tribesperson accused of murder was viewed as senseless for responding to a perceived slight of honor in a way that may have been more in line with the old customs. He then is constructed as mad by those in power who stand in judgment of him. Perhaps in this case the defendant is suffering a mental affliction, but on the other hand, given the colonial treatment of Eddorsi and bin Abdullah, it is hard to feel confident of this, given how liberally the label appears to be used in the records to describe a broad swathe of individuals not conforming to the new colonial justice.

WOMEN IN THE CACHE OF CRIMINAL CASES

In the sample of cases, there are few that deal with tribal notions of women's honor; however, we know from other sources that honor killings and complicated issues of extramarital affairs (in which men would not permit women to divorce per religious law) came to be handled by colonial authorities. It appears, though, that unlike in cases of murder and attempted murder involving men, crimes against women were not considered criminal affairs so readily. In the cases involving women as direct victims that are in the sample, one is the case involving Al-Hajiri. Another is the attempted rape of Mrs. Balan, wife of K. Balan, which took place on November 15, 1938, by Deradas David, in violation of sections 354 (assault with intent to outrage modesty) and 451 (trespassing) of the Indian Penal Code.[28] Both the defendant and the victim's husband were British Indians and BAPCO employees. BAPCO put up the defendant's bail on December 20, 1938. Meanwhile, several witnesses against the defendant, aside from the victim, surfaced, but the defendant maintained his innocence and alleged that the witnesses were personal enemies. Although Indian notions of honor may have been an issue in the case, no such information is even hinted at, aside from the charge, and so the meaning of the offense is mostly lost.

Another incident generates two criminal cases in the sample and features women as victims and defendants.[29] In the first case, Khuda Rahim Herawi, and four accomplices (all Persian men), reportedly raped Atkeh bint Marzook, a Somalian woman, on the incitement of Wahdeh bint Muhammad and Makkiyah bint Salim. The men had visited the two women's brothel and, according to the judgment in the case, deliberately raped the complainant on August 2, 1924. The motive stemmed from Rahim's relationship with the victim, having asked her to live with him, and she rebuffed him. Also, the two female dependents reportedly had a grudge against the victim and encouraged Rahim to commit the crime in order to maintain control over her within the brothel. Specific details as to the nature of that encouragement, beyond operating a brothel, could not be found.[30]

In a memorandum, the captain of the state police indicated to the political agency's court that "[bint Salim] hid one woman named Sharifa bint Mubarak in her house for illegal purposes. Sharifa's husband['s] brother requested Makiyah to give their women (Sharifa) to them but Makiyah refused to do so. Makiyah was a pimp and used to induce women to have illegal intercourse with me."[31]

The two Somali women were noted for having run a house of ill repute, which the defendant and accomplices were visiting at the time of the offense. Bint Salim was charged and convicted of violations of sections 498 and 376 and 110. According to handwritten notes in the case file, she had previously been deported for keeping "an immoral home." Bint Salim was sentenced to four years imprisonment and 100 rupees or two months imprisonment, as well as eighteen months imprisonment, and 100 rupees or two months imprisonment. She was deported after serving her time, but later contested that deportation as illegal since she claimed Bahraini citizenship (having been born "near the telegram office in Bahrein"). According to the case file, bint Muhammad received six months imprisonment, and a fine of 300 rupees or two months imprisonment. The Persian men received the following sentences: one was given five years imprisonment; and the rest received two years imprisonment and 100 rupees or two months imprisonment.

The Court showed disdain for defendant bint Salim, starting out the finding in the case with: "In the first place it is not possible to overlook the fact that the accused is a notorious procuress of women, whose house is used for immoral purposes. Her character is notoriously bad. This being so no reliance whatever can be placed in her statement that she merely sheltered [bint Marzook] . . . "[32] The record has more editorial comments from police and court personnel against bint Salim as a prostitute than it reveals toward the rapists. Although it cannot be certain that the case file is complete, it nonetheless leaves the impression that disdain for prostitution ran hotter for colonial administrators than rape.

CONCERN ABOUT HONOR KILLINGS AND OTHER VIOLENCE AGAINST WOMEN

As early as 1906, colonial administrators expressed concern over Bahraini treatment of women by Sunni tribal communities. This type of concern is a common theme across colonial societies, "[C]olonial rulers found themselves scandalized, shocked or outraged by local customs," and exerted their moral superiority through criminalizing and punishing the behaviors.[33] Famous examples include the British colonial criminalization of *suttee* in India,[34] a custom by which a widow fatally throws herself on her husband's funeral pyre, or of concubinage in Hong Kong.[35] In analyses of pictorial and literary artifacts produced by Westerners about Muslim women, scholars have labeled the Western gaze "gendered Orientalism" with women portrayed as passive victims or hyper-sexualized in depictions of harems.[36] Anthropologist Lila Abu-Lughod cautions that although cultural accounts of crimes against women hold water, reducing the cause of such crimes to "tradition" alone inappropriately blames a society for relatively rare phenomena, which also involves family dynamics, individual decision-making, and many other factors. This reductionist thinking acts to stigmatize a culture rather than the act of violence and is often used to justify other projects of power and control by the state.[37]

Here, I take a cultural approach to crimes about gender and honor as a particular manifestation of patriarchal gender relations which when viewed from the colonial, Western perspective takes on a reductionist gloss propelled by a divergent culture-based sense of moral outrage. In doing so, I recognize that colonists invented these crimes as a category of criminality, taking them from the private sphere into the realm of the criminal investigation and adjudication by the state. At the same time I do so recognizing that femicide is a serious crime that should not be taken lightly. In any case, there is no evidence from the colonial record that local leaders demanded action by the state on these incidents (often they criticized the state for involving itself in these private matters); however, as we shall see below, victims themselves sometimes exhibited individual agency and approached colonists for assistance in managing honor-based violence in their family lives.

Both Shi`a and Sunni communities share a general Islamic foundation in that these types of crimes can be categorized as often involving improper sexual relations, such as *zina* (adultery), a *hudd* punishment in shari'a law. There are *hadith*s (recorded sayings of the Prophet Muhammed) that support the killing of adulterers if four witnesses can come forth to corroborate the charge. Further, tribal customs around women's honor (*'urd* in Arabic, *erz* in Farsi) share similar worries about the socially damaging effect that improprieties have on family, tribe, or clan reputation.[38] Because Sunni *qadi*s were often hierarchically below tribal sheikhs, tribal custom had as much to do with Sunni responses as jurisprudence. According to H. R. P. Dickson, *'urd* is directly connected to the reputation of the family and if sullied "nothing short of killing the errant woman will restore it."[39] Although this is likely an ethnographic exaggeration and frames errant women as falling into a taboo of sorts, anthropologist Mary Douglas might note instead the importance of the observation in that it conveys the "grave concern"[40] tribal societies had for supposedly sullied women. At the very least, we can see that such women stir passions, and that errant women have fomented a kind of "gender trouble" if she has behaved inappropriately, subverting the performativity[41] of tribal gender identity as honorable behavior through a divergent performance that contradicts the normative expectations. The cultural problem becomes how to cancel the stain upon the family's honor, and there may be limited scripts within the tradition to do this short of violence. As Abu-Lughod described in her ethnographic exploration of Egyptian Bedouin, although in principle honor killing appears to be the only way to restore kin honor, it is still a rare occurrence, and the practical situations she heard about showed that clans managed this type of trouble through marrying off women to people outside the community or relocating the entire family.[42]

In Bahrain, the "Nora" case exemplifies the tensions between the supposed moral do-gooding of the colonialists and the local problem of allegedly errant females. In 1906, "Nora," a divorced woman, received refuge at the

Political Agency by an Indian Assistant who sheltered her. Her lover had thrown her out of his house where she had been living for approximately two years. Hearing that the political agency provided her asylum, her father then complained bitterly to the agency. Political Agent Francis Prideaux attempted to mediate the situation between "Nora" and her father, but his efforts failed, and the agency was soon facing a petition from tribal Sunnis and the Sunni *qadi* for the right to adjudicate the case. No judicial action was reportedly taken, but when "Nora" was later taken to the American Mission Hospital for a medical check, she escaped and disappeared, never to be seen again.[43]

In subsequent correspondence, Political Resident Percy Cox suggested that such cases be turned over to Arab notables and Sheikh Isa, until further social and legal reforms could take place. He stated that it was true that tribal authorities often failed to respond firmly in such cases, but that, at least under the current political structure, it was a matter for the Sheikh and his subjects.[44] Under the OiC reforms, there were almost no provisions related specifically to women. The law referred only to the need for males over age twenty-one to register with the government for themselves, and on behalf of their wives, household women, and minor children, during an accounting of who was to be a Bahraini citizen and who was a foreigner under the new citizenship laws.[45]

In his memoirs, Belgrave recalled that though murders were rare in Bahrain during his tenure, when they occurred they often involved female victims of honor killings.[46] Whether the cache of criminal cases is not truly representative of the universe of PA cases, or that cases touching on female honor found themselves almost exclusively in other judicial venues (the Bahrain Court or religious courts) is not known. Aggregate accountings of criminal cases recorded in the OiC annual reports did not regularly feature a breakdown by charge, but rather in outcome of case (acquittal, conviction, discharged, etc.). Even speculation about honor-based offenses from charges of rape and attempted rape, or murders of women, cannot be made from within the sample. Among cases with female defendants or victims (about a third of the criminal case cache), casual judgments about sexual impropriety factored into a few of the cases, but they were not treated explicitly as honor killings by colonial administrators. It was not the involvement of women, and alleged impropriety, alone which put a case into that category in their minds, but rather the involvement of multiple male relatives either in the perpetration of the crime, or in the concealment of it from authorities. For example, in the Al-Hajiri case described earlier in the chapter, there was little social support for the violence even though the case involved femicide during a sexual encounter. As such, colonial administrators did not appear to categorize it as an honor-based crime, and in fact, found it to lack any discernible motive at all.

When we look at other sources besides the sample, we find reference to a number of cases in the honor crimes category. Advisor Charles Belgrave focused on responding to honor killings in the 1930s. In his annual report from 1937 he explained:

> there are still a number of Arabs living in [Hidd] and Muharraq who consider they are justified in murdering their female relations if the woman brings shame on the family. A few of the very old-fashioned Arab even consider that because the Government does not ignore such murders it is encouraging immorality. The [qadis] though ultra conservative in their outlook, disapprove of men taking the law in their own hands and murdering women who misbehave.[47]

He provided the following example from an incident in 1938:

> A murder took place in Hidd, a girl drowned by her father for the usual reasons, but the father escaped arrest and took refuge in [Qatar]. The reputation of [Hidd], as being a place where women are frequently murdered, is notorious.[48]

Cases of violent crime numbered 393 the same year that the above murder occurred,[49] however, it is unknown how many of these violent cases featured honor-related offenses. Hidd and Muharraq during this time period were Sunni strongholds and to the extent that honor played into the reported violence, it was the tribal manifestation of it. Although the Sheikh and the *qadi*s supported the criminalization of honor killings, at least tacitly, local opposition to using the law in this way was palpable.[50] In nearly every case commented upon by Belgrave, members of the victim's family resisted state involvement in the matters.

Groping in the margins of Belgrave's diaries and the annual reports, we can see numerous cases of alleged honor killings, but we are left with only a few words as clues to the nature of these offenses. In addition to implicating entire families of men, they almost exclusively take place in Sunni communities. For example: "There was a pearl merchant from [Qatar], a rascally old fellow who as I heard later is known to have murdered two wives, a real Blackbeard."[51] In 1932, Belgrave took evidence of one of four men who murdered a girl in Muharraq; the other three culprits had fled to the mainland.[52] The same year, Belgrave wrote in his diary that a girl in Hidd nearly got murdered.[53] And in 1934: "A murder case in Muharraq, the victim is a woman of the town, she was found in the sea tied in a sack."[54] The latter case generated more comment as Belgrave spent many days questioning mostly female witnesses in the victim's family. He discovered that two groups of men were in a rivalry for the affections of the victim. He ultimately decides to deport the men (to the Arab mainland) rather than prosecute them because he was worried that his forensic evidence was weak.[55]

In another case shortly thereafter, the Emir of Muharraq reported that he suspected another woman had been murdered in Hidd by a brother who tried to kill her two years previously.[56] The woman's father told authorities that she had gone to Saudi Arabia to visit relatives, but it was also determined that she was rumored to have had an affair with a married man.[57] Belgrave soon received further information and dug up the floorboards of a house in Hidd looking for the woman's body.[58] Initially, the wrong part of the house was searched, but the diary explains that later the body was found.[59] "A young sister of the missing girl told police that she had been murdered [and] buried under the floor of a house—these cases make me very angry especially as it is difficult to find the truth."[60] In further disclosures, the victim's sister stated that her husband and her brother were the culprits. Although the motive was not clear, Belgrave implied that it stemmed from the victim's perceived sexual impropriety and a threat to the family's honor (*'ird*). He wrote:

> It is a difficult matter, the men considering it right to kill women relations who go wrong, this we cannot allow, but it's true that if men have no authority to punish their women then there are more goings on. The [*qadi*'s] idea is that the solution would be to refer all cases about women to the [*shari'a*] court which would try them by [*shari'a*] law which in extreme cases order women to be killed by being stoned to death, that again is a thing we could never tolerate.[61]

The mention of stoning to death, though a sanction in *shari'a* law had not been practiced in Bahrain, so this reference probably is based on a more generalized colonial concern for Muslim-based punishments as being unduly harsh, at least on paper. The more contextualized argument made by colonial administrators in Bahrain had to so with an alleged cultural or social license to murder through drowning or strangulation in honor-based situations:

> There is some agitation in the [Hidd] among the Arabs—always a tiresome lot who more or less say they wish to be allowed to murder their female relations as much as they like. It makes me very angry.[62]

According to Belgrave, the people in Hidd who support violence based on traditional notions of *'ird* wrote a petition to the Court, underscoring how valued the murderous practices allegedly were. However, no record of the petition itself could be found. Meanwhile, The Bahrain Court found the two Hidd men guilty of the murder of the woman under the floorboards and recommended to the Sheikh (who had sentencing authority) that they receive the death penalty; he did not agree with the sentence but agreed to implement a year later, in order to give time for the local community to calm down from having been the target of the state's investigation.[63] This softness on the part of the Sheikh could also be connected to Sunni forgiveness as discussed in the previous chapter: the Sheikhs exhibited reluctance to implement harsh punishments against Sunni offenders, a disposition they did not show for Shi`a offenders. Because these types of crimes, when they occurred, often occurred in Sunni communities, the murder of Sunni women often went unpunished because it would uncomfortably implicate Sunni men in the context of a Sunni chauvinistic state apparatus. As Belgrave describes another such example, on January 23, 1935, Sheikh Hamad gave orders to release a prisoner "who last year attempted to murder his sister" and had been sentenced to five years, but had only served one and a half.[64]

Complicated issues related to extramarital affairs also came to be handled by colonial authorities, and touch on gender-based honor and sectarianism. Between the religious courts, the criminal courts and the civil courts, it appears that it was difficult to know exactly where these issues around adultery belonged. Technically, the Sunni and Shi`a qadis were empowered to conduct marriages and grant divorces according to their respective legal schools.[65] For example, in the year 1945, there were nine cases of adultery known to police, involving ten defendants, and resulting in eight convictions.[66] Belgrave reports that he often heard such cases and engaged in mediation and other informal settlements so as not to bog down the courts.[67]

In one example of this informal processing, however, a member of the Al Khalifah was once again implicated in murder:

> There is a report of a murder . . . but the divorced wife of the Shaikh's brother[-in-law]. An Arab girl started playing up with the men [and] eventually captured the affection of Rashid bin Mohamed. His wife objected [and] complained to his mother. The old lady gave a picnic, invited the girl [and] about 20 others at a spring then, it is said, order[ed] two of her slave women to drown the girl. They did so. I got the girl's brother, but he didn't seem to know much about the show.[68]

Further inquiries led to the problem of bringing in an Al Khalifah as a person of interest in the case:

> The sheikh called in the afternoon with Sheikh Mohamed about the affair of the girl at [Riffa'], very fussed at the idea of Parke [Commandant of Police] sending for one of Sheikh Mohamed's divorced wives to give evidence. Ladies of the Khalifa family, it appears, can NEVER appear in Court, if, as is not unlikely, one of them murders someone I wonder what would happen—according to their idea—nothing, in this case the Khalifa lady is said to have ordered the girl to be drowned.[69]

Unfortunately, the diary is silent as to the outcome of this case, and no other records could be found. However, from this commentary, we see a lack of punitive response for a Sunni perpetrator and member of the royal family, connecting crimes against women to the sectarian discriminatory context in which they occur.

The concern over violence against women by Western officials like Belgrave was common across the British Empire. In his diaries, he often expressed anger about cases of femicide, an emotion that he does not express often in his writings. In the British colonial world, women often became markers for cultural anxieties and cultural difference and policies and programs about them often became key aspects of modernizing projects.[70] Women also were often treated in a monolithic way, as if their marginalization and exclusion from public life, as well as their vulnerability to violent victimization, meant the same things across cultural contexts. Instead women's roles are produced through social relations, which have historical and cultural specificities in different times and places.[71] Critically speaking, universalist approaches reflect an uncomfortable dynamic of Western arrogance, namely that women from indigenous communities need saving from their own men by colonial authorities. This perspective completely discounts local communities' agency in managing these social problems and also discounts the prevalent problem of domestic violence in Western societies as well. Lila Abu-Lughod confronted this when she posed the question "Do Muslim women need saving?" in the context of contemporary Western societies, aptly pointing out that since colonial times, the obsession with honor crimes as a reason for Western intervention in Muslim communities cannot be separated from other political agendas of imperial power and control.[72]

Belgrave's concern for violence against women in the Bahraini context is also illuminating when compared to his relationship to violence in general. By his own account, he was a violent man in the sense that he favored harsh punishments and performed public displays of brutality on behalf of the colonial state. There are several moments in his diary in which he relishes such escapades. He regularly beat police officers as punishment for violations of police policy: "[Police] Fort before breakfast, beat some men. I seem to have a lot of beatings now a days."[73] He beat suspects[74] and prisoners.[75] He ordered the public beating of thieves by police.[76] And, he took over an execution when the executioners hesitated: "the firing squad were nervous and I had to use my revolver . . . "[77] In 1945, after anti-Semitic sentiment had been whipped up in Manama, Persians and Omanis attacked Jewish shops in the suq. The police and Belgrave allegedly took on the attackers. In a dramatic description of engaging in combat with the rioters, Belgrave wrote: "I gave a lot of men something to remember [and] by the end of it my fists were almost raw from contact with peoples' noses [and] faces."[78] Therefore, it was not the violence per se that affronted him, but its meaning and context, as a response to domestic and interpersonal disagreements in the private sphere. In the British-educated sensibility that Belgrave brought to his duties, men unleashing violence against woman is abhorrent, but violence by elite men seemingly has its place in civil society, particularly if perpetrated in defense of the social order of the colonial state. Again, the violence itself is not the problem so much as its moral interpretation by the colonial state.

Shi`a Femicide

Cases with Shi`a victims of femicide appear less often in the colonial record, sparse as it is. Given the Al Khalifah dismissal of Shi`a as less than deserving state subjects, and the colonial acquiescence to that over time, if there was a bias in the scant empirical evidence we have, it would probably implicate more marginal groups like Shi`a in the so-called problem of honor-based violence against women. Instead, the violence reportedly erupts from within Sunni-allied communities, and in one case implicated the royal family. It appears from this analysis that notions of honor are less violence-provoking in Shi`a Bahrainis than Sunni Bahrainis, recognizing that such violence overall is actually relatively rare.

In the Shi`a community, the religious qadis are not hierarchically inferior to the community leaders, but are in fact, the top leaders themselves, answerable only to higher clergy, often ayatollahs outside of Bahrain. Within the Jafari legal tradition largely adhered to at this time in Bahrain (though other schools are present), Shi`a have differed among themselves as to the response to honor killings. In contemporary commentary, A. Hashemi, for example, argues against leniency, tracing honor killings back to pre-Islamic customs and the maintenance of patriarchy, and ultimately opining that honor killing is best categorized as vigilantism that threatens public order.[79]

Only two cases of Shi`a violence around sexual impropriety and women could be found in Belgrave's diaries, in contrast to the many cases documented as originating in Sunni communities. In March of 1935, Belgrave mentioned a murder in Sitra in which one man killed another by rifle after quarrelling about a woman.[80] The next month, the shooter was found guilty and executed.[81] Note here that there is no evidence of procedural delay for this Shi`a defendant as in the case involving the Sunni perpetrator in Hidd in 1935.

Another case occurred a few years earlier, on June 8, 1929, when the state police arrested a man who murdered a Shi`a "lady friend"[82] who had been living with him while her husband was away pearl-diving. As Belgrave noted of the villagers: "None of them appeared to take it very seriously and the girl's father, the chief witness, evidently enjoyed talking and made the most of taking evidence."[83]

> They murdered the wife of the *natur* [pearl diver] apparently as she bossed the house and they were afraid of her and tired of her. I can't make out why the husband didn't just divorce her which he could have done easily. I know of the man quite well, he carries all the letters from Mespers [Mesopotamia Persia

> Corporation Limited], he always seemed a most decent old fellow. The brother has confessed but the *natur* denies it. They killed the woman by throttling her with a rope, while one of them held a cloth over her mouth, in a hut within a few feet of other people in the middle of the day. It's an interesting case, it will be held at the Agency as they are Persians.[84]

The apparent lack of major concern over the matter by the woman's father may be a quirk in this particular case, or could have a cultural foundation. If the latter is true, the root of Bahraini Shi`a being less emotionally explosive around issues of sexual honor may have stemmed from their historic experience as part of the larger Indian Ocean community of merchants, pearl divers, and sea-farers. As mentioned, that culture has been characterized by historians as tolerant of difference, which may have extended somewhat to gender relations and the maintenance of patriarchy. Sexual honor still mattered, and certainly the religiously pious would take it seriously based on Muslim law. Patriarchy was a major feature of the society in all groups. However, the cultural pressure that would incite violence may have been less present in these coastal communities (among the "people of the sea") than in the interior tribal ones ("the people of the land"). In fact, we know that given the long absences that people of the sea often took for pearling, innovative sexual arrangements were common, from men with wives in many ports to women seeking companionship while husbands were away. Moreover, if we take Belgrave's account of the victim's male relatives' motivation entirely at face value, the motive for the violence may have stemmed from a more mundane anger around being "bossed," and though perhaps not a gender-free provocation, perhaps not involving sexual honor per se, but merely patriarchal control. In any case, what the cache of criminal cases and the secondary sources, which mention cases with female victimization, indicates is that Shi`a women were more likely to be killed by Sunni men (in Dawasir home invasions, for example, as we see in chapters 2 and 4) than Shi`a men. For Sunni women, however, they were more likely to be killed by their male relatives, also Sunni men. For Shi`a women, this is contrary to most criminological data across time and place, which place the greatest danger to women at the hands of their relatives, regardless of identity. However, in the context of a socially and politically fragmented society in the midst of sectarian mass violence, which is confronted in the next chapter, the noted trend of how Shi`a women are in danger, begins to make more sense as a problem not of everyday criminal justice as it might seem at first glance, but as one of civil unrest and war. Were it not for the political problem in Bahrain, Shi`a women would be in most danger from Shi`a men, albeit at a seemingly lower rate than Sunni women. We turn now to the sectarian nature of the new criminal adjudication and how violence against Shi`a, and the creation of a Shi`a criminal class, factor into the institutionalization of sectarianism in the Bahraini criminal justice system.

NOTES

1. Case no. 3 of 1925 (India Office Records, R/15/3/6998).
2. Petition from Ahmad Juma'a Al-Lail [India Office Records, R/15/3/6998, September 29, 1926].
3. Elias 1939: 325.
4. Elias 1939: 314.
5. Pierre Bourdieu, *The Sense of Honour in Algeria*. Cambridge University Press (1979): 95–132.
6. Mohammed Abu-Nimer, "Conflict Resolution Approaches," *American Journal of Economics and Sociology* 55 (1996): 35–52.
7. Lienhardt 1950:68.
8. Dickson 1949: 132.
9. Dickson 1949: 57–58.
10. Lienhardt 1950.
11. Dickson 1949: 440–441.
12. Amani M. Awwad, "Gossip, Scandal, Shame and Honor Killing: A Case for Social Constructionism and Hegemonic Discourse," *Social Thought & Research*, (2001): 39–52.
13. Case no. 22 of 1933 (India Office Records, R/15/3/7011).
14. Sessions case *King Emperor v. M. ad-ds* (India Office Records, R/15/3/11574, February 15, 1933).
15. Letter from Political Agent to Political Resident (India Office Records, R/15/1/306, February 3, 1933).
16. Strobl 2010.
17. Wakil statement in *King Emperor v. M. ad-Dowseri* (India Office Records, R/15/3/11574).
18. Case no. 6 of 1937, *Police v. Mahmud bin Abdullah Basri* (India Office Records, R/15/3/7013).
19. Criminal case no. 131 of 1939 (India Office Records, R/15/3/7019).
20. Sulayman Khalaf, "Settlement of Violence in Bedouin Society," *Ethnology*: 29 (1990).
21. Belgrave, personal diary, July 18, 1939.
22. Belgrave, personal diary, July 23, 1939.
23. Memorandum from Abdullah bin Abdur Rahman Al Khalifah to the PA Court, "Re: Judgment against Shari bin Said Al-Hajiri" (India Office Records, R/15/3/7019, July 30, 1939).
24. Case no. 131 of 1939 (India Office Records, R/15/3/7019).
25. Belgrave, personal diary, July 18, 1939.
26. Elias 1939/2000: 366.
27. Elias 1939/2000: 368–369.
28. Criminal case no. 194 of 1938 (India Office Records, R/15/3/7006).
29. Criminal case no. 252/1310 of 1924 (India Office Records, R/15/3/6995); Criminal case no. 685/1322 of 1924 (India Office Records, R/15/6996).
30. Judgment in criminal case no. 252 of 1924 [India Office Records, R/15/3/6995, August 15, 1924].
31. Memorandum no. 47/15 Commandant of the State Police to Political Agent [India Office Records, R/15/3/6995, July 31, 1927].
32. Finding in criminal case no 685 of 1924, Major C. Daly, [India Office Records, R/15/3/6995, August 14, 1924.
33. Bracey 2006: 86.
34. Spivak 1999.
35. Bracey 2006: 86.

36. Lila Abu-Lughod, *Do Muslim Women Need Saving?* (Cambridge: Harvard University Press, 2013).
37. Abu-Lughod 2013: 114.
38. Irene Schneider, "The Concept of Honor and Its Reflection in the Iranian Penal Code," *Journal of Persianate Studies* 5 (2012): 43–57.
39. Dickson 1949: 55.
40. Douglas 1966: 81.
41. Judith Butler, *Gender Trouble: Feminism and the Subversion of Identity*, 2nd Ed. (Routledge, 1999).
42. Abu-Lughod 1986: 286–287 note 16.
43. Radhi 2003: 23–24.
44. Radhi 2003: 23–24.
45. Radhi, 2003: 35.
46. Charles Belgrave, *Personal Column* (1960): 101.
47. Government of Bahrain, "Annual Reports, Volume II" (1987): 10.
48. Government of Bahrain, "Annual Reports, Volume II" (1987): 17.
49. Government of Bahrain, "Annual Reports, Volume II" (1987): 17.
50. Strobl 2010: 127.
51. Belgrave, personal diaries, August 3, 1926.
52. Belgrave, personal diaries, June 26, 1932.
53. Belgrave, personal diaries, November 19, 1932.
54. Belgrave, personal diaries, December 12, 1934.
55. Belgrave, personal diaries, December 16 1934 and January 10, 1935.
56. Belgrave, personal diaries, June 1, 1935.
57. Belgrave, *Personal Column* (1960): 101.
58. Belgrave, personal diaries, June 1, 1935.
59. Belgrave, personal diaries, June 6, 1935.
60. Belgrave, personal diaries, June 1, 1935.
61. Belgrave personal diaries, January 8, 1935.
62. Belgrave, personal diaries, June 10, 1935.
63. Belgrave personal diaries, July 30, August 1, and August 18, 1935.
64. Letter from Advisor Sir Charles Belgrave to Political Agent (India Office Records, R/15/2/573, January 23, 1935).
65. Letter no. 404 from Charles Belgrave to Sheikh Ali bin Jafar bin Muhamed (India Office Records, R/15/1/343, July 17, 1935).
66. "The Police" in Annual Report 1945–1946. [Government of Bahrain. *Annual Reports, Volume II*. London: Archive Editions Limited, 1987.]
67. Belgrave, personal diaries, November 15, 1928.
68. Belgrave, personal diaries, August 15, 1927.
69. Belgrave, personal diaries, August 27, 1927.
70. Lila Abu-Lughod "Feminist Longings and Post-Colonial Conditions," in *Remaking Women: Feminism and Modernity in the Middle East*, ed. Lila Abu-Lughod (Princeton University Press, 1998): 3–13; Afshan Jafar, "Woman, Islam and State in Pakistan" *Gender Issues* 22 (1995): 35–55.
71. Chandra Talpade Mohanty, *Feminism without Borders: Decolonizing Theory, Practicing Solidarity* (Duke University Press: 2003).
72. Lila Abu Lughod, *Do Muslim Women Need Saving?* (Cambridge: Harvard University Press, 2013).
73. Belgrave, personal diaries, February 17, 1930.
74. Belgrave, personal diaries, February 15, 1930; January 28, 1935.
75. Belgrave, personal diaries, October 1, 1940; March 1, 1945.
76. Belgrave, personal diaries, August 10, 1933.
77. Belgrave, personal diaries, April 22, 1935.
78. Belgrave, personal diaries, December 4, 1945.
79. As quoted in Schneider 2012.
80. Belgrave, personal diaries, March 23, 1935.

81. Belgrave, personal diaries, April 8 and April 22, 1935.
82. Belgrave, personal diaries, June 8, 1929.
83. Belgrave, personal diaries, June 8, 1929.
84. Belgrave, personal diaries, October 9, 1929.

Chapter Four

Sectarian *Tashwish*

Anti-Shi`a Violence and Sunni-Dominated Policing

In 1922 and 1923, the political agent, Major Clive Daly, routinely documented that he received complaints by Shi`a against the Al Khalifa family for bolstering Sunni wealth by illegally seizing *Baharna* property. To boot, Sunni allies of the royal family enjoyed immunity from the taxation charged to Shi`a people. This policy of tax discrimination became a major source of Shi`a frustration, leading to unrest in the country. In petitions, groups of *Baharna* questioned the fact that they were the only group being charged the date-garden and fish taxes, despite technical applicability to people of a variety of identities; the *raqibah* (neck-tax or poll tax) collected arbitrarily from Shi`a males; and a special tax for *Muharram* festivities, one of the most important Shi`a holidays.[1] The ruling family allegedly reformed the tax laws in response, but they failed to completely erase their discriminatory nature. Bahraini Shi`a were not passive acceptors of this or any other colonially-backed institutionalization of the Sunni-dominated system. In 1923, opposition groups demanded the abolition of *sakhra* (forced labor), and petitioned against arrests without warrants, the adjudication of criminal cases in the Bahrain Court by members of the ruling family, and poor prison conditions. They also again mentioned that Sheikh Hamad let his camels loose to graze over Shi`a agricultural plots, disrupting cultivation efforts. There was little response to the petition, according to colonial records.

On May 10, 1923, sectarian disturbances between "Persian" (Shi`a) and "Nejdi" (Sunni tribal) individuals culminated in eight dead and dozens wounded. Some were slain by police.[2] Telegrams from Bahrain to the political resident emphatically pleaded for a "gunboat [to] visit here as soon as possible and stay till the end of Ramazan [sic] it would have a steadying effect."[3] Here we see that mass political violence was difficult to contain using the internal security resources available to colonial authorities.

Later, authorities uncovered that the proximate cause for the violence was a dispute over a criminal matter: a stolen watch. A young boy pilfered it from a Nejdi man (identified as "Qusaibi") in the *suq* and sold it to a Persian jewelry shopkeeper. When Qusaibi asked for its return, the Persian shop-owner refused unless Qusaibi paid him three rupees. Unable to agree, both men consulted a nearby mediator. However, the Persian and a friend arrived to the mediator's house staggering from dagger wounds; a group of Nejdis trailed behind. The mediator called for assistance from the Political Agency, but in doing so, unintentionally sparked a riot between Qusaibi's group and the group of Persians.

Daly, the political agent, declined to try anyone in the Qusaibi matter in PA Court for fear of arousing further criticisms of British interference in local matters, fueling the fire of opposition to the OiC reforms.[4] He had recently been harshly criticized in Egyptian newspaper editorials, read in the Gulf, for implementing the reforms.[5] Underscoring tensions was the recent forced abdication of Sheikh Isa that had led many of his loyalists to demand an end to the British in Bahrain.[6] The royal family also did not favor prosecution in the matter, allegedly fearing Saudi retaliation (as Dawasir allies).

From the above we see that sectarian passions flared among ordinary Bahrainis negotiating a discriminatory colonial–Al Khalifah state. The operation of the state exhibited sectarian tendencies in its very foundations, a routine *modus operandi* of the "people of the land" against many of the "people of the sea." As will be argued below, the nature of the new criminal adjudication, although seemingly based on a secular rule of law, solidified the institutional sectarianism that remains today. This occurred in at least four ways. First, the colonial state aided and abetted external allies and internal elites who raided Shi`a villages and perpetrated mass violence; these events were not separate from the events that also served to pacify Sunni tribal contestations discussed in chapter 2. Second, the colonial state did not protect Shi`a victims from violence, and in at least a few instances, state actors (members of the Al Khalifah ruling family) perpetrated massacres in examples of state violence. Third, the colonial period features a peculiar form of restorative justice that in practice was extended only to Sunni perpetrators, and represents the absorption of tribal notions of forgiveness into the bureaucratic fold of colonial justice. What is officially forgiven in large part is Sunni violence against Shi`a. Finally, the colonial state institutionalized a Sunni-dominated police force in order to maintain the political hegemony of the Al Khalifah and their Sunni allies. It also absorbed into the state and its security apparatus renegade members of the royal family who were directly responsible for anti-Shi`a violence.

SECTARIAN VIOLENCE: AIDING AND ABETTING AMOUNTS TO NO PROTECTION

Sectarian violence occurred within the nexus of the Dawasir tribe, the Khawalid branch (also known as the Khalids, relations of Sheikh Khalid) of the Al Khalifah family, Sheikh Isa, Sheikh Abdullah, and various additional Sunni allies. The nexus is evident through the case files on the Dawasir home invasion crimes, which will be taken up again in order to drill down into the sectarian nature of those events; two violent rampages in Sitra; the attacks on the village of 'Ali (mentioned above), and other related events.

We know that members of the Dawasir tribe victimized Shi`a villages in Tubli, Farsiya, Wadiyan, Senabis, and Garaya attacks per the criminal case files. In the early 1920s, Sheikh Hamad received many complaints that Dawasir tribes, originating from the mainland, were regularly attacking and plundering Shi`a communities; according to the record, Sheikh Hamad did little to protect them. This pattern of failing to protect Shi`a communities from Sunni violence has haunted Bahrain since the Al Khalifah arrived and is a factor in state-building that academic scholarship has not taken into enough consideration, having unduly favored available Sunni-centric narratives. At minimum the lack of protection acts as royal complicity, but could amount to as much as the state aiding and abetting the violence, or the state being intentionally blameworthy itself. All these options present themselves in the colonial record.

The alliance with the Dawasir, and its routine raids on Shi`a people, from within and from afar, reveal at minimum a tacit acceptance of anti-Shi`a violence by Al Khalifah and colonial interests. Sheikh Hamad's branch of the family may have ultimately accepted the violence as a management strategy. By permitting the Khawalids to maintain a Dawasir connection, this could have acted as a bulwark against a larger takeover by the tribe or other mainland forces, including the Al Saud. At the same time, the violence tamped down internal (Shi`a) threats in a brutal way, but had the advantage of plausible deniability on the part of Hamad's branch. In any case, the treatment of the Dawasir tribe by British and Al Khalifah authorities is telling about how tenuous the monopoly on legitimate violence was for the colonial state in its early administrative stages; without the British backing the royal family, the royals may have been unable to maintain their rule. As long as Shi`a and oppositional Sunni demands were held in check through the threat of British naval power, some form of Al Khalifah power could be sustained. At the same time, the dynamic is more complicated given the Sheikhs Isa-Hamad successionary struggle. The Dawasir refused to pay any taxes or patronage to Shiekh Hamad. Putting together the events discussed in chapter 2 around the successionary struggle, it was likely the case that both the Khawalid and the Dawasir were supporters of the deposed Shiekh Isa and/or the ambitious

Shiekh Abdullah, an assertion supported by testimonial evidence documented in the criminal case files. Sheikh Hamad's relationship with the Dawasir was a delicate balancing act as the sectarian violence unfolded.

'Ali and Sitra Sectarian Attacks

We begin with the Dawasir rampages on the Shi`a village of 'Ali in May and June of 1923, the latter of which saw several people killed and wounded.[7] Regarding the first attack, authorities pleaded for a gunboat to visit Bahraini waters hoping its presence would curtail the violence, which was all the more horrible because it targeted Shi`a during Islam's holiest time of its calendar year.

> Yesterday sunnis [sic] of Budaiyeh and Raffah attacked Shiahs [sic] of ['Ali], houses burnt and several casualties. To-day [sic] situation improving believed to be in hand, though religious feeling still running high.[8]

Although no criminal case files have been preserved related to the 'Ali violence, sources reveal that colonial authorities placed Dawasir Chief Ahmad bin Abdulla al-Dossari and his son on trial for the attacks in the Bahrain Court, ultimately convicting them and ordering a fine of 15,000 rupees with 13,000 of the rupees directed to victim compensation. Commenting from Bushehr, the political resident thought this was light punishment noting that the Dawasir in general "have been guilty of many similar crimes against the [*Baharna* and *'Ajam*] in the past."[9] Overall, the attacks signaled that Sheikh Hamad could not or would not protect Shi`a. This suggested that he was challenged in managing the opposition to his administration, and that he would only prosecute sectarian violence when pushed by the political agency or by popular demand.[10] Further, there were repercussions for even the weakest attempts at bringing perpetrators of anti-Shi`a violence to justice. Two Shi`a were later murdered on the road between Budaiyah and Diraz as payback for testifying against the Chief al-Dossari at trial.[11]

The next major act of sectarian violence was The First Sitra Outrage of September 18, 1923, happening chronologically after the 'Ali attacks and the home invasion in Tubli, but a few months before the Garayah attack. The outrage involved the Khalids, who raided Sitra, a primarily Shi`a island, killing one person. It allegedly occurred after a member of the Khalids found one of their camels wounded on the island, which the Al Khalifah considered their domain and patrolled by their *fidawi*. However, other sources report that the deeper reason behind the attacks was discouraging the British-initiated OiC reforms, which in its early stages were supported by Shi`a leaders. The Khawalid branch opposed the reforms because they feared the diminishing power of tribal rule.[12] The Khawalid may have also been engaged in a specific vendetta against Major Clive Daly, the political agent at the time, whose influence under the new OiC laws had grown as tribal governance declined. Such violence in Bahrain embarrassed the political agency and certainly delayed, though did not ultimately prevent, plans for continued administrative reform.

At the demand of the Political Agency, in order not to appear slack against tribal transgressors, Sheikh Hamad tried Sheikh Ibrahim and his two sons a few days after the First Sitra Outrage. The agency court was fined 2,000 rupees and ordered him to vacate his holdings in Sitra and move to Riffa'. His son, Sheikh Ali bin Khalid, was banished for life (but his sentence was later reduced to ten years), and additional sons and relatives were banished for less time or imprisoned.[13] Most of the perpetrators relocated to Dhamman in Al-Hasa on the Saudi mainland. Although no criminal case files could be found detailing this trial, the punishment of the perpetrators was short-lived. Although it was another example of anti-Shi`a violence, colonial authorities' mild concern for the sectarian pattern was met with Al Khalifah indifference. The *Baharnah* felt that the punishment was very lenient.[14]

Learning about the Dawasir relocation, the political resident received permission from New Delhi to write Ibn Saud about the situation—but not to warn him about Dawasir proclivity to harm local Shi`a (of which Al-Hasa had many). Rather, the letter cautioned the Saudis that it would be against the Saudi-British treaty relationship if the tribe used the Al-Hasa coast as a base of operations to continue attacks on Bahrain, [15] a protection of Bahraini Shi`a indirectly, but not an official recognition of the problem of anti-Shi`a violence in general. The stated concern was that Dawasir attacks on Bahrain were attacks on its sovereignty. Here we see the primacy of sovereignty over the safety of the inhabitants on Bahrain. We can recall Steinmetz's theoretical notion of the transfer of sovereignty to foreign control as paramount to the colonial project.[16] Asserting sovereignty in this situation seeks to essentially create the modern boundary of Bahrain and to attempt to break the region of its tribal complexities (such as the more porous *dirah* system described in chapter 1) in favor of fixed territories and nation-states. Because the boundaries are new and fragile, as a metaphor for the fragility of the colonial state itself, they must be "constantly policed."[17]

The need to maintain boundaries to perform sovereignty resurfaces in 1927, when the Dawasir requested return to Bahrain from exile. Colonial agents and Sheikh Hamad's branch of the family were apprehensive given the Dawasir's past. Again, the major talking points in the historical record are not concerns with Shi`a welfare, but rather the threat the Dawasir have on the sovereignty of Bahrain, unwilling as they are to accept the OiC reforms and the European-style rule of law evidenced by their continued use of tribal violence. Some sources also disclose that the Dawasir were secretly agents of Ibn Saud in support of his expansionist claims on Bahrain. Sheikh Hamad revealed to colonial authorities that Sheikh Khalid traveled to Dhamman that year specifically to meet with the Ibn Saud and the exiled Dawasir about taking control of Bahrain.[18]

As Belgrave explained, however, soon Sheikh Hamad was angling for the return of the Dawasir despite the danger to his realm:

> I personally consider the return of the Dowasir [sic] is a great mistake, they oppressed their divers [and] the Bahrainis [and] were arrogant [and] truculent . . . [The Sheikh] wanted to show me a letter from Bin Saoud, Sultan of Nejd, approving of the return of the Dowasir to Bahrain, [and] also to discuss the question of their rights. He looks at it all in quite the wrong way [believing] that the Dowasir are the oppressed prodigal sons, naturally they are all getting at him to grant them favours [sic].[19]

Ultimately, the Dawasir were granted permission to return probably due to what an earlier colonial agent had chalked up to the problematic practice of "subsidizing the mainland Bedouin whenever they came to [Bahrain] to renew their assurances of loyalty and service."[20] The Dawasir's perpetuation of the customary tribal warfare made the British uneasy and they did not trust the tribe; however, Sheikh Hamad likely interpreted the Dawasir within the context of traditional tribal patterns and was more willing to tolerate the back and forth loyalty of the tribe, as long as his branch of the Al Khalifah were ultimately the more powerful of the two in any negotiations—and with the British behind them, they were. Sheikh Hamad had mastered using his British protectors in order to control Dawasir and other competition, staving off the dire threats to his power and authority, while also maintaining the complicated alliance for purposes of discouraging and punishing internal enemies.

The Al Khalifah relationship to Dawasir violence, however, grew to be more than tacit acceptance of their sectarian attacks and began to take shape as state-sanctioned violence. On the night of January 7, 1924, Sheikh Khalid and his relations teamed up with Dawasir tribesmen and "murdered a lot of [*Baharna*]"[21] in Wadyan, Sitra, an event known as the Second Sitra Outrage,[22] happening chronologically after the Garayah attack but before the one in Farsiya and the assassination attempt on Sheikh Hamad. During the Second Sitra Outrage, the perpetrators killed several Shi`a and wounded more. It started as a home invasion on Abdul Hassan's household; both he and Hajji Radhi were murdered. The massacre, however, began to take on a more arbitrary sheen when the perpetrators moved on to shooting random Shi`a villagers in the streets. Allegedly, the crime was timed to occur while Sheikh Hamad was out of the country on a hawking trip to Lingah.[23] The pretext for the attack allegedly was that residents of Sitra had testified against Sheikh Khalid for the First Sitra Outrage and deserved punishment.[24] Other causes have been attributed to the Shi`a not paying their rents to the Khawalids;[25] or the intimidation of Shi`a who hoped to gain greater rights under the OiC reforms;[26] or it was an indirect revenge on Major Clive Daly and the British for putting the OiC reforms in motion,[27] or an attack on Sheikh Hamad for taking the throne from Sheikh Isa (or Sheikh Abdullah). The textual evidence points to all of the above as motivating factors for the anti-Shi`a violence, amounting to an arm of the Al Khalifah perpetuating collective punishment on a particular sect-defined group as part of their larger struggle for tribal power and control.

The ruling branch of the royal family were loath to condemn the anti-Shi`a violence or to do much about it. Reading between the lines, anti-Shi`a violence was part of the family's operant framework. A *Baharna* victim after the Garaya attack approached Sheikh Hamad, imploring him to respond (a request corroborated by a police officer), but the Sheikh "did nothing," allegedly because the witness would not give the specific names of the perpetrators. In reality the witness knew the names, but feared being killed if he gave them. The chilling effect that the routine anti-Shi`a violence had affected the community's willingness to take steps to intervene or stop the violence to the extent they could. Immediately after the Garaya attack, a victim reported that "I did make a noise then, but no one came out. Bahrana [sic] are too timid to come out in danger."[28] Regarding the testimony in the Second Sitra Outrage and related events, one witness to the massacre, Ahmad bin Haji Husain bin Eid, stated "This is the first time I come to give evidence about the robbery and murders in question . . . We have no protection except since recently the Government is protecting us so I come to give evidence." [29]

Notably, the Garyah victims knew their Dawasir attackers. The records seem to suggest that the identity of the perpetrators were something of an open secret and ostensibly something the Hamad branch of the Khalifah clan also knew. As one victim explained, Dawasir co-defendant Mulla had a cultivation plot in Garayah given to him by Shiekh Khalid; when tending it he used to stay with another Khalid who lived nearby. The victim also reported that the perpetrators were routinely in Sitra to buy dates, and that Musaid lived and worked in Al-Hamriyah.[30] At the very least, this information solidifies the social closeness of the Khalids and the Dawasir henchmen.

Testimony in the Dawasir cases by the defendants themselves also point to the deliberately anti-Shi`a nature of the attacks. In the Garyah investigation, Mulla admits "I wanted to cause loss and trouble generally in the village of *Baharna* and did this as Shiekh Isa had told me to cause (*tashwish*[31]) and I was his paid servant as also a servant of Sheikh Hamad before."[32] Interestingly, the implication here is that Mulla was no longer a servant of Hamad, but had allegiance to Isa and Abdulla. Musaid testified that "I knew . . . from the beginning that the object was an armed attack upon the house of a *Bahrani* [singular of *Baharna*] and I joined him . . ."[33] In the Farsiya case, the Indian Assistant asked Mulla the following:

Q: Have you any quarrel with the Baharnah, that you should take part in a murderous attack on them?
A: I have no quarrel with them and I did not know that they were to be killed.
Q: Then what did you expect?
A: I thought that bin Ghattam [organizer of attack along with Sheikh Ibrahim] was merely trying to drive the *Baharnah* out of the village.

Mulla also testified that Sheikh Ibrahim bin Khalid acted as the messenger of the order to attack the Garaya household on behalf of Sheikh Isa. It is this statement among the colonial files that most directly connects the players in the Sunni opposition front to the events in Sitra. It also shows the key roles that anti-Shi`a violence plays in their construction of political protest. A similar statement at trial in the Wadiyan/Second Sitra Outrage case by co-defendant Musaid also fingers Sheikh Isa as behind the events along with Sheikh Ibrahim.[34] In the Tubli case, many witnesses said Mulla told them the event was by order of the "Shuyuck" (probably meaning Sheikh Isa) even though at one point he stated: "I did this only for the *tam'a* (greed) Hamud bin Subah offered me. I had no *damm* (blood) to revenge no property to recover." Co-defendant Muhasin insisted that Mulla told him that "the Shayukh had ordered the Araibi's house to be attacked and Araibi killed . . ."[35]

In 1924, following the Garayah attack and the Second Sitra Outrage, the royal palace was overwhelmed by large crowds of *Baharna* demanding justice. In response, Sheikh Hamad agreed to try the Sheikh Ibrahim bin Khalid, Salman bin Khalid, and Abdur Razzaq, a distant relation, in the Bahrain Court, but within days of the attack, they had fled the country; Sheikh Hamad tried them *in absentia*. The Khalids and Razzaq received the death penalty and the state confiscated their property.[36] The political agent noted in his annual report for 1924 that Sheikh Hamad only passed the death sentence knowing that the recipients had absconded and it could not be carried out.[37] Later, these events would be the subject of another criminal prosecution after they were allowed to return to Bahrain, trickling in in 1927 and 1928 ("The town of Budeiyah is gradually being re-inhabited by members of the Dawasir tribe who returned one by one from Dhammam,")[38] and many were convicted in 1929 (see chapter 2).[39]

THE DAWASIR HENCHMEN AS *GHAZZU*

In the early 1920s, Political Agent Major Daly often wrote about the abhorrent conditions of the *Baharna*,[40] influenced by petitions from Shi`a leaders who also voiced these concerns formally.[41] At this point in time, it was not yet clear whether the emerging nation-state would grant more rights to Shi`a subjects. Sheikh Hamad, in being closely connected to the colonial project, was the sheikh who was perceived to likely liberalize in this way (although this did not end up happening). The Shi`a supported the administrative reforms initiated under Daly's watch as a potential way out of the crippling political and economic order under their Al Khalifah overlords. Yet, at this moment, the Sunni opposition, among its many concerns, also sought to hold on to the Shi`a subjugation that had enriched them and given them a people over which to be royal (a position the tribe did not have historically until they moved to the Gulf littoral in the events of the first disruption).

Consistent with the basic thesis of Sewell's event-as-theoretical-category,[42] the criminal cases and related sectarian violence constituted the extended moment when the fundamental power shifted from one mode of government (tribal) to another (colonial). The discursive landscape, at least in the criminal cases and related India Office files, exudes the tension in its simultaneous procedural detail and contextual richness in some ways, and silence in others, primarily around the true sectarian nature of the crimes. The meaning of the Dawasir tribal raids against Shi`a also speaks to the cultural heritage of armed retainers (*ghazzu*). If Mulla and Muhasin had been brought on as heavies in the contest between the axis of Isa-Abdullah-Khalids-Dawasir versus that of Hamad and colonial authorities, then part of the transaction may have involved Isa and/or Abdulla[43] backing the Dawasir in raids against Bahraini Shi`a subjects, with any spoils being a payment for their services. According to Dickson, "Raiding is the breath of life for the Badawin [sic]. Prevent him from raiding and he becomes the most melancholy of men."[44] Perhaps Dickson over-dramatizes here, but the importance of raiding, in the traditional sense, is to satisfy "greed for camels" (the most prized resource historically), to establish masculinity and authority, and to foster a sense of unity among men in a tribal alliance. In the witness statement in the Garaya case, the patriarch of the household explained that the perpetrators intimidated him greatly, chocked him with his own *ghutrah* (headpiece cord), and robbed him and his wife of 4,200 rupees, two gold bangles, and two gold nose-pieces, as well as making off with coffee and tobacco.[45] Clearly, at least part of the motive for the attack was to accumulate goods as in a typical tribal raid. Dickson is clear in noting that the raids are not meant to be fought to the death and victims are not expected to stand their ground, but rather desert their camels if they fear an uncertain loss in the violence. The object of raids is camel stock, not loss of life. With Mulla and Muhasin, however, we see very violent behavior and loss of life (but on the other hand, under customary law, it is the obligation of the victim to surrender, rather than for the attacker to hold back).

All this is not to stigmatize the Al Khalifah branch of the Bani 'Utba or the Dawasir as being the only tribes in the region continuing raids into the twentieth century. As colonization is taking root, there are references to other tribes operating in this fashion. In 1933, the political agency became concerned that members of the 'Ajman tribe were planning a raid on another tribe in Saudi territory by way of a Bahrain landing. Officiating Political Agent Everald Gastrell communicated worries about this to Sheikh Hamad, who replied that if the 'Ajman did arrive they would not be encouraged to raid.[46] Although a lot is left unsaid in the record, one could surmise that because the branch of 'Ajman in question was allied with the Al Khalifah, a certain respect, non-interference and even hospitality, was required of the Al Khalifah—even when the 'Ajman could cause a problem for British control and Al-Khalifah-British sovereignty.

PARDONING THE KHALIDS AND THE DAWASIR

After Sheikh Hamad passed judgment in the Bahrain Court on one of the Khawalid relations, that relation returned to Bahrain without permission, despite being banished. Belgrave observed that the Sheikh was "lamentably unfirm [and] practically told him that he was sorry to have to give him six months' hard [labor], but hoped he would get off easy in prison.[47] Sheikh Hamad's leniency for the transgressions of the Khalids and the Dawasir, and his allowance for their return to Bahrain, warranted particular note in colonial records:

> Daly used instantly to say that it would be ruination to let them back, now there is an intrigue afoot, [and] the Sheikh has been got at, to let them return. He tried to get me to reply for him [and] when I wouldn't said he thought it might be a good thing. Myself I think it's madness. [48]

And later:

> The Shaikh came in afterwards very delighted at having arranged for the Dowasir [sic] to return. Some of them came in, many pretty speeches [and] embracing, but he didn't tell them the terms on which they were to return.[49]

Sheikh Hamad hoped to repair the convicted Dawasir tribesmen's reputations. Related to defendants Muhasin, Mulla, and Musaid (the Tubli case), Sheikh Hamad at one point disavowed that they could be the culprits in the matter, citing a religious piety rationale: "The Sheikh talked with quite exceptional stupidity even for him. He constantly said the accused people couldn't have done anything wicked because they never missed their prayers they were good people."[50] And Sheikh Hamad and other members of the Khalifah family attended the wedding party of Hamud bin Subah's son (Subah was implicated in the Tubli case by the Bahrain Court, "along with the bride's father," not named[51]). Bin Subah served as a presiding judge in the *majlis al-urfi* for several years by royal appointment.[52] In addition, Belgrave's diary has a reference to another crime involving gang theft and murder ordered or committed by bin Subah that was described as never prompting "any trial or enquiry."[53] In any case, Bin Subah had not been convicted in the Tubli case either. "We are satisfied that the evidence that [Sheikh Hamud bin Subah] was actually at the murder is not sufficient, the only evidence being that of one man who says Hamud ordered him to do it."[54]

And, advocating for the return of two more members of the Khalid branch from exile:

> Lately the two Khaleds [sic] have been worrying him from the mainland [and] the Shaikh thinks that because they have been having such an uncomfortable time [and] are living on dates in a grass hut the judgment should be reversed [and] they should be allowed to return. [Political Agent Cyril Barrett], to my mind very weakly and unwisely, has agreed that there should be a new trial before the four [Qadis]. The Shaikh is delighted [and] says he hasn't ever been so pleased so his murdering relations are to be allowed to return [and] to be tried again, in the meantime he is trying to persuade the relations of the murdered people to deny their evidence so that there need be no trial at all.[55]

Government documents indicate that the Khalids had been corresponding with the Sheikh since their exile to negotiate their return and the Sheikh had been working to make it happen. The Sheikh hoped to reconcile the aggrieved *Baharna* community and the Khalids, but appeared to be doing this by trying to persuade *Baharna* witnesses to recant their statements against the Khalids.[56]

When Ibrahim and Salman Khalid returned in April of 1928, the Sheikh held a *majlis*. The Shi`a qadi, Hasan bin Marzuq, representing the children of the Khalid's victims, Abd Ali bin Rajab, a *Baharna* leader, and Belgrave also attended. The discussions led to Marzuq agreeing to drop criminal charges against the Khalids after "they had received assurances from the Shaikh to the effect that the Khalids would not indulge in offenses against them in the future."[57] Around the same time, the Sheikh arranged for the Khalids to recoup the land confiscated from them after their offenses.[58] The Sheikh also restored the monthly allowances to the Khalids from the Bahrain Government, which were provided to all members of the royal family. The political resident observing from a distance, expressed great hope that the settlement sent the proper message that the royal family could not commit violence against *Baharnah* in the newly formed state. "I consider it advisable to accept the compromise which the *Baharnah* have made and so terminate the incident. So doing is more likely to bring the Khalifah and *Baharnah* together than keeping open a source of dislike and distrust between them."[59] Another colonial communication shows that the political agency was favorable to the original request for clemency in 1925.

> I have given the matter a good deal of consideration and am inclined to agree with Hamad that relations having so much improved between the Sunnis and [the Shi`a], clemency in this case may be advantageous rather than otherwise, and would tend to pacify any revengeful feeling which may linger among [Sheikh Ali bin Khalid's] relatives and, if they give up all hope of getting him back, might induce them to break out.[60]

As aforementioned, a retrial of the Khalids and the Dawasir was not ordered until new evidence against them surfaced the following year (the 1929 cases). Yet, the eventual pardoning of the Khalid branch of the Al Khalifah had repercussions that cannot be overly stated. In essence, despite British hope initially in the 1920s that sectarian violence could be criminalized, that hope is eroded through the royal insistence on pardons. Eventually, political agents place sectarian harmony on the back-burner of their hopes and dreams as their anxieties become channeled toward other seemingly more pressing issues such as Persian claims to the island and the development of the burgeoning oil industry.

Further, their gradual restoration of the Khalids into the ruling regime spawned two inter-related outcomes: Sheikh Hamad was able to absorb the Khawalid branch of his family back into the fold as partners rather than opponents, and simultaneously a vehemently anti-Shi`a wing of the family was legitimized. From here begins the long cover-up of Sunni-centric narratives in the creation of the Bahrain state and the swinging of the royal family into subsequent sectarian positions than may not have otherwise occurred.

Still known today as the "Khawalid," two descendant brothers, Khalid bin Ahmed and Khalifah bin Ahmed, form a hardline within the royal family, the latter serving as Minister of Defense and commander-in-chief of the Bahrain Defense Forces.[61] The Khawalids stand in opposition to initiatives that would reform Bahrain in order to share power with Shi`a citizens, and they are widely seen as the masterminds of the kind of frequent repressions, from citizenship removal to dissident arrests, in post-Arab Spring Bahrain. Their political ally and nephew, Ahmad bin Atiyyat Allah, was implicated in the infamous Bandar report, named after whistle-blower Salah Bandar. He spent $6 million on an elaborate spying operation targeting Bahrain Shi`a political activists in London. He also financed phony non-governmental organizations (NGOs) hatched to cultivate anti-Shi`a sentiment in social media, designed the plan to quickly naturalize Sunni immigrants to Bahrain in order to swing sectarian demographics in Sunni favor,[62] and subsidized costs related to conversions from Shi'ism to Sunni Islam.[63]

THE SUNNI PRIVILEGE OF RESTORATIVE JUSTICE

Synthesizing events related to the above pardons, we see that some key prosecutions in the 1920s were fundamentally about the intertwining of the elements of a crisis in tribal succession and a perpetuation of sectarian violence. Sheikh Hamad was often coerced into prosecution by the colonial authorities. Yet, we see him also attempting to interpret these criminalizations from the vantage point of customary practice. It is this perspective which gives rise to a culture of Sunni forgiveness and pardons, carved out from within the formal system, acting as a stand-in for non-judicial, tribal resolutions.

The observed Sunni leniency can be understood as a vestige of tribal custom brought into the formal system at the discretion of the ruler, leading to a colonial hybridity in the application of criminal justice. Under waning tribal custom, surrender and subjugation were important acts in achieving political stability after a political contest. Applied here, we can see that once Sheikh Hamad would receive an oath of allegiance from a Sunni tribal guilty party, he often accepted this in lieu of punishment. For, under the tribal system, contests that successfully reorder political loyalty to the satisfaction of the victor have accomplished their goals, and no further punishment is needed. It is also a matter of honor, for in not accepting a surrender or in not protecting a surrendered person, honor can be diminished or lost. As ethnographer Dickson explains: "a [tribesperson] surrendering to another either in battle or raid, or if pursued and overtaken, is safe and entitled to good treatment . . . the matter is finished, and the person has accepted surrender must go bail for his captive with his life. He has given him his *wejh* (face), and it would go hard with any member of his own tribe who harmed the prisoner later, and so blackened the protector's face."[64]

Through British eyes, however, this leniency was dangerous, serving to show weakness in ruling, and not effectively deterring or punishing bad behavior. In the British world of post-Enlightenment rational-legal justice, proper order maintenance necessitated the codification of law, and the lack of follow-through on punishments threatened colonial codification and modern development. We see the Raj's frustration in this regard:

> . . . as long as we are responsible for the administration of Criminal Justice with regard to foreign subjects in Bahrain, we must also accept some responsibility for seeing that the elementary principles of justice as understood in other countries is observed.[65]

According to Belgrave and other colonial observers, even in ordinary cases, the pardoning of defendants was a routine event; according to this analysis, Sunni people overwhelmingly constituted the pardoned. For example, Sheikh

Hamad declined to follow through on Khalid bin Feraj who was deported for writing anti-English articles in Cairo Newspapers from abroad. Sheikh Hamad allowed him back in Bahrain, while Belgrave railed against it in his diary, calling it a sign of weakness.[66] Sheikh Hamad also cancelled the banishment order of a thief after the head of the thief's unspecified Sunni tribe asked him to do so.[67] In 1935, Belgrave lamented Sheikh Hamad's "tiresome habit" of releasing prisoners during the Eid holiday, calling it a "dangerous business."[68] In one instance in 1935, the Sheikh gave orders to release a prisoner who had attempted to murder his sister and had been sentenced to five years in the Bahrain Court, but had only served a year and a half. In the same order, he let go another prisoner serving five years for theft. That same year, he urged the Political Agency to release a rapist convicted in its court, Said bin Abdul Hui.[69] In a note to a political agency file, an unknown employee of the political agency wrote: "if people once got the idea that they could beg releases from [Sheikh Hamad] it would make it very difficult for him and bad for justice."[70]

Meanwhile, the attitude toward Shi`a defendants was not one of understanding or forgiveness at any stage of the criminal process. As Belgrave observed:

> I went to see the Sheikh [about the case of a Sunni Arab stabbing a *Baharna* person], he as usual took sides against the Baharna, not even having seen or heard the parties.[71]

Belgrave also wrote early on in his career in Bahrain that a local confidante told him: "the Khalifah consider that a [*Baharna*] is worth less than a dog and in the old days they showed it by oppressing them and shooting them and murdering them."[72] Across the cases in the cache from the India Office Records, a pattern emerged of Shi`a defendants being treated more harshly. For example, as will be shown in chapter 5, punishment and deportation for low-level offenses almost always were attached to *Baharn*a, Shi`a, and/or Iranian defendants. But admittedly, given the minute nature of the sample relative to all cases known to have been prosecuted, such a pattern can only be asserted with caution.

THE RISE OF THE COLONIAL POLICE AND SECT-LOYALTY

For a Sunni hegemonic colonial state, it would make sense that the tendency would be to lean toward a Sunni-dominated police force; however, in the early days of the modern police force, colonial authorities attempted to bring Shi`a into policing; this was soon met with elite resistance. Sheikh Abdullah reportedly drafted "a gang not yet identified" (which may or may not have been the Dawasir heavies) who were shooting police posts in Manama from a distance "presumably with the object of terrifying the police and inhabitants who are much disturbed . . . Anonymous letters and threatening municipal officers and police [were] also received."[73] This same year, Sheikh Abdullah was accused by Sheikh Salman to be behind the fatal shooting of a police officer.[74] The potential absorption of Shi`a into the political and civic life of the colonial state deeply irked the Sunni opposition and the newly minted police force served as a major symbol of the abhorrent liberalization project.

The Attempt on Major Daly's Life

A question that may never be answered for sure based on the historical record is whether the Sunni opposition was behind the attempt on Major Daly's life in October of 1926. The incident served to undermine the new police force in the country, a major aim of the opposition Sheikhs and their minions. One month before the assassination attempt on Sheikh Hamad, a levy sepoy (lowest rank, soldier in the Indian Army) killed two of his colleagues and injured Daly. The case was tried as a violation of sections 302 (murder) and 324 (voluntarily causing injury through use of a dangerous weapon) of the Indian Penal Code.[75]

Although evidence for this point of view is admittedly scant, many speculated at the time that the aims were political and related to the same groups involved in the sectarian attacks in Sitra and 'Ali. Just a month before, Political Resident Francis Prideaux had visited Bahrain to hold talks with three Dawasir chiefs, Abdul Latif bin Ibrahim, Isa bin Sa'ad, and Ahmad bin Abdullah bin Hasan who were lobbying for members of their tribe to return from exile for past transgressions. Allegedly, they balked when the condition was presented that they must pay the same taxes and would have the same rights as "their Bahraini tenants and negro drivers."[76] Bin Hasan, in particular, could not tolerate these conditions of purported sect equality and encouraged other chiefs to reject them.[77]

The attempt on Daly's life occurred at the Police Fort when a British Indian captain, Subredor (second highest rank among Junior Commissioned Officers in the Indian Army) Niaz Ali Khan, was shot and killed. The victim and another sepoy were speaking with Daly when Daly was struck by a bullet fired from the outside and through a window. Another shot nicked Daly's ear while an approaching Indian officer, Havrildar (highest ranks among non-commissioned officers) Nuur Daad, was also shot and killed.[78] As the attack continued, Daly was bayoneted in five places on his body. The perpetrator, Ismail bin Shah Murad, a Baluchi sepoy with Omani citizenship, surrendered shortly thereafter, and told his jailers that he wished he had killed three more people.[79] Later, he told investigators that he committed the offense because he was angry at the ill treatment he received by Khan, his supervisor.[80]

According to Belgrave's interpretation of events, the perpetrator did not mean to target Daly,[81] but rather was angling for Khan, Haji Salman bin Jasim, and other high-ranking members of the corps in a planned "plot,"[82] allegedly organized by an unspecified *mullah*, perhaps acting as an agent of an unknown or unspecified group with political aims. The political resident sent two of his assistants to Bahrain to investigate the situation, and to relieve Daly from his duties so he could convalesce.[83] Although their findings are not recorded, correspondence indicated that many men in the force knew the attack had been planned.[84] Murad was tried for murder after being certified "perfectly sane," through an unspecified evaluation.[85] He was sentenced to death by firing squad,[86] and executed on September 21, 1926.[87]

Sect-Loyalty

The 1930s saw the rise of the social construction of Shi`a as a criminal class (described in the next chapter), and the restoration of the Al Khalifah family after its successionary struggles, uniting under the Sheikh Hamad branch of the family. From here, the state sought to actively create a modern police force that was sect-loyal and willing to maintain a Sunni and Al Khalifah hegemony. The development of modern policing cannot be divorced from Sheikh Hamad's larger political compromise with the Khawalid branch, restoring them to the fold despite their deep sectarian animosity; unfortunately this branch becomes tasked with developing policing and other security apparatuses, thereby putting the final nail in the coffin of a once potentially sect-diverse police force.

C. J. Jeffries theorizes the police develop in the colonial setting as part of the project of creating "self-governing nations" and so the "British colonial project [was] a partnership on nation-building."[88] As he explains, there are generally three main phases in the rise of British colonial policing in a territory. The first is an improvised phase in which the basic essentials of law and order are secured. The second is a semi-military constabulary that is modeled upon the Royal Irish Constabulary/Royal Ulster Constabulary (RIC/RUC)[89] in which the focus is on suppressing social and political unrest and mass violence. The third phase is a conversion to a civilian police force with an emphasis on policing by local people. Police deployment at this stage is seen as one that handles internal security; however, can be used whenever an armed response is needed if imperial forces are not available.

Jeffries meant this framework to describe the formal British colonies that participated in the empire-wide Colonial Police Service (CPS), a recruitment, training, and promotional framework designed to provide a career pathway for people policing the empire. The CPS set standards and consistency on pay, pension, and rank. Bahrain, operating under the administrative fiction of not being a full British colonial possession, did not employ CPS officers.

However, many former and future CPS officers flowed through the ranks of Bahrain policing. Moreover, the development of policing in the country roughly comports with what Jeffries identifies[90] through the second stage; Bahrain, however, never managed to make policing a truly local affair as characterized by the third stage (as still today over half of the force are Sunnis hailing from other countries[91]). Another theory puts forth that policing evolved in a more ad hoc fashion than Jeffries envisioned, responding to local acceptance or rejection of colonial rule.[92] Intentionality in the identity of police recruits, often from a particular ethnic group in order to control another, characterized British colonial policing of its often politically-fragile regimes.[93]

Improvisation: The First Police Forces

The first attempt at colonial control of policing in Bahrain was initiated by Political Agent Terence Keys. In 1914, he asked, or perhaps demanded, that Sheikh Isa modernize his order maintenance regime after the murder of a "Christian merchant,"[94] which proved that British reliance on their navy to quell unrest in Bahrain was ineffective. British naval ships were not always immediately available, so a local force, answerable to the colonial administration, was necessary to keep law and order. But, officials felt that the *fidawi*, though local, could not be trusted to operate in a purportedly just framework characterizing a developing nation-state.[95] To revisit tribal and Al-Khalifah customs, order maintenance was the purview of the *fidawi*s, or armed attendants of the Al Khalifah sheikhs who divided up the archipelago into domains of control among them. As we have earlier explained, this structure of control is a type of feudalism. Shi`a villages belonged to particular Al Khalifah sheikhs who acted as a lord and exploited the villages for tax collection and economic gain (in the domains of date cultivation, fishing, and pearling).[96] *Fidawi*, Sunni men, often of Baluchi and African descent, acted as the foot soldiers for the Al Khalifah sheikhs, maintaining the feudal structure. They were notoriously violent toward indigenous populations.

At this time, influencing the Al Khalifah in internal matters such as policing was a matter of subtle coercion; the OiC laws were not yet in play, though being envisioned and drafted in the halls of the India Office. Keys' job was to cajole Sheikh Isa into agreeing to change course away from reliance on his own tribal forces. According to colonial records, the Sheikh initially agreed, reportedly only concerned that funds should be made available to support a state-sponsored police force. Customarily he had funded the *fidawi* and *natur*s through a tax on shops in Manama, but sought to expand this tax to all households if he was to grow the security apparatus of the country. The agent found this agreeable[97] and proceeded to weed out some of the "low class '*naturs*'" serving the Sheikh, and to enlist thirty men deployed by the Political Agency. He also established three "police *chowkis*" (the Hindi vernacular for police stations).[98] Later, in 1920 or 1921, depending on the source, the Manama municipality raised its own force; it employed many individuals of Persian descent.[99]

The Short-Lived Levy Corps

After the OiC reforms were implemented in the early 1920s, the two colonial criminal courts shared police as their source of cases and as their enforcement arm. This unique arrangement, based on the dual administrative control exercised by the Sheikh and his advisor on one hand, and the British political agent on the other,[100] was not without its problems. The Levy Corps, established in 1924, cooperated heavily with the British Raj and the Political Agency for supplies, training, and recruitment. They were centralized and militarized, based on the Royal Irish Constabulary (RIC) who were effective in political situations in which opposition to British rule was robust.[101] Although not a constabulary per se, it follows Jeffries' second phase theoretically because it was a semi-military force that was tied to the empire, and employed by imperials transplants, rather than locals. Technically this force, however, was under the purview of the Bahrain Government (represented by the Sheikh and the advisor).[102]

According to an annual report, the Levy Corps was created primarily to handle armed attacks against Bahrain sovereignty such as from the Dawasir.[103] Another agency report explains that the Levies would "support [Sheikh Hamad's] prestige and enable him to exert some authority," a similar rationale that led to the early force initiated by Keys. The creation of the Levy Corps is also attributed specifically to the sectarian violence of the Second Sitrah Outrage.[104] Interestingly, no mention is made of the Sheikh's and his family's *fedawiyyah* in many of the documents at this time related to the development of modern policing. Despite being increasingly ostracized from the colonial project, many sheikhs still maintained their own armed retainers as a customary practice even as modern policing development. These *fidawi*, numbering 114 men by 1933 often hailed from Baluchistan and Sunni Muslim communities in Africa. They were considered part of the *bani khudayr* (literally, the "green stock" or "green tribe"). They had no tribal affiliation or had lost it,[105] but were considered loyal subjects to the Bani 'Utba.

According to Belgrave, the Levy Corps was 200 strong in 1926 and primarily were Baluchis and descendants of African slaves recruited from Muscat (similar to the identities of the *fidawi*). Baluchis, seemingly loyal to colonial administrators as British subjects, were preferred because they would act independent of tribal loyalties (but were nonetheless acceptable to Sunni tribes). At the same time, many administrators noted their inefficiency precisely because they were not locals, often unable to speak local languages (Arabic and Persian) and lacking cultural competencies necessary for the job. In addition, most of them could not read and write in their own languages or English. Compounding these problems was a reported lack of discipline and motivation.

As Jill Crystal notes, the British Empire in general relied on an "ethnic" policing model in the Middle East. A minority within a colony would be utilized to police a majority, the idea being that ethnic cleavages could be used to maintain British control over subjects. They could employ locals without fear of ceding local control.[106] In these early days of modern policing, we have shown that the greatest threat was perceived to be intra-Sunni and/or intra-Khalifah threats to sovereignty; therefore, the local ethnic group utilized appeared to be Persians and/or Shi`a people outside the sphere of tribal politics, but still local. However, the cultural biases against these people by elites and in Bahraini society in general, coupled with the Al Khalifah disdain for its Persian and/or Shi`a subjects problematized British efforts to "give" policing to Persians and/or Shi`a.

The corps did not last long, brought down from the instability related to the events in attempted murder of Daly. Afterwards, Daly reported to the political resident that although the murderer was apprehended, the loyalty of the Levy Corps was in question. Fearing an insurrection, Britain redirected two man-of-war naval ships to Bahrain, the first arriving on August 14, 1926. This "had quieting effect on town and levies, and effectively prevented any further trouble."[107] Meanwhile, a ripple effect continued. In late August of 1926, the wife of the political agent, the advisor, and the director of customs were threatened by an anonymous letter linked to the political opposition to colonial rule. And, although the details are scare, there was a shooting attempt on the lives of a political agency interpreter and an ethnically Persian policeman. According to Belgrave, Daly himself called for the disbanding of the Levy Corps.[108] The political resident also made this request to the Government of India, faulting the incident on the commandant. "A reliable commandant could have perhaps sorted sheep from goats but it is clear that no one present can do this."[109] The Government of India approved the dissolution of the force and recommended repatriation of the levy officers. Although this may have been a brief symbolic victory for the Dawasir, the Khawalid, Sheikhs Isa, and Abdullah, and others who abhorred the police.

We know that many Sunni Arab Bahrainis resented the Persianization of the force. In November of 1926, Shaikh Abdullah formed his own force to meet demands for change, patrolling the roads by night, after a series of burglaries sent panic through the country "as people have no faith in the Persian nature [of the] police."[110] One can't help but wonder, however, whether these burglaries were a reference to the home invasions and sectarian violence ('Ali attacks, Sitra outrages, etc.) that he was allegedly behind, along with Sheikh Isa and the Khawalid, in the first place. It once again begs the question of whether his own part in the sectarian violence had the instrumental purpose of delegitimizing Sheikh Hamad's rule (through Sheikh Hamad being unable to provide for public safety), while also stepping in to save the public from that very violence. In any case, the levels of Persian and/or Shi`a participation in policing would never recover.

The Creation of the State Police: A Failed Attempt to Localize

The new State Police formed the same year, absorbing the Manama municipal police and replacing the Levies. Only three of the original Levies, perceived of as loyal to the government, were invited into the new force.[111] Belgrave was sent to Lahore in British India, with Havildars Bahadur Kahn and Nader Khan and Clerk Faizal Hussein to recruit a hundred new Punjabi, Muslim officers.[112] The new officers in the new state police, however, had problems. In the early summer of 1928, the acting police commander, Captain L. S. Parke, dismissed a Lance Naik (lowest level on non-commissioned officers) for gross insubordination and unsatisfactory conduct in the early summer of 1928. This apparently led to retaliation by the ranks, in support of the dismissed officer. They filed a petition with the Political Agency demanding more leave and better rations. As a result, Captain Parke met with the twenty petitioners and heard their complaints. He summed them up:

> The whole thing appeared to me to be most trivial, but convinced me at the same time that they had been induced to and inspired from the outside to make "fitna" on account of resentment at several unsatisfactory persons having been sent from Bahrein [sic].

Fitna is an Arabic word with many meanings, including religious ones, but in this particular context it probably means revolt. The latter appears to also refer to a situation in which the dismissal and deportation of some Indian sepoys or staff at the Political Agency angered the Indian assistant to the political agent, Bahadur Sayid Siddiq Hassan and the postmaster, although details are not clear.[113]

In November of 1927, Sir Denys Bray, Foreign Secretary of India in the Foreign and Political Affairs Department took a tour, stopping in Bahrain. Speaking on state security, he felt that British interference was "over-advertised" in the police because of the number of British Indians and the likeliness of their uniforms to that of an Indian regiment, making "it look as if the present state of Bahrain depends for its security on the Indian bayonet alone."[114] Although one might think Bray was arguing for local police, his alternative suggestion, given the lack of a local interest, was to bring in Arabs from Yemen, probably because they would be loyal to the Sunni regime and appear less foreign.[115] In 1929, the police were placed under

Charles Belgrave as Commandant and there were 100 Indian officers, and a few local constables, mostly Persian. In the late 1920s, a few Persian or Shi`a Bahrainis were still included in policing, a trend that would change drastically within a decade, as colonial administrators take on the ethnic and sect-based discrimination preferred by the now-united Al Khalifah royal family. By the early 1930s, the make-up of the force had shifted to forty-four British Indians and seventy-nine Arabs. They were recruited from outside Bahrain, primarily from the mainland, including Yemen. In 1932, despite efforts to the contrary, it was again noted that there were not enough locals in the force at this time; many local Arabs and Sunnis took no interest in recruitment efforts. The composition of the force at that time was sixty-five British Indians, mostly Punjabis, and thirty unspecified locals.[116]

In 1936, the Political Agency issued a notice that under Article 70 of the King's Regulation of the Bahrain Orders-in-Council, local officers to be formed into a Special Police Officers' force were to be recruited among residents in Bahrain "for the preservation of peace and good order."[117] The recruits were to have all the powers, privileges, and protections of a police officer and perform the duties as assigned by the Commandant of Police. Despite this notice for the localization of police, complaints surfaced as to the dearth of local recruits. Many locals reportedly refrained from interest in policing because of the socially undesirable groups (foreigners) on the force.[118] According to an annual report, in 1936, the state police had three hundred officers, mostly non-commissioned. An additional six British police were on hand to assist public security efforts. Meanwhile, 153 *natur*s remained in play, including 36 who were working directly for the British Royal Airforce in the region.

Upon reflection, the brief Persian inclusion in policing may have been due to the social justice perspective Daly brought to his job. Clashing with many members of the Al Khalifah, including Sheikh Isa, he was suspicious of the threat of tribal politics on the colonial state and its goal to stabilize the country. He also showed a strong sympathy for the plight of the *Baharna* and *'ajam* as the social, economic, and political underdogs of Bahrain. Unlike many later colonial administrators, his reports directly detailed sectarian tensions. For example, in a report, under the subheading "Justice," he elaborated on Sunni-Shi`a tensions being fomented by the Al Khalifah and other Sunni elites, and that justice for Shi`a would not be possible if the Al Khalifah gained full control of the burgeoning justice system. He believed British intervention in this regard was necessary in any reform efforts, or else Shi`a would be at risk of systemic injustice.[119] It does not appear that he was wrong.

However, subsequent administrators, in cultivating closeness with the Al Khalifah rulers, began to take on the sectarian discrimination and hierarchy of the social and political milieu of Al Khalifah and the Sunni tribal elites.

Their interest in maintaining Al Khalifah stability and cooperation in order to pacify the region for larger imperial economic interests overrode any social justice inclinations. Although administrators sometimes noted the injustice of the sectarian oppression, very little was ever done to rectify it, placing such potential efforts at a very low priority. By the 1930s, when Iranian claims to Bahrain threatened British and Al Khalifah sovereignty, the Iranian/Persian and/or Shi`a dissatisfaction with the sectarian colonial state takes on a more radical sheen. Having a class of people increasingly being constructed as a criminal and even seditious group cooperating with an external threat made them highly undesirable candidates for police positions. Soon Persians and Shi`a began to be selected *against* in police recruitment. The British and Al Khalifah built up a force of British Indians readily trained and available from the subcontinent; all elites were now cooperating in building a Sunni-dominated state whose order maintenance regime would increasingly conflate external Persian threats with a so-defined criminal class of Shi`a and Persian Bahrainis.

NOTES

1. Al-Tajir 1987: 37–36.
2. Belgrave 1960; Al-Tajir 1987: 43.
3. Telegram Report no. 60/c [India Office Records, R/15/2/86, May 13, 1923].
4. Major Clive Daly, Confidential Memorandum no. 62A/c (India Office Records, British Library, May, 13, 1923, R/15/2/86).
5. Al-Tajir 1987: 43–44.
6. Belgrave 1960.
7. Telegram Report no. 60/c (India Office Records, R/15/2/86, May 13, 1923).
8. Telegram Report no. 60/c (India Office Records, R/15/2/86, May 13, 1923).
9. Al-Tajir 1987: 57.
10. Al-Tajir 1987: 57.
11. Al-Tajir 1987: 35–38.
12. Nebil Husayn, "Mechanisms of Authoritarian Rule in Bahrain," *Arab Studies Quarterly* 37 (1): (2015) 35 [32–53].
13. Al-Tajir 1987: 58.
14. Al-Tajir 1987: 58.
15. Al-Tajir 1987.
16. Steinmetz 2008.
17. Mitchell 1988: 167.
18. Memorandum no. 415/18, Political Agent to Political Resident (India Office Records, R/15/2/108, January 20, 1925).
19. Charles Belgrave, Diaries, entry dated March 26, 1927.
20. Letter no. 279 from Francis Prideaux, Political Agent to Percy Cox (India Office Records, r/15/2/28, 1905).
21. Belgrave, personal diary, February 4, 1928.
22. Despatch no. 90, C.A. Gault to Selwyn Lloyd (Papers of Charles Dalrymple Belgrave, 1926–1947, University of Exeter, United Kingdom, 148/2/1, 1956).
23. Al-Tajir 1987: 67.
24. Al-Tajir 1987: 67.
25. Belgrave, personal diary, April 29, 1927.
26. Husayn 2015: 35.

27. Al-Tajir 1987: 58–59.
28. Indian Assistant's handwritten account of witness interviews in case no. 62/397 of 1929 (India Office Records, R/15/3/7002).
29. Indian Assistant's handwritten account of witness interviews in case no. 64/398 of 1929 (India Office Records, R/15/3/7003).
30. Indian Assistant's handwritten account of witness interviews in case no. 62/397 of 1929 (India Office Records, R/15/3/7002).
31. The Indian Assistant translated the word used by Mulla, *tashwish*, as trouble, but it also has the meaning of muddling, confusing, deranging, disturbing, or bewildering.
32. Indian Assistant's handwritten account of witness interviews in case no. 62/397 of 1929 (India Office Records, R/15/3/7002).
33. Indian Assistant's handwritten account of witness interviews in case no. 63/397 of 1929 (India Office Records, R/15/3/7001).
34. Indian Assistant's handwritten account of trial in case no. 64/398 of 1929 (India Office Records, R/15/3/7003).
35. Indian Assistant's handwritten account of trial in case no. 63/397 of 1929 (India Office Records, R/15/3/7002).
36. Al-Tajir 1987: 67; Memorandum no. 415/18, Political Agent to Political Resident (India Office Records, R/15/2/108, January 20, 1925.
37. Annual Report, 1924 (India Office Records, R/15/2/296).
38. Belgrave, personal diary, March, 1928.
39. Case no. 64/398 of 1928 (India Office Records, R/15/3/7003).
40. Khuri 1980: 93.
41. Gengler 2015: 59; Khuri 1980.
42. Sewell 2005.
43. The notion that Sheikh Abdulla was behind the attacks is implied by an entry in Belgrave's diary which explains that Abdulla was placed on the judges' panel for the Dawasir and Khawalid court cases because he would "…condemn the men to shield himself, and if [the defendants] accused him in Court he is quite clever enough to suppress any such idea." This appears to suggest Abdulla's role as a co-conspirator in some or all of the sectarian attacks was known and that Belgrave and the Al Khalifah ruling family were involved in obfuscating that fact. The diary entry goes on to state that because of this it was a "good move" to add him as a judge to the criminal cases. [Belgrave, personal diaries, February 2, 1929; Jones 2013.]
44. Dickson 1949: 341.
45. Indian Assistant's handwritten account of witness interviews in case no. 63 of 1929 (India Office Records, R/15/3/7002).
46. Belgrave, personal diary, July 14, 1933.
47. Belgrave, personal diary, July 26, 1926.
48. Belgrave, personal diary, September 15, 1926.
49. Belgrave, personal diary, March 23, 1927.
50. Belgrave, personal diary, August 13, 1929.
51. Belgrave, personal diary, July 17, 1929.
52. Belgrave, personal diary, September 3, 1929.
53. Belgrave, personal diary, August 7, 1927.
54. Belgrave, personal diary, August 13, 1929.
55. Belgrave, personal diary, January 30, 1928.
56. Al-Tajir 1987: 90.
57. Al-Tajir 1987: 91.
58. Belgrave, personal diary, February 14, 1927.
59. Letter no. 203–S from Political Resident Lionel Haworth to the Foreign Secretary, Government of India (India Office Records, 15/2/88, May 16, 1928).
60. Memorandum no. 415/18, Political Agent to Political Resident (India Office Records, R/15/2/108, January 20, 1925).
61. Kristin Smith Diwan, "Royal Factions, Ruling Strategies and Sectarianism in Bahrain," in *Sectarian Politics in the Persian Gulf*, edited by Lawrence G. Potter, 143–177. (Oxford: Oxford University Press, 2014): 146.

62. Concern about the number of Sunni citizens in Bahrain is not a new anxiety affecting public policy. In reference to agreeing to allow the exiled Dawasir to return to Bahrain in 1927, Political Resident Colonel Haworth indicated to the Indian government that "the [Al Khalifa] are a Sunni people governing a Shi`a population and they do not desire to weaken themselves by the expulsion of a powerful Sunni support." [Letter no. 87–S from Political Resident Colonel Haworth to the Foreign Secretary of the Government of India (India Office Records, LPS/10/1042, March 27, 1927).]

63. Husayn 2015: 35.

64. Dickson 1949: 125.

65. Confidential letter from Political Resident Trenchard Fowle to H.A.F. Metcalf, Foreign and Political Department, Government of India, Simla (India Office Records, R/15/2/573, July 1, 1935).

66. Belgrave, personal diary, January 4, 1929.

67. Belgrave, personal diary, February 20, 1928.

68. Belgrave, personal diary, January 24, 1935.

69. Direct order 838/6A from Advisor to the Bahrain Government, Sir Charles Belgrave, to Political Agent Colonel Percy Loch (India Office Records, R/15/2/573, January 23, 1935).

70. Note to file (India Office Records, R/15/2/573, January 30, 1935).

71. Belgrave, personal diaries, August 29, 1935.

72. Belgrave, personal diary, August 19, 1929.

73. Memorandum from the Political Agent to the Political Resident (India Office Records, R/15/2/1394, January 12, 1922).

74. Memorandum no 52/c from the Political Agent to the Political Resident (India Office Records, R/15/2/1394, January 22, 1922).

75. Judgment, *King Emperor vs. Ismail bin Shah Murad* (India Office Records, R/15/2/137, August 16, 1926); Indian Penal Code, sections 302 and 324.

76. Al-Tajir 1987: 86.

77. Al-Tajir 1987: 86.

78. Belgrave 1960.

79. Belgrave, personal diaries, August 4, 1926.

80. Letter no. 1 of 1926 from Political Resident to Government of India (India Office Records, R/15/2/137, August 21, 1926. Judgment, *King Emperor vs. Ismail bin Shah Murad* (India Office Records, R/15/2/137, August 16, 1926).

81. Belgrave, personal diaries, August 6, 1926.

82. Belgrave, personal diaries, August 5, 1926.

83. Telegram to Political Agent from Political Resident (India Office Records, R/15/2/137).

84. Letter from Political Agent Clive Daly to Political Agent in Muscat (India Office Records, R/15/2/137, August 26, 1926).

85. Judgment, *King Emperor vs. Ismail bin Shah Murad* (India Office Records, R/15/2/137, August 16, 1926).

86. Belgrave 1960; Judgment, *King Emperor vs. Ismail bin Shah Murad* (India Office Records, R/15/2/137, August 16, 1926).

87. Letter from Political Resident Frances Prideaux to Secretary of State for the Government of India, Simla (India Office Recrods, R/15/2/137, September 25, 1926).

88. Jeffries 1952: 273.

89. The force was the Royal Irish Constabulary (RIC) until the partition of Ireland in 1922 when it was disbanded. Britain maintained control of Northern Ireland and commissioned a similar force called the Royal Ulster Constabulary (RUC).

90. Jeffries 1952.

91. Staci Strobl, "The Roots of Sectarian Law and Order in the Gulf," In Frederic Wehrey (Ed.), *Beyond Sunni and Shia: The Roots of Sectarianism in a Changing Middle East*. (London: Hurst & Co.: 2017): 228.

92. B.A. Cole, "Post-colonial systems." In R. Mawby (Ed.), *Policing Across the World: Issues for the 21st Century*. (London: UCL Press, 2013): 88–108.

93. Jill Crystal, "Criminal Justice in the Middle East," Journal of Criminal Justice, 29, 6 (2001): 469–483.; Strobl 2011.

94. Political Agent Terence Keys, "Exhibit from Administrative Report," for 1914 (India Office Records, R/15/1/299, 1915).
95. Khuri 1980: 114.
96. Diwan 2014: 149.
97. Political Agent Terence Keys, "Exhibit from Administrative Report," for 1914 (India Office Records, R/15/1/299, 1915).
98. Political Agent Terence Keys, "Exhibit from Administrative Report," for 1914 (India Office Records, R/15/1/299, 1915).
99. Annual Report on the Operation of the Order-in-Council for the year 1921 (India Office Records, R/15/1/305, 1921).
100. Al-Tajir 1987: 262–263; Khuri 1980: 85.
101. Jill Crystal, "Criminal Justice in the Middle East," Journal of Criminal Justice, 29, 6 (2001): 469–483.
102. Letter no. 1044/9/A from Commandant of the Levy Corps to Advisor Charles Belgrave (India Office Records, R/15/2/1202, June 16, 1926); Letter no. 668/6/2 of Political Agent to Advisor Charles Belgrave (India Office Records, R/15/2/1202, July 9, 1926).
103. Annual Report of the Bahrain Government, 1350 (India Office Records, R/15/2/306, 1932): 90.
104. Report of the Political Agency, no. 209/9/1 (India Office Records, R/15/1/339, August 31, 1924).
105. Peterson 2014: 239.
106. Jill Crystal, "Criminal Justice in the Middle East," *Journal of Criminal Justice*, 29, 6 (2001): 469–483.
107. Confidential memorandum from Political Agent to Political Resident (India Office Records, R/15/2/137, August 14, 1926).
108. Belgrave, personal diaries, August 16, 1926.
109. Naval message, "Resident 520" (India Office Records, R/15/2/137, August 21, 1926).
110. Letter no. 120/9/10 from Political Agent Clive Daly to Political Resident Francis Prideaux (India Office Records, November 17, 1926).
111. Letter no. 136/9/10 from the Political Agent to the Political Resident (India Office Records, R/15/2/137, December 14, 1926).
112. Letter no. 108/9/10 from Political Barrett to Recruiting Office for Punjabi Musulmans (India Office Records, R/15/2/137, October 19, 1926).
113. Letter from Captain L.S. Parke to Political Agent Cyril Barrett (India Office Records, 15/2/137, August 17, 1928).
114. Notes on reforms in Bahrain, Sir Denys Bray, Foreign Secretary to the Government of India (India Office Records, R/15/2/127 November 6, 1927).
115. Notes on reforms in Bahrain, Sir Denys Bray, Foreign Secretary to the Government of India (India Office Records, R/15/2/127, November 6, 1927).
116. Annual Report of the Bahrain Government, 1351 (India Office Records, R/15/2/308, 1933): 90; Khuri 1980: 115.
117. Notice, Bahrain Special Police Officers Regulations, 1936 (India Office Records, R/15/1/306, December 8, 1936).
118. Khuri 1980: 115.
119. Memorandum no. 28/C from Political Agent Clive Daly to the Political Resident Arthur Trevor (India Office Records, R/15/2/1394, February 11, 1923).

Chapter Five

"Mad, No House, No Money"

Sect-Based Citizenship and Crime

Was Makkiyah bint Salem a Bahraini? In 1929 it was hard to say for sure, wrote colonial administrators. When she was arrested for abetment of rape, reportedly in connection with her brothel, she was tried in the PA Court as a British subject due to her allegedly Somali citizenship. Convicted of the crime, she was sent to serve her five years of imprisonment in Karachi as there was no women's prison in Bahrain. Afterward, Karachi authorities sent her back to Bahrain, but at the port she was briefly detained for lack of passport or permission to enter. On May 12, 1929, Advisor Charles Belgrave wrote to the Political Agency, believing her to be a British subject based on her having been originally sentenced in the PA Court. He stated: "I suggest she is an undesirable person to be allowed to return here and pending your instructions she is being detained on board."[1] In deferring to the political agent's judgment, and pending investigation, Belgrave provided her with a temporary passport. Meanwhile, bint Salam claimed to have been born in Bahrain in 1894 near the telegraph office in Hala. Her occupation was listed as "tailor" and at one point she owned property (it had been sold to cover her criminal fines). Ultimately, her fate is unclear though it appears she was repatriated to Bahrain because the political agent asked the adviser to accept 45 rupees for the repatriation costs.

In the 1920s and 1930s, there was often confusion over who was Bahraini and who was not. In the context of a developing nation-state, such distinctions cut to the very core of Bahraini national identity. Because the Bahrain Government administered Bahrainis, and the Political Agency handled British subjects and foreigners, the distinction was also important on a practical level. But the notion of Bahraini citizenship was only newly being constructed, and administrative mistakes occurred often. The two courts often pursued prosecutions for the same event, even when co-defendants were not of mixed background, and retried cases in the other courts if the original court placed a defendant in the wrong jurisdiction. Further, they often disagreed with defendants as to their self-identified citizenship, detaining people at ports or not detaining them, erroneously. Bint Salem, if she indeed was Bahraini all along, should never have been tried in the PA Court as a non-Bahraini, but should have been handled by the Bahrain Court.

Who was Bahraini was legally unclear and in flux during this period. Bint Salem is only one example of the administrative confusion that did not match her lived experience of being Bahraini, born and raised. In fact, by the 1930s, dozens of people were being deported from the country despite having strong ties, including being born there and/or having significant family connections. These people believed they were Bahraini, but the Bahrain Government either disagreed, was not sure, or simply did not care. Whereas many of these allegedly ambiguous people had committed criminal offenses, like bint Salam, many others were conveniently disbelieved because they were Shi`a and/or Persian.

In the sectarian worldview of the Al Khalifah, who could tolerate and even forgive murdering Sunnis, Shi`a and Persians were increasingly constructed as foreign populations despite their indigenous presence on the island and by the mid-1930s were essentially defined as a criminal class. As a result, Bahraini Shi`a and Persians were often caught up in the criminal justice system for low-level crimes, like begging, and faced the disproportionate possibility of being deported to countries they hardly knew or never had known at all. These social and legal constructions of Shi`a and Persians as foreign and criminal, though being locally embedded, were a secular exacerbation of larger regional anti-Shi`a attitudes by Sunni clerics since at least the eleventh century, condemning Shi`a as *rafidah* (rejectors of the truth) and not really Muslims.[2]

THE "VILLAGE OF OPPRESSION" AND THE SOCIAL CONSTRUCTION OF A CRIMINAL CLASS

Many times the criminal case files refer to "Persians" without sect identity. We can understand this, however, in terms of the social hierarchy with the "Persians" at issue being the Shi`a ones. At the bottom of the hierarchy were the Shi`a Persian (*'ajam*) along with indigenous Shi`a Arabs, or the *Baharna*. As Al Tajir sums up: "Relations between the Persians and local Arabs were to a large extent influenced by the religious sect to which they belonged."[3] According to Belgrave, Sunni Persians enjoyed a type of exceptionalism in colonial Bahrain; their role in the tribal alliances and merchant classes, and their sect adherence, ingratiated them to the Al Khalifah and colonial authorities. Many Sunni Persians harbored anti-Persian and anti-Shi`a attitudes themselves.

In an interesting passage in Belgrave's diary, elite social attitudes toward a Persian lower class are revealed in this vignette about a particular village:

> Dined with de G[renier, Customs] . . . I never quite trust de G's dinners. The cook is such a very messy looking fellow, a Persian, and lives in a very dirty Persian village where all the coolies were deported from Manama by [Political Agent] Daly. They call it Thulmabad, meaning the village of oppression, but its official name is Adilabad, the pleasant village. When I first came here, only hearing the first name, I mentioned the name in a proclamation, rather a faux pas.[4]

Significantly, the village is uncritically constructed as a source for urban indigents and the passage reveals the contextual eliding of Persian, poor, dirty, bad, and relocatable into one cultural nugget. *Thulma* can also be translated as an irreparable loss and is related to the Arabic verb denoting the discrediting of one's reputation and honor. The *mathlum* are people whose honor has been defiled. Calling the village "Thulmabad" was remarkable to Belgrave only because it showed the limits of his ethnographic acuity when he first arrived. But, its implications here extend to signaling that a whole village was labeled problematic for being Persian and poor. Belgrave seems to buy into the label given his review of the cook from the village. In a previous diary entry, he admitted flatly to disliking Persians. The context for that admission was the land confiscation cases in the courts, the product of Persian and Shi`a complaints of Sunni confiscation of their properties.[5]

Although the Al Khalifah harbored a distinct anti-Shi`a and anti-Persian bias, this bias fit into the larger British worldview and could be tacitly accepted or even explicitly justified. Throughout the empire, colonial administrators often made use of domestic-imperial analogies to decide how to privilege some groups over the other, creating lower classes in the colonies as they did with the indigent classes back home in London; in the colonies, they often cultivated a sense of familiarity and closeness with one group while alienating others. Objectionable behavior in one group often evoked articulations that they were similar to the underserving poor in Britain, uncivilized, uncultured, and disproportionately criminalized.[6] Heavily influenced by the Al Khalifah and Sunni tribal elite constructions of Persian and/or Shi`a as an undeserving underclass, and understanding the situation in Bahrain through the pretentions of their own cultural perspective and social class within Britain,[7] colonial authorities often actively reified the social injustice, or at least turned an administrative blind eye to sectarian oppression being cemented into the foundations of the new nation-state.

THE LEGAL CONSTRUCTS OF CITIZENSHIP

In colonial Bahrain, the law around citizenship and deportation has its foundation in OiC section 21(1) indicating that British subjects could be deported from Bahrain on the discretion of the political agency for a period of two years:

> When it is shown by evidence on oath, to the satisfaction of the [Political Agent's] Court, that any British subject has committed, or is about to commit, an offence against this order, or is otherwise conducting himself so as to be dangerous to peace and good order, or is endeavoring to excite enmity between the people of Bahrain and His Majesty's power and authority, the Court may, if it thinks fit, by order until its seal, prohibit that person from being within the limits of this Order during anytime therein specified, not exceeding two years.[8]

The social disdain for Shi`a and Persians increasingly led to their official exclusion from civic life and eventually, their legal right to be in the territory, under the above clause of being "dangerous to peace and good order."

The example of locally reinforcing the imperial OiC law was the Decree of 2nd Rajab 1347 (December 14, 1928). It required all ethnic Persians to have passports endorsed by a British official to enter the country. Previous legitimate documentation, an *ilm-o-Khobar*, or notification of personal information often corroborated by a Bahraini higher in the social hierarchy than the holder, would no longer be accepted.[9] This meant that the diffuse authority of social and economic networks, the legacy of the Indian Ocean proto-capitalist society, would heretofore be supplanted by a centralized, colonial authority conforming to Al Khalifah and Sunni elite preference, as well as the global influence of an emergent international passport system. Replacing the old customs appeared to be the express purpose of Advisor Belgrave. He felt that allowing Persians to pass freely from Iranian ports to Bahrain acted as a tacit admission that Bahrain was a part of Iran, obviously contrary to the interest of Bahraini sovereignty.[10] However, in performing sovereignty in this way, Belgrave and Sheikh Hamad disenfranchised many people who called Bahrain home, or one of their homes if semi-nomadic, and where their extended family had long had roots. The centuries-long history of welcoming semi-nomadic Persians with ties to multiple locations on the Gulf littoral was ending. This same year (or the next, depending on the source document), the Bahrain Government began issuing passports to those it defined as citizens, valid for two years and then renewable for eight. It cost 8 rupees to complete the application process.[11]

As Bahrainis began to experience the administrative determinations of being judged a citizen or not, often ad hoc in nature and based on Al Khalifah notions of social inclusion as defined solely by tribal networks and alliances, complaints about arbitrariness ensued, necessitating a subsequent imperial codification. In 1937, this law was supplemented by King's Regulation No. 7, which provided for permanent deportation and was extended to foreigners as well as British subjects. The law plugged a gap in section 21(1), which did not provide a clear framework for deporting people who simultaneously were non-British and non-Bahraini (foreign to Bahrain and the British Empire). It also allowed for deportation for longer than two years, something that had been done in practice, but had dubious legal footing.[12] In a memorandum from the political agent to the political resident, "putting undesirables on a ship and repatriating them by executive order" was characterized as legally ambiguous, but nonetheless "the old established custom" among colonial administrators in Bahrain.[13]

Ostensibly to sort through some of the confusion about citizenship, but also a targeted message to the Persian community, on February 2, 1929, the Government of Bahrain issued a proclamation (*'alan*) calling for all Persians to register with the Political Agency. The order explains that anyone of Persian heritage, but who was born in Bahrain, would be considered Bahraini unless they registered as foreign with the Political Agency.[14] As the political resident contextualized in response to inquiries from Whitehall (London):

> The real virtue of the Proclamation is that children of Persians (who are the chief foreign community residing permanently in Bahrain) become subjects to the jurisdiction of the Bahrain Courts, for *they* do *not* [emphasis in original] register in the Agency, and so in the process of time the British Protected Persian (who is a perfect nuisance and a fruitful source of petty litigation in the Agency Court) will by a natural process cease to exist.[15]

Nevertheless, section 21(1) was echoed in the Bahrain Nationality of Law of 1937, in which Sheikh Hamad declared that Bahrainis are those born in the country, whether before or after the issuance of the law, or born abroad but having a paternal father or grandfather born in Bahrain. Article 3 specified who was not Bahraini: someone who was born in Bahrain, but whose father registered him or her otherwise within two years of age, a child who registers otherwise at age 18, or if Sheikh Hamad cancelled the person's citizenship.[16] The latter clause underscored the government's right to deny citizenship and does not provide a specific reason for any denial, relying instead on the discretion of the Sheikh. Article 4 of the law indicated that women take the nationality of their husband, thus a Bahraini woman marrying a foreigner would lose their citizenship.[17]

The King's Regulation No. 2 of 1937 clarified citizenship as attaching to those born in Bahrain or whose father was born in Bahrain. In practice, birth or paternal birth was no guarantee when claims were made by defendants identified as Persian or Shi`a. A double-standard of citizenship proof is evident in the readiness to deport or deny citizenship to Persian, Iranian, or

Shi`a—an observation corroborated by secret political memorandum of the day which points to an official policy of trying to relieve Bahrain of "an undesirable element" who might support Iranian claims to the island.

> In view of the peculiar circumstances of Bahrain, particularly with reference to the Persian pretentions, Foreigners although enjoying all the benefits of British protection, would if they were totally immune from deportation [and] so disposed, be able to make a tremendous amount of difficulty . . .[18]

From the criminal and political discourse around citizenship cases, the treatment of Shi`a and Persians/Iranians as a criminal and seditious class, not belonging to the country even when they were born in it, is clearly evident. The policy construed deportation as connected to combating Persian claims to the country, thus criminalizing Persian and/or Shi`a identity and doing so under the banner of sovereignty and security.

Citizenship is a major defining aspect of the control of movement within a territory, which along with territorial control itself, and a monopolization on the use of force, are markers of the emerging nation-state. Citizenship fundamentally grants a right to be in a territory. Who has that right is a cornerstone of national identity, in addition to providing for control of the social milieu of the territory itself. On the flip side, nation-states also construct their identity based on who they exclude or contain as undesirable individuals. Controlling movement requires an elaborate bureaucracy to embrace some and expel others through law and policy around citizenship definitions and requirements, passport and visa issuances, and deportation.[19] Given that by the 1930s, much of Bahrain's deportation machinery churned out Persian/Iranian deportees (the strong majority of which were of Shi`a identity), we can see this group being constructed as an excluded element within society. Having already here noted their political and social isolation from the colonial Al Khalifah state, deportation served as a further means of social and political control of this community, as well as a way to cull the numbers of Shi`a inhabiting the Bahraini archipelago and claiming citizenship.

IRANIAN CLAIMS TO BAHRAIN AND ITS EFFECT ON CITIZENSHIP DETERMINATIONS

At the time, the colonial Al Khalifah government was concerned over the controversy of Iranian claims to Bahrain that had been taken to the League of Nations and debated in the spring of 1928. This spurred paranoia about Persian intrigue in the country that could threaten British sovereignty and control. The Political Resident writing to the Foreign Secretary in Simla remarked that he was "fearful of the retaliation of Persia of the oppression of a [Shi`a] population," and that misrule in this regard would be the only weak link in defending against Iran at the League.[20] The exploration of oil in Bahrain and the belief that the country was resting on a "goldmine"[21] would exacerbate Iranian-Bahraini-British relations, giving Iran an economic impetus to claim as much of the Gulf littoral as it possibly could.

Iran utilized diasporic Persians and Bahrainis in the Gulf to make its historic claim based on the domains of the Safavid Empire. Iran, having officially changed its name from Persia in order to conjure up a nationalist identity under the Pahlavi Dynasty,[22] was engaged in a performance of dominance in the region. Meanwhile, it was testing the loyalties of inhabitants of its Gulf coastline by breaking the power of local *shayukh*s who maintained ties to the Arabian side of the Gulf, and nationalizing maritime trade.[23] The pressure on these coastal communities to conform to Iranian nationalism, including young men taking up military conscription, led to a combination of voluntary migrations and involuntary expulsions. The people of the Iranian coast reunited with extended family in other parts of the Gulf outside the Pahlavi territory, including Bahrain. Iran did not officially give up its claim on Bahrain until 1970.[24]

The British, for their part, never recognized Persian claims on Bahrain as having any validity since the 1783 arrival of the Al Khalifah.[25] However, based on tribal accounts in the region, the Al Khalifah foothold on Bahrain was shakier than British articulations and Persia often threatened to take back the territory throughout the nineteenth century;[26] in 1859, the Al Khalifah submitted briefly to the control of both the Ottomans and the Persians, which from the British point of view necessitated the subsequent trucial agreements to bring the archipelago into protectorate status (which it held unto the colonization process of the OiC reforms). In general, British colonial policy in the Gulf "backed regional enclaves" such as those in Bahrain or other trucial states over that of the "Iranian center," despite governing the Gulf from Bushehr, clearly in Persian territory.[27]

In 1928, Iran targeted the estimated 8,000 *Baharna* of Mohammerah, in its territory, forcing them to officially renounce any Bahraini nationality they claimed and then conscripted men into the Persian army. In retaliation, Sheikh Hamad excluded all Persian representatives in public bodies, brought Persian schools under the control of the government, and banned the wearing of Pahlavi hats. The political resident was not sympathetic to Sheikh Hamad's decrees, but supported them, explaining that if the Persians decided to cease their bad treatment of Bahrainis, Bahrain would reciprocate by easing the policies instituted against Persians.[28] Three years later, a symbolic contestation between Britain and Iran took place at Basaidu (Qeshm island) when a Persian officer took down the British flag there. A few days later, officers from the HMS Brideford put the flag back up.[29] Although in 1935, Britain would relinquish claims to the Gulf island,[30] the back and forth flag-raising at Basaidu, and the subsequent detention of an Iranian customs officer operating there, characterized the unstable territorial boundaries and sovereignty between the powers now competing for control of territory and oil in the Gulf littoral.

And:

> the fabulous stories current about Bahrain's prosperity attracts many indigent immigrants there and created a situation with which the Shaikh's administration now had to deal.[31]

A major factor in the flows of Persians was the collapse of the pearl industry. By the late 1930s, cultured pearls from Japan had flooded the international market and greatly reduced the demand for Gulf pearls. Many Shi`a and Persians had been employed as divers, but now found themselves out of work. The oil industry, however, provided opportunity for these out of work divers, and many streamed into Bahrain for this purpose. The many Persians initially employed by BAPCO (Bahrain Petroleum Company) complicated the contestation with Iran. In 1933, Bahrain Government's publication of a notice requiring all Persian to register or else be treated as foreign subjects irked the leadership of BAPCO. In their pursuance of clarification about deportation of BAPCO employees, there is reference to a case entitled *Gulshan* (no criminal case file could be found in the records), ostensibly someone deported despite having stable employment with BAPCO, much to BAPCO's chagrin.[32] By 1939, records reveal that in large part sedentary indigent Persians had been expelled from Bahrain, and the majority of action on this front would now derive from people arriving in the country without proper documentation.[33] It is important to note that the legal constructions discussed in this chapter come on the heels of the Khawalid-Dawasir sectarian violence that, according to the criminal case files, admittedly had the purpose, at least in part, of driving Shi`a out of their communities and perhaps out of the country. We turn now to the documentary evidence we have about an express state policy to remove indigent Persians and Shi`a as a means of diminishing Persian and Shi`a populations in the country.

DEPORTATION CASES: A STATE OFFENSIVE AGAINST "PERSIAN PRETENSIONS"

Two criminal case files from the cache provide detailed reporting on instances of deportation. A third case also provides insight into the complications of Persian Bahrainis proving their citizenship or right to be in the country. Additional files in the India Office Records also contain information on a series of deportation cases in the PA Court. The low-level crime of begging acted as the pretextual prosecution for which to deport undesirable

Shi`a and Persians. Finally, the deportation of Sheikh Khalaf offers another window on the deportation landscape during the period of interest.

We start with a violation of passport regulations. In this case, the accused, Mahmud bin Haji 'Abd ul-Nabi Bushiry, a Persian, entered Bahrain without a passport in 1929.[34] The accused's father fought Customs and the Political Agency on behalf of his son, asserting that his son could disembark in Bahrain based on *kaifi khudat* or *a la hawa*, meaning that he could do so without identity papers and on his own responsibility. This was argued to be the necessary approach because his son reportedly could not get a visa to Bahrain while in Iran, and apparently when he exited Bahrain in the first place, he was not warned of the consequences of failing to have the proper permission to return. Because of the "clerical error" involved in departure from Bahrain, Political Agent Geoffrey Prior ultimately discharged the case. The importance of the case, however, rests with the customs asserted by the defendant's father. Like the *ilm-o-khobar* documentation aforementioned, Persians in Bahrain seem to have been relying on the old customs of *a la hawa*, or relatively free travel along the Gulf coastal ports, and are caught off guard by the new centralized, administrative approach to citizenship and travel.

Turning now to the deportation files, as early as 1927, a Persian individual was deported to Lingah under OiC conceptions of citizenship and criminality. A memorandum on the matter noted that he was "an incorrigible thief and an undesirable."[35] By the early 1930s, the records begin to point to massive deportations of indigent Persian from Bahrain. In one sweep, 547 Persians were arrested with 117 of them prosecuted, resulting in seventy-seven deportations. Soon thereafter, another cohort of forty-four indigents were deported to ports along the Gulf Coast, including Qatif.[36] From the criminal case files, we found that on May 9, 1938, the Passport Department of the Bahrain Government presented the PA court with forty-three Iranian individuals apprehended by the State Police for violation of passport regulations per King's Regulation No. 2 of 1937.[37] The political agency interviewed each defendant and all allegedly admitted to entering Bahrain without "passes or permission." They reportedly had no work, place to live, or means of support in Bahrain. Investigators often remarked on language skills in order to evaluate citizenship claims. The agency engaged in brief inquiries into each defendant that could not have lasted more than two days (based on when the list came from the Bahrain Court, and the order to deport, finalized the following day).

On May 10, 1938, the political agent authorized the removal of twenty people from this case (as well as an additional twenty-two Persians listed as being deported from other cases that are not preserved[38]). The following day, the list was sent by Express Mail to Political Residency in Bushehr. This was followed by approval from the External Affairs Department of the Government of India in Simla on May 27, 1938. Once approved, the State Police Passport Department was tasked with physically removing the individuals. Interestingly, the deportations appeared so common as to be done en masse and by a long list. Very few days were spent investigating the defendants' claims that they belonged in the country, suggesting that the administrative apparatus was politically oriented to remove as many Persians in as short of an amount of time as could be accommodated.

One particularly dubious judgment occurred in relation to defendant Hasan bin Ahmed, whose occupation was listed as a carpenter, and whose employment was corroborated. Under the reasoning that Persians should be deported for being "indigent," Hasan bin Ahmed does not fit this description, having been employed earning 10 to 12 annas a day (although approximately ten days a month his corroborator indicted that there was no work for him). Apparently, the political agency did not believe that this was sufficient employment, and deported him anyway.

Of the fifteen people in this case who gave their years in Bahrain, the average amount of time was nine years, ranging from one year to twenty-two years. One defendant's amount of time in Bahrain was unknown and four other defendants merely indicated they had been in the country "a long time." As such, nine years probably underestimates the cohort's true average time spent in Bahrain. If we impute the highest number in years, twenty-two, as "a long time" in this sample, and add information about a defendant who claims to have been on the island since birth and that his age is 35, the average time jumps to nearly 13 years in the country before deportation.

One defendant, whose amount of time in Bahrain was noted as unknown, could not be identified beyond the appellation "Mundu." He was noted to be "mad," with "no house, no money." Though he claimed Bahraini citizenship, the Indian Assistant dismissed the claim since his spoken Arabic was poor: he was "obviously Persian." However, we note here that there were communities in the archipelago whose native, and sometimes only language was Persian, though admittedly it was quite common for Bahraini-Persian people to also speak Arabic. Regardless, language alone was not an accurate indicator of having been born in Bahrain or not, but that was considered enough in this case.

Madness featured in another Persian Shi`a deportation noted in a file summarizing deportations in the late 1920s. Belgrave explained to the political agency:

> There is a man called Hassan bin Ali born in Mohammerah, therefore presumably a Persian subject, though his father was a Bahraini. He is mad, certified by the Medical Officer as subject to frequent outbursts of madness. It takes the form of setting fires to things. Thinking that he was a Bahrain subject, I have kept him under supervision in the [Police] Fort. His wife and family are at

> Mohammerah, but he also has a brother and relations here. I suggest that he is a suitable subject for repatriation to Mohammerah. He is said to be well known there and has a house in Ferij Al-Neggarin in Mohammerah.[39]

The second case from among the cache of criminal case files ensnared seventeen "indigent," Shi`a/Iranian defendants who stood accused of Breach of Passport Regulations prohibited by King's Regulation No. 2 of 1937.[40] The State Police initially apprehended the defendants for begging in the *suq*. Advisor Charles Belgrave handled the begging cases from the Bahrain Court to the PA Court for deportation proceedings on May 25, 1939.

> The Bahrain Government is having much difficulty in preventing undesirable persons not only from unlawfully entering Bahrain; but public nuisance; and submit that drastic measure be taken to deter others from similar action.[41]

According to the Bahrain Government, each defendant was interviewed and all allegedly admitted to entering Bahrain without "passes or permission." Nine of the people were considered Iranian/Persian (a proxy for Shi`a) by the Bahrain Court (another one, considered "Najrani" was most probably Shi`a based on the population in Najran). Ultimately, seven people were deported, of which four were either Persian/Iranian or Najrani. The other three deportees hailed from Oman (two people) and Al-Hasa in Saudi Arabia. Of course, it is very possible these three were also Shi`a, but we can't know for sure from the records.

One of the deported Iranians, Hassan bin Sultan had come to Bahrain twenty years previously working as a laborer. He claimed he was not a beggar, but had irregular work. He reported a stable place to live. Another of the deported, Ibrahim bin Hasan, had been a pearl diver, but after a dispute with his *nakhuda* (boat captain) ended up without work. He admitted to begging in the suq. Another of the deported, Ghulam Husain, explained that he worked as a mason and was not a beggar. From the limited personal information of the deported, it appeared that at this time in Bahrain, work status, or criminal history was not consistent across the cases and suggests a criteria for deportation other than the ethnic identity of the accused, and the lack of a financially stable relative to support the individual. Although in the case of the deported Ahmad bin Hussein, the Najrani defendant's, support of a family in Quraibi was not sufficient to prevent his deportation.

Furthermore, a "secret" file documenting deportation lists twenty-five cases administered from October 19, 1936 to April 26, 1938. Twelve of these cases involved Iranian individuals, six relate to people of unknown origin (not recorded), and the rest of the cases feature people hailing from Iraq, Portuguese India, British India, and Saudi Arabia. Iranians/Persians overwhelmingly topped the list of known individual identities of deportees. One of the cases referenced in this file is the case with forty-three defendants described above. We know from that criminal case file, that twenty of the forty-three defendants were Iranian. Taking into consideration only the known Iranians, and as a very conservative estimate, the file shows that at least 27 percent of deportees were sent "back" to Iran. Given that no other single known category of deportees is greater than 2.4 percent (Portuguese Indians), this represents a disproportionate focus on Iranians, based on the sample. From a sectarian point of view, this is also a very conservative estimate, as well, as there are many likely Shi`a from among the unknowns and knowns (if we use Iranian as a proxy for Shi`a identity). For example, people connected to the case included twenty-seven divers, which although unrecorded, likely involved many Persian/Iranian and/or Shi`a people.

The records also show that two hundred Persian families were expelled from the island in 1938. These families were living in "atrocious conditions amounting to savagery," which allegedly justified their relocation, purportedly to better conditions among their ethnic compatriots in Iran. When Iran complained about this deportation, the Political Residency explained that indigents in general were repatriated based on their lack of means of support in Bahrain[42] and that care was being taken to make sure each deportation was permitted by law, the King's Regulation of 1937.[43] In June of the same year, 36 additional Iranians were deported after trying to enter Bahrain.[44] The scale of the deportation operations themselves could exacerbate the political problem they were designed to solve:

> Indigent Persians are constantly trickling into Bahrain and unless the State is to be flooded with them they must, of course, be deported. I would suggest that they should be deported in smaller batches, so as to attract less attention, and the more out of the way they are deported to the less likely they are to make complaints that will reach Tehran. But perhaps you have already evolved some policy on these lines.[45]

By 1939, however, the problem was not construed as deportation batches that were too large. Rather, too many cases were being retried due to wrong identifications and, therefore, being handled by the wrong court and wasting valuable administrative time and resources; correct information was arising very late in the proceedings. Writing to the advisor, the political agent inquired as to whether a policy should be written to address the problem.[46] Agreeing, the Bahrain Government issued a new proclamation:

> any transfer of cases between Bahrain and Agency Courts will be allowed on the grounds that the nationality of any of the parties to the case exempts them from jurisdiction of the Court before which they are appearing, unless this claim is raised at the beginning of the first hearing of the case (or the first hearing after the publication of this notice). If no such claim is raised, the

> parties will be held to have accepted the jurisdiction of the Court; this will also govern the procedure for appeal.[47]

Despite more specific and legally binding codification around citizenship and deportation, the confusion noted at the top of the chapter with Makkiyah bint Salem was not abating. This suggests that the rule of law, though superficially well-developed, was actually being trumped by purely political concerns with removing "Persian pretensions" from the archipelago, making the courts a continual site for ethnic and sect-based conflict.

IRANIAN COMPLAINTS ABOUT HARSH CRIMINAL JUSTICE TREATMENT OF PERSIANS

The Foreign Minister of Iran took on the case a Bahraini-Persian named Muhammad Ali Ghulam, using it as an example of the Bahrain Government's ill treatment of Persians, folding it into the overall case to the League of Nations that Bahrain should belong to Iran. Although Ghulam's criminal file was not preserved in the cache of criminal cases in the India Office Records, we do know some details about this PA court case. According to the Iranian Foreign Minister, Ghulam was discriminated against when he was treated by the criminal justice system more harshly than others, having been fined 100 rupees for attempting to provide his sick mother with a half bottle of contraband cognac to ease her suffering.[48]

Political Agent Percy Loch responded to internal inquiries about the case, providing the facts as known to the PA Court. Ghulam had visited a steamer with two Persian friends and returned with a ginger ale bottle of liquor, determined to be brandy. When questioned by officials, he first stated that the bottle contained mineral water, but then indicated it was medicine. He told the Court that the brandy was for his sick mother, but the Court investigated and found that there was not such a prescription from a doctor (though his mother was indeed in the hospital). Loch stated that giving Ghulam only a fine for the offense was actually a show of leniency, not discrimination or harshness.

> The Bahrain Government is determined to prevent the growth of the drink evil, which threatens, unless sternly checked, to assume serious proportions among the very cosmopolitan population of Manamah.[49]

Unfortunately, we do not know the charges filed against Ghulam to note what the IPC punishment would have been, nor do we have good information as to the average sentence given by the PA Court for these types of offenses.

The Iranian Foreign Minister also complained about prohibitions placed on Meshedi Hussein, son of Ali Kazim Busheri, and Meshedi Abbas of

Kazaruni and his brother, all of them from the merchant class in Bahrain. The Bahrain government instructed that they were not to frequent one another's society at night,[50] suggesting that they were plotting against Bahrain for Iran. However, the political agent denied any such action, which would interfere with the merchants' right to associate with each other.

The Foreign Office in Tehran also reported that the Government of Bahrain was dismissing all Persians employed by BAPCO.[51] A year later, they refined their complaint to allege that the dismissal of Persian workers was used as a way to pressure Persians to change their citizenship to Bahrain.[52] Political Agent Gordon Loch denied these claims, indicating that as a private, American company, the Bahraini government did not engage in managing employment there. He also opined that making transparent to the Iranians that BAPCO was American-owned (though British imperial in the sense that its official corporate registration was in Canada) may make them more inclined to renew their claims to Bahrain.[53]

By 1938, the Iranian government had taken notice of the deportations from Bahrain; indeed the batches had been too large. Iranian authorities complained to the Foreign Office in London about the poor treatment of Bahrainis of Iranian or Persian descent. Iran reportedly likened the expulsions to the "savage act" of deportation undertaken by the contemporaneous Soviet Government. The political resident responded to London's inquiries about the complaints reaffirming the Sheikh's rights to deport in order to administer his country, and underscoring that the true problem was Iranian claims that Bahrain belongs to it.[54]

BEGGING AS A GATEWAY TO DEPORTATION

To further understand the deportation cases in context, we need to focus on the "begging" charge that brings the potential deportees to the attention of authorities in at least one of the criminal cases noted above, but also routinely noted as a pretext for removal within the deportation files. Begging as criminal behavior is a colonial invention, and concern with it appears to attach to modernizing or industrializing societies. William Chambliss' analysis of low-level vagrancy laws theorized that changes in the focal concerns of such laws reflected changes in social and cultural needs. Based on an analysis of the history of Anglo-American vagrancy laws, he found that elites with a vested interest in capital development (having a ready supply of laborers) constructed vagrancy laws, which came to be rationalized on the basis of discouraging the idleness of people who could hypothetically work. The charge of vagrancy was consistent through many years, but the definition of vagrancy and the practical implementation of vagrancy laws shifted significantly.[55]

Similarly, we see a shift in the meaning of begging in Bahraini society during the colonial era, from tolerant and even welcoming attitudes to criminalization. Customary, religious, and commercial law in Bahrain did not specifically outlaw this practice before the OiC reforms. In fact, giving money or other assistance to a beggar could be an opportunity for *zakat* (charity), one of the five main pillars of Islam. In Arab tribal culture, the term *zakat*, however, refers to the payment that chiefs of tribes receive annually from their male subjects, traditionally based on the number of camels and/or sheep possessed.[56] *Zakat* often in practice connotes mandatory contributions, required either by a tribe, a religious sect, or government. Beggars in the *suq* more than likely relied on *sadaqah*,[57] or voluntary alms aside from *zakat* that many Muslims also feel was a key aspect of being a good Muslim.

In the Shi`a tradition in Bahrain, *'ashura* celebrations also featured charity, specifically a collection of food and other items at the *ma'tam* (place of community and worship for Shi`a) for distribution to the poor. In this tradition, *zakat* is the term for donation to the *'asyad* (plural of *sayyid*; religious devotees who take an ascetic path to practicing Islam and often claim to be a direct descendants of 'Ali); Shi`a believe donations to the *'asyad* are mandatory under the faith. *Sadaqa*, meanwhile, are donations to the poor in the larger community, which are merely recommended.[58]

Therefore, noticing poor beggars in the *suq*, for example, particularly during holy times of the year, represents an opportunity for religious practice rather than a social problem or disease. The Al Khalifah themselves contributed to Shi`a *ma'tam*s at *'ashura* as a charitable gesture.[59] And, the *waqf* system of property as endowed charity for use by the people could also be considered a *sadaqa*-like venture,[60] though it was managed by the state after the OiC reforms, and was subject to intense criticism and a cite for sectarian discrimination beyond the scope of this book.

Going back further, beggars in the Indian Ocean culture (specifically the Gulf and the Swahili Coast) were not considered social problems either; they contributed to the richness of life and were tolerated as part of the communities they inhabited. In *Tales from Al-Hoora*, an old neighborhood of pearl divers and intellectuals in Manama, "Santool," a homeless man who frequented those streets, was someone who had the respect of the neighborhood despite his travails. Prone to drinking, thieving, and squatting, children followed him in the streets in the 1940s and 1950s. "We would chase him until he turn[ed] back and shower[ed] us with deluges of curses which we have not and shall not hear anything similar to them." The neighborhood social club provided him with lodging and personal supplies, and would have continued to do so indefinitely, but surprisingly, he disappeared two weeks after the arrangement, never to be seen again. In the telling of the story, there is nothing but jovial remembrance, and although the narrator explains that had Santool not succumbed to desire, he may have been the great lute player he once appeared destined to become, he was not constructed as any type of social or criminal problem. In fact, he stole the club's radio upon vacating the neighborhood, and every time the club members remembered their missing radio, they laughed fondly.[61]

Similarly, in earlier colonial times, it was the custom for passers-by to give beggars a handful of dates when they could. Belgrave documented in 1944 that the Bahrain Government had absorbed this practice by popular demand, handing out dates daily to seven hundred "deserving" indigents (although there was no information provided for what qualified someone as deserving) during World War II when there was a date quota in effect.[62] Beyond the customary and religious notions of helping the poor, which are common to many societies, begging in the *suq* simply was not seen as a problem per se by Bahrainis, but rather an integral part of the social fabric of life.

However, under the colonial conception, begging was a sign of social disorder and a lack of modern development. We see this attitude in bold relief in Belgrave's diaries.

> A tiresome beggar followed us all the way down to the Police Station so I handed him over to the Police and gave orders for him to be deported on the next boat. He was very old. If I catch one every Friday we should be gradually rid of them.[63]

In the annual report for the Muslim year 1350 (1932) in the Police section, it was noted briefly that a "large number" of prostitutes and beggars had been repatriated to ports from which they came.[64] The shifting sands of who should be removed and why extended beyond beggars and even to upstart clerics, as described below.

THE REMOVAL OF SHEIKH KHALAF

In an early case of Shi`a deportation, Sheikh Al Asfur Khalaf, the first official Shi`a *qadi* under the OiC reforms,[65] was accused of bribery and banished to Iraq for two years in 1927.[66] It appears he was considered a Bahraini at this time since he was deported by the Bahrain Government and not the Political Agency—though he claimed he was not born in the territory, but rather in Bushehr, arriving in Bahrain in 1920. While banished, he was instructed to tour the Shi`a holy places in Iraq (Karbala and Najaf). This was punishment, or perhaps a form of forced spiritual rehabilitation, for continuing to accept bribes from his community members (even after promising colonial officials he would not do that anymore five years previously). He initially came to the authorities' attention having decided a case in favor of Nasr bin Maji Muhammad after receiving a 1,000-rupee bribe from him.

Sheikh Khalaf also reportedly enriched himself by dipping into *zakat* and *sadaqat* monies designated for the poor, and extorted a high price out of Shi`a who requested his services from divorce and marriage proceedings. As complaints about his conduct collected, the colonial administration became frustrated with the pattern of corruption.[67]

However, legal historian Hassan Ali Al-Radhi suspects that the accusations stemmed from the Sheikh's independent streak and clashed with Belgrave. Khalaf was likely resting on the Shi`a custom of *qadi*s: relying on gifts from their community for their livelihood. Perhaps he could not conform to the new civil servant system for *qadis*.[68] The Bahrain government worked with Iraq's security sector to keep tabs on the *qadi* in exile and to make sure he was not continuing his corrupt practices there. Iraqi authorities ultimately gave a positive report on the Sheikh's behavior.[69]

In 1931, Sheikh Khalaf sent word as to his desire to return to Bahrain briefly. Sheikh Hamad initially refused. Hamad believed that Sheikh Khalaf was angling to be fully reinstated in Bahrain, having made a deal with Persian authorities to be their agent in the archipelago.[70] Further, in the context of the many permissions given to Sunni agitators to freely return to the country over the years as part of an unofficial policy of Sunni forgiveness (see chapter 4), the disallowance of Khalaf likely involved a sectarian bias, although we cannot be sure from the content of the file. In any case, the Political Agency overrode the Sheikh's refusal and authorized Khalaf's return, ostensibly taking him to be a Persian subject and therefore under agency control. Political Agent Cyril Barrett granted Khalaf three months to close out his affairs in Bahrain and then return to Iraq.[71]

Khalaf popped up again, however, in 1933, referred to in correspondence as the return of the "notorious Shi`ah ex-Qadhi [sic]." The Agency inquired of the Bahrain Government as to how he entered the country.[72] According to Belgrave, for several years he had been traveling mysteriously under a Bahraini passport, and he now claimed he was born in Bahrain though of Persian origin, contrary to agency intelligence about his origins. In a 1934 letter about his return, the political agent, refers to "the unfortunate way he was helped by us in 1933."[73] However, it is not clear from the file as to what exactly is meant by an "unfortunate" decision. The letter does state that "[f]ortunately his power for evil seems to have diminished."[74] An undated report in the file does reveal that sometime between 1931 and 1933, when he showed up again, he had been in Bushehr selling his shops, and sent a servant to Bahrain to sell his land there, and travelled to Lingah to visit relatives, telling them he hoped to settle in Iraq. Apparently, his last noted arrival in Bahrain coordinated with a time in which Bushehr was decommissioning the *ulema* and Khalaf had reason to lay low.[75]

The shifting notions of citizenship of Persian, Shi`a subjects are evident in the treatment of Sheikh Khalaf over the time period of interest. Initially in the 1920s, Sheikh Khalaf's Bahraini-ness was not in question, even though he reported then having only been in the country a few years. He had an official post as a Shi`a *qadi*, and his two-year banishment was related to alleged criminal conduct, not lack of citizenship. By the 1930s, however, his identity is considered to be foreign by the Political Agency, perhaps conveniently in order to justify its continued control over his movement. But the Bahrain Government claims him as a national, and he was noted as having procured a Bahraini passport. The record never provides a clear disposition and Sheikh Khalaf's Bahraini-ness seems to rely more on shifting politics than the rule of law. Looking at it this way, we can see how individuals caught in these sectarian politics came to be deprived of citizenship, the legacy of which continues today.

The First *Bidun*

Many of the deported people in the colonial files may have been the first *bidun*. Today, the *bidun*, meaning "without" in Arabic, refers to a group of mostly Shi`a individuals who claim Bahraini citizenship, but the state disagrees and refuses to grant it. Residing in Bahrain, they are unable to receive a passport to travel, and do not have citizenship in any other country. Therefore, they are stateless and between identities in a very literal example of post-colonial drift. According to the International Observatory on Statelessness, there are approximately 1,300 stateless Bahrainis.[76] There had been a few thousand more prior to the tenure of the current King Hamad who granted citizenship as part of the reforms characterizing the early years of his rule.[77]

A TRIBE NOT A STATE

Circling back to the beginning of this saga, we can see the cultural logic in the construction of indigenous people and/or Shi`a and/or Persians as foreigners if we again consider the tribal influence on order maintenance in colonial Bahrain. In essence, Sheikh Hamad, other Al Khalifah leaders, and the Sunni elite drew upon customary notions of who was in and out of the tribal circle of alliances, utilizing the increasingly Westernized modality of the new criminal adjudication to reinvent their prior historical constructions of social order. Although a post-colonial scholar could merely blame the British for inventing the legal codification of an unequal society, it was just as much, if not more, the clinging to the customary order maintenance regime of the Al Khalifah that gave rise to the sectarian framework still operating today. In the colonial deportation cases, the plethora of Sunni pardons in criminal cases, and the lack of protection from and even tacit acceptance of anti-Shi`a violence by criminal justice authorities (who themselves were overwhelmingly Sunni), we see a neo-tribalism. Bahrain in the colonial period through today clings to the basic formulation of the shaikhly world of the pre-twentieth century reforms, suggesting the continued political power of tribal Sunni networks of power and control. According to anthropologists who documented Sunni tribes in the pre-oil Gulf, Bedouin encampments were circular, or a series of linear stations, but the inner circle or inner line always consisted of the sheikhs and their families, the next was their relatives and followers, and the outer tents were for slaves and servants. Being *'asil* or from a tribe of pure, hereditary descent, claiming origin from the patriarchs, Qahtan and Ishmael, remains a palpable part of the lore of elite Sunnis in the Gulf, even though it is not necessarily adhered to in the present day. Likewise, *wasta* (or clout in a practical sense of having power over others to get what you want) continues to be related to having *'asil* or being in favor with those with *'asil*, often in the ruling classes.

It seems a fitting metaphor for the present organization of the Bahrain state, then, to say it functions more as a tribe than a state. Though it is not moving through a negotiated *dirah* (geographic sphere of migration and influence), but now finds itself in a fixed territory, its inner and outer circles of social inclusion and exclusion are historically embedded. Fuad Khuri came to a similar conclusion in his classic, *Tribe and State in Bahrain*,[78] in which he argued that the social organization of the Bahrain state was "tribalism" and was characterized by kinship exclusiveness, collective control of tribal behavior outside of public office, and "claims to legitimacy of rule on the basis of historically earned rights without resort to public delegation."

Being neo-tribal is a complicated political stance for Bahrain because its main Western allies are firmly embedded in an international legal and political order of aspirational multicultural democracies. Bahrain has never recovered from the first disruption when the interior tribes moved into it. Indeed its contemporary, nationalist identity (*al-turath*), is a Sunni tribal narrative. Upheavals subsequent to the coming of the Al Khalifah are derivative of this original problematic expansion and occupation, which robbed the original Bahraini inhabitants of their safety, security, and at times, right to exist (long before the Iranian Revolution of 1979 which erroneously gets outsized attention as the origin point for Bahraini Shi`a dissatisfaction). The metaphorical outer encampment are populations of expatriates Sunnis who people the security sector, the South Asian housemaids who cook and clean, the international poor who labor to construct the financial towers and world trade centers, and the Western expatriates who consult and bank as an army of Belgraves for the post-modern era.

The very legitimacy of the ruling family as belonging to Bahrain itself is in question every time a Shi`a dissident asserts his or her rights, questioning the overlay of Sunni command and control over his or her life. It is a performance of Foucaultian governmentality, or the use of power to establish discipline over even the minute individual conduct. The Bahraini criminal justice system finds itself being utilized to quash the on-going and quite-grounded critique of Sunni-chauvinistic rule, big or small, despite constitutional and democratic overtures by the state. The first disruption of the eighteenth century remains contained in the colonial and post-colonial codification of the second disruption—one criminal case at a time.

NOTES

1. Case no. 685 of 1924 (India Office Records, R/15/3/6996, December 5, 1929).
2. Vali Nasr. *The Shia Revival: How Conflicts Within Islam Will Shape the Future.* (New York: W.W. Norton & Co., 2006): 53–54.
3. Al Tajir 1987: 220; It is important to note here that Bahrainis of Persian extraction were Shi`a, but there was a small community of Sunni Persians; this smaller group tended to be more powerful and a part of the merchant class cooperating with the colonial-Al Khalifa government.
4. Belgrave diaries, March 20, 1929.
5. Belgrave diaries, February 13, 1929.
6. Paul Knepper, *The Invention of International Crime: A Global Issue in the Making, 1881–1914,* (Palgrave MacMillan, 2010): 50; David Cannadine, *Ornamentalism* (Oxford: Oxford University Press, 2001): 4–5.
7. Kwarteng 2011: 7.
8. Orders in Council (India Office Records, R/15/1/299).
9. Criminal case no. 80 of 1938 (India Office Records, R/15/3/7015).
10. Belgrave diaries, November 7, 1928.
11. Administrative Report for the Years 1926–1937, Government of Bahrain (India Office Records, L/PS/18/B463): 41; Annual Report for the Government of Bahrain, 1348–1349 (India Office Records, R/15/2/306).
12. King's Regulation No. 7 (India Office Records, L/PS/12/3329, 1937).
13. Memorandum no. ORC 995 from Political Agent Terence Keys to the Political Resident Arthur Trevor (Indian Office Records, R/15/1/299, May 20, 1915).
14. Public Notice [*'alan*] (India Office Records, R/15/2/150, February 2, 1929).
15. Letter no. 1262–s of 1933, Political Resident to Whitehall (India Office records, R/15/2/150, September 30, 1933).
16. Al Tajir 1987: 223.
17. Al Tajir 1987: 224.
18. Confidential memorandum entitled "Deportation of Foreigners under the Bahrain Order in Council," from the Political Agent (India Office Records, R/15/2/104, undated, circa 1924).
19. Torpey 2000.
20. Letter no. 365–s of 1929, political resident to foreign secretary (India Office records, R/15/2/127, August, 28, 1929).
21. Telegram from Secretary of State for Foreign Affairs in London to Political Resident (India Office Records, R/15/2/492, May 16, 1934).
22. Abbas Amanat, *Iran: A Modern History*. New Haven, CT: Yale University Press, 2017.
23. Najmabadi 209: 139–140.
24. Amanat 2017: 144.
25. Kelly 1980: 54, 178.
26. Kelly 1980: 179.
27. Amanat 2017: 644.
28. Al-Tajir 1987: 220–222.
29. Telegram no. 766 Political Resident to Political Agents at Bahrain, Kuwait, Muscat (India Office Records, R/15/2/491, September 7, 1933.
30. Koroush Ahmadi, *Islands and International Politics in the Persian Gulf: The Abu Musa and Tunbs in Strategic Context* (London: Routledge, 2008): 69.

31. Telegram no. 266 from Foreign Minister in Tehran to Secretary of Foreign Affairs in London (India Office Records, R/15/2/494, July 1, 1938).

32. Telegram, Foreign Minister to Tehran to Political Resident (India Office Records, I/O/R/150, May 6, 1933).

33. Direct order no. C/578 (India Office Records, R/15/2/494, September 25, 1939).

34. Criminal case no. 142/1022 of 1929 (India Office Records, R/15/3/7006).

35. Memorandum from Political Agent to Bahrain State Police (India Office Records, R/15/2/1394, 1927).

36. Deportation file (India Office Records, R/15/2/494).

37. Case no. 80 of 1938 (India Office Records, R/15/3/7015).

38. Within the additional 22 Persians, there are listed a "Muhammad bin Ahmad" and a "Abdulla bin Muhammad," the same names as one of the original 43 Persians who was in the order of deportation in the case (issued May, 10, 1938) and reportedly did not go on to be deported. Had they gone on to be deported, the figure would be that 22 Persians were deported out of the 43 arrested. However, it is not clear whether the Muhammad bin Ahmad and the Abdulla bin Muhammad deported in the additional cases (documented on May 27, 1938 in two document both entitled "Bahrain Order in Council, 1913 in criminal case file) reference the same individuals in the case of the 43 Persians or not. For purposes of my quantitative figures generated to describe this particular case, I did not include Muhammad bin Ahmad and Abdulla bin Muhammad. [Criminal Case no. 80 of 1938 (India Office Records, R/15/3/7015).]

39. Memorandum from Advisor Sir Charles Belgrave to Political Agent (India Office Records, R/15/2/1394, September 18, 1927).

40. Case no. 92 of 1939 (India Office Records, R/15/3/7017).

41. Letter from Government of Bahrain Passport Division to Political Agency (India Office Records, R/15/3/7017, May 25, 1939).

42. Telegram no. 244 from the Political Resident to the Political Agent (India Office Records, R/15/2/494, June 12, 1938).

43. Telegram from Political Resident to Foreign Minister in Tehran (India Office Records, R/15/2/494, June 12, 1938). Reportedly, Bahrain did not deport Persian female dependents if they had means of support through a Bahraini family with citizenship. However, "undesirable women" accused of working as prostitutes were readily deported. On May, 16, 1927, 27 such ethnically Persian and/or Shi`a women were deported, followed by five more approximately a week later. [Memorandum no. 375/15 from Captain of the State Police to Advisor Sir Charles Belgrave (India Office Records, R/15/2/1394, May 18, 1927); Memorandum no. 391/15 from Captain of the State Police to Advisor Sir Charles Belgrave (India Office Records, R/15/2/1394, May 23, 1927).]

44. Telegram no. 108 from the Political Agent to the Political Resident (India Office Records, R/15/2/494, June 14, 1938).

45. Confidential letter no. C/463 from Political Agent to Political Resident (India Office Records, R/15/2/494, September 24, 1939).

46. Memorandum from Political Agent to Advisor Charles Belgrave (India Office Records, R/15/2/1824, February 4, 1939).

47. Public notice (*'alan*) no. 3/1358 (India Office Records, R/15/2/1824, March 4, 1939).

48. Letter no. 5774 from the Iranian Minister for Foreign Affairs to His Majesty's Minister (India Office Records, R/15/2/150, May 1, 1933).

49. Letter no. 5774 from the Iranian Minister for Foreign Affairs to His Majesty's Minister (India Office Records, R/15/2/150, May 1, 1933).

50. Letter no. 5774 from the Iranian Minister for Foreign Affairs to His Majesty's Minister (India Office Records, R/15/2/150, May 1, 1933).

51. Telegram R'27, no. 34, H.M.'s Minister in Tehran to Political Resident in Bushehr (India Office Records, R/15/2/150, May 6, 1933).

52. Letter from the British Legation to Tehran to the India Office in Simila and the Political Agency in Bushehr (India Office Records, R/15/2/150, May 19, 1934).

53. Letter c/190 from Political Agent Gordon Loch to Political Resident in Bushehr (India Office Records, R/15/2/150, June 4, 1933).

54. Telegram from the Political Resident to the Foreign Office (India Office Records, L/PS/12/3327, June 11, 1938).
55. Chambliss 2001.
56. Dickson 1949: 440–441.
57. Filippo Osella and Osella, Caroline, "Muslim Entrepreneurs in Public Life Between India and the Gulf: Making Good and Doing Good," *Journal of the Royal Anthropological Society* 15, 1 (2009): S207.
58. Khuri 1980: 81–82.
59. Thomas Fibiger, "Ashura in Bahrain," *Social Analytics* 54, 3 (2010): 40 [29–46].
60. Amy Singer, "Soup and *Sadaqa*: Charity in Islamic Societies," *Historical Research* 79, 205 (2006): 317.
61. Khalifah Sulaibeck, *Tales from Al-Hoora, Bahrain*, 2nd ed. (Al Sayah Public Relations, 2004): 65–66.
62. Memorandum no. 1391–50 from Advisor Charles Belgrave to the Political Agent in Bahrain, Dates Quota, 1944–45, Bahrain and Trucial Coast, (India Office Records, R/15/2/785, July 12, 1944).
63. Belgrave, personal diary, May 10, 1929.
64. "Police," Annual Report of the Bahrain Government, 1350 (India Office Records, R/15/2/307, June 9, 1932): 3.
65. Al-Radhi 2003: 51.
66. Memorandum no. 952/24 of 1345 (1927) from Advisor Charles Belgrave to Political Agent (India Office Records, R/15/2/112, April 27, 1927).
67. Undated notes in "Sheikh Khalaf" file [India Office Records, British Library, R/15/2/112].
68. Al-Radhi 2003: 54–55.
69. Letter from King Faisal to Sheikh Hamad, July 24, 1928 [India Office Records, British Library, R/15/2/112].
70. Belgrave diaries, November 10, 1928.
71. Letter no. 32 from Political Agent to Political Resident (India Office Records, R/15/2/112, March 21, 1931).
72. Letter no C/556 from the Political Agent to Political Resident Trenchard Fowle (India Office Records, R/15/2/139).
73. Letter from the Political Agent to the Political Resident (India Office Records, R/15/2/139, January 27, 1934).
74. Letter from the Political Agent to the Political Resident (India Office Records, R/15/2/139, January 27, 1934).
75. Report 30/12033 (India Office Records, R/15/2/139, undated).
76. International Observatory of Statelessness. Bahrain. http://www.nationalityforall.org/bahrain
77. Peterson: 2014. Likewise, the colonial origins of the *bidun* of Kuwait, a much larger stateless group in the Gulf, are clear. They are a group of more than 100,000 stateless people who did not register in 1961 when colonial Kuwait formally issued passports. An estimated 45% to 60% of the *bidun* in Kuwait are Shi`a. Naturalization of these people would change the official metric as to the sectarian makeup of the country (although this would not give it a Shi`a majority). [Matthiesen, *Sectarian Gulf*, 2013: 108.]
78. Khuri 1980: 236.

Conclusion

Bahrain and Transitional Justice

In 2006, as I was winding down fieldwork on women and policing in Bahrain—the subject of my dissertation—my main contact within the police force asked me to refrain from mentioning Shi`a identity. The contact explained:

> It would not be good for the country to talk about Shi`a and Sunni. We have to see ourselves as one people and [academic] work that focus[es] on sectarian problems just makes everything worse for us.

I would not have had access to my police interview subjects, nor been permitted to sit in police stations to observe their workings ethnographically without this person's blessing. We had never talked about not mentioning sectarian matters, and an early survey I was authorized to distribute to a sample of police directly asked them their sectarian identity. After months of fieldwork, I found that sect matters a great deal to the course of justice in Bahrain, probably more than any other factor critical and cultural criminologists typically consider (such as class and gender; though in reality these characteristics are embodied in humans in bundles and so fundamentally intersect and interact), and not sect in a particularly religious sense, but how these sect identities developed socially within tribal and maritime Gulf societies. Although my dissertation focused on gender, the part of me trained as a journalist recognized that the "real" story about criminal justice in Bahrain was the discriminatory policing of Shi`a communities.

Why at the end of my fieldwork did my contact have concerns about sectarianism being mentioned in my work? Word may have gotten around that as part of my fieldwork, I interviewed women in the community, Shi`a women who reported on arrest and torture they were subjected to at the hands of police after they had been perceived to be engaging in political activism.[1] They had fallen afoul of the discursive rule that a Shi`a person asserting her rights is a dangerous person, no different than the colonial authorities' notion of Shi`a being a class "dangerous to peace and good order."[2]

Word may have also gotten around that I had attended the recent '*ashura* festivities, the most important Shi`a holiday characterized by parades and reenactments of the martyrdom of Hussein Ali at the Battle of Karbala in 680 CE. At '*ashura* time, I received a text message from the U.S. State Department's emergency network warning me that Americans should avoid '*ashura* due to dangerous anti-American demonstrations. I immediately thereafter received another one from a Shi`a network reminding me to enthusiastically attend '*ashura* celebrations. I took the advice of the latter and though many gatherings and parades occurred throughout the urban warren of Shi`a Manama, I happened to wander into a Hezbollah demonstration featuring chants of "Death to America." People near me saw me for who I was, an American, but I never felt unsafe. One gentleman merely asked me to consider covering my head (in *hijab*: though this was not required by law and many Bahraini women don't). Perhaps I was spotted at this rally by Bahraini authorities who then worried about where my research was heading.

In any case, I told my contact as politely as I knew how that I understood the concern, but that in my professional opinion one could not understand criminal justice in Bahrain without understanding sectarian identity. My contact seemed dismayed and politely asked me to reconsider. I have long thought about this conversation and certainly it rubs up against the ethical problems of fieldwork: stakeholders have their own conceptions of the harm that research publications can cause. Was it my own American bias that saw the true harm as being the hidden history of Shi`a oppression? What if it does "make everything worse" to focus on this problem? From an American point of view, the exposure of hidden truths is an honorable pursuit in the cause of social justice and the performance of democratic ideals, but from a Sunni Bahraini point of view, it was a badge of shame, drudging up cleavages and besmirching the reputations of authorities.

I am reminded of the dangerous colonial period of Major Clive Daly, the political agent in Bahrain from 1921 to 1926. He was the most sympathetic to the Shi`a cause among the parade of colonial agents over the years. According to the records, he endeavored to reverse the patterns of discrimination and abuse. But did his advocacy for change make things worse? There is some indication that his attempt to tackle the problem may have factored into the increased violence during that period. His institutional moves toward social justice often coincided with very violent and even potentially genocidal (the Second Sitra Outrage) responses by the opposition to reform. As explained by a witness in the Farsiya case: "Our village was being taxed by Abdullah in Ghattam whose estate it is, and some time before the murders, Major Daly had ordered that we should pay no tax at all and we had stopped paying the tax for fish and prawns."[3] Do calls for reform of sectarian discrimination lead to more violence? This is certainly the kind of fear on which perpetrators of collective punishment rely: that the status quo sectarian oppression can be maintained through fear of physical retribution when it cannot be discursively muted; in this case, fear and violence are perpetuated by the state and an extended group of (often Sunni) vigilantes loyal to the state.[4]

One aim of this book has been to correct what I see as an over-adoption of the Sunni historical narrative by Western academics, which has unwittingly aided the sanitization of the importance of sectarian considerations from the criminal justice and larger political science literature. Although there are some notable exceptions, the rational choice framework that seems to belie much of Gulf Studies (that elites are making political choices to construct sectarian groups in certain instrumental ways) fails to properly contextualize why perpetuating sectarian divisiveness even works in the first place. It was "invented" long ago and the current environment is a structural adaptation growing from the roots of a very sectarian cultural milieu. Without understanding the meaning of sect identity in Bahrain over the *long d urée*, scholars miss that sect is a highly subjective and emotional matter for Gulf people and a seemingly "natural" part of the way they order their world. The feelings behind sectarianism, the passions and fears it stirs among ordinary people and elites alike, is part of the operant discursive framework; it is the precedent, not the antecedent, although it now exists in a kind of feedback loop; it is a strong cultural force (after the first disruption); it is not a political artificiality, but a heartfelt anxiety that cannot be easily put aside or shoved under the rug. Focusing on Bahraini criminal justice historically allows us to see the problem in a very illuminating way. As this book describes, the sectarian discrimination and violence has been made all the more problematic by colonialism, and more recently, the forces of globalization, both of which shored up the state, and were complicit in state legitimacy being derived, at least in part, through the perpetuation of sectarian discrimination and violence.

Although this book hopes to make an academic point, the fact remains that as a non-Bahraini it may be easy to drudge up a violent history and not to have to live the present consequences myself. I am not likely to be put in jail for writing this book, but a Bahraini Shi`a writing the same words would likely be incarcerated or worse. Regardless of the very real collective punishment that the state serves up unimpeded, Bahrain will not have social peace unless it bravely descends into the muck and mire of the problem. The "us" my contact said for which "everything would be worse" is the status quo elite. The fundamental problem in Bahrain is that the "us" is narrowly construed, attaching only to Sunni elites and a small cadre of Shi`a tokenized notables who rule with the un-critical military support of the U.K. and United States.[5] A more honest perspective on the outsized role of sectarian discrimination and violence in the country will not be worse for a majority of Bahrainis, certainly not in the long run.

Another aim of this book, then, is to suggest that calls from the outside for sectarian justice in Bahrain should be comprehensive, show commitment from key Western allies, and involve specific consequences for the cycle of collective punishment that historically follows any liberalization efforts. Although many Americans and British are sympathetic to the civil rights struggle of Shi`a Bahrainis as represented by the events of the Arab Spring, the fact that the criminal justice system became more punitive afterwards, and there were no political consequences from the U.S. or U.K. governments, is a depressing failure. A greater commitment to encouraging reform is absolutely necessary in order to maintain the public safety of a majority of Bahrainis who, just like in the 1920s and 1930s as this book has outlined, remain problematically criminalized, disproportionately victimized, and increasingly stripped of citizenship, with no sign of abatement.

There can be no equitable criminal justice in Bahrain without confronting the sectarian nature of the political system. The post-independence *turath* (cultural heritage) narrative, focused primarily on Arab Bedouin (Sunni tribal) heritage,[6] speaks volumes as to the privileged sectarian identity in the country—and that privilege extends quite readily into who is arrested, how they are investigated and adjudicated, and the extent of their punishment. White-washing the disruptive nature of the "the people of the land" to the way of life of "the people of the sea," exacerbated by colonialism, serves to maintain the sectarian state of affairs through historical denial. The outcomes in the criminal justice system's records since its very beginnings hinge on sect identity through sect-based mass deportations and pardons, sect-based collective punishment and violence, and a lack of commitment to the safety of Shia communities in the Bahraini-British colonial state. The present day sectarian order maintenance strategy is an extension of decades of the same policy, disguised as secular criminal justice and the rule of law. It would be a step too far to equate today's political cleavages directly to an easy binary of the peoples of the land and sea. Yet, the lack of resolution of the original disruptions that, broadly construed, put together these two peoples in an unequal and problematic way is being acted out again and again, embedded in the very cultural and social fabric of the country, and may amount in practice to a form of apartheid.[7]

In recent evidence that sectarian discrimination remains the modus operandi of the Bahrain state today, in July 2017, five activists were killed by police outside prominent Shi`a cleric Sheikh Isa Qasim's house when they collected to protest the stripping of his citizenship and pending deportation.[8]

In September of the same year, three relatives of a Shi`a human rights activist, and advocacy director of the Bahrain Institute for Rights and Democracy, Sayed Ahmed Al-Wadaei, were charged with planting a fake explosive device. Human Rights Watch reported that prosecutors presented no evidence linking the family to the alleged plot and that the convictions appeared to be retaliation for Al-Wadaei's criticism of the ruling family. In 2015, the government stripped Al-Wadaei of his Bahraini citizenship; he is currently based in London.[9] Meanwhile, Nabeel Rajab, one of the most prominent human rights activists, has been in custody for speech crimes since July 2016, after using Twitter to question the sectarian discrimination and human rights violations of the Bahraini government, as well as the on-going war in Yemen.[10] And Maryam Al-Khawaja, previously detained and imprisoned herself for non-violent activism,[11] continues to shine a light on human rights violations in Bahrain. In particular, she keeps her long-imprisoned father, Abdulhadi Al-Khawaja, director of the Gulf Centre for Human Rights and serving a life sentence, in public awareness though her Twitter handle, @angryarabiya. The list could go on. Meanwhile, the American and British alliance with Bahrain has never been stronger. President Trump recently permitted the sale of $9 billion in U.S.-manufactured arms to Bahrain[12] and the British have re-established a military base there[13] after vacating theirs (later bought by the Americans for the Navy's Fifth Fleet) shortly after Bahraini independence in 1971. The cycle of discrimination and violence will continue in light of Western support, and Gulf Cooperation Council (GCC) commitment to the discriminatory status quo.[14]

The persistence of sectarianism in Bahrain, however, does not amount to hopelessness, but it does mean that solutions are not easy. They must be as foundation-shaking as the two historical disruptions themselves. Transitional justice,[15] that directly confronts such past violent fissures, provides a pathway forward. Sect-silent solutions around building general capacities for democracy, equality, and economic participation for Shi`a—though helpful—will not enable the collective healing from a traumatic sectarian past that can produce a more sustainable and healthy state. The Shi`a of Bahrain have been subjected to violence and discrimination for generations, yet this fact has never been fully admitted by the royal family. A royal apology about the past is almost certainly the only way to authentically start a path toward change (though admittedly this is a tall order). Models of transitional justice often rely on such apologies, or their processes call for apologies, in order to help ruling elites re-establish trust with a group historically marginalized and abused.

A transitional justice process in Bahrain should allow victims of past sectarian discrimination and abuse at the hands of the criminal justice system to give a voice to their experiences and for evidence of the institutionalized sectarianism within police and security forces to be produced publicly. There would be immunity from criminal prosecution for people describing their role in past abuses. Like in South Africa, Morocco, and more recently in Tunisia, such a process should be truth-seeking rather than punishment and revenge-oriented in order to break the cycle of fear and violence. In Morocco, the truth-seeking forums were televised and confronted the arbitrary detentions of members of the opposition movement from 1956 to 1999 before an independent arbitration commission (made up of Moroccan academics, rights advocates, and former political prisoners). The process unearthed information about twenty thousand separate incidents of disappearances, rape, torture, and murder.[16] As the first example of transitional justice in the Arab world, the panel made recommendations that the responsibility for the human rights abuses rested with the state, and the Prime Minister should make a public apology, and Morocco should commit to security sector reform. However, these recommendations were never implemented, and in the end, the greatest accomplishment of the process was the awarding of over $100 million in victim compensation, primarily to families of the missing, numbering seven thousand recipients. A formal apology from the state was never made.[17] Although the process failed to create widespread reform, it has been considered successful as a means of acknowledging the victims and their families. Many of the problems the process encountered can be learned from, such as the strained relationship between the independent human rights observers and the arbitration panel, and the short application deadlines, which left some victims out of the process who may have otherwise participated.

A potential Bahraini process should involve neutral international organizers to help facilitate what will be emotional, controversial, but hopefully transformative, testimony. However, the panel itself should be international and independent, rather than merely the observers (as was the case in Morocco). Relevant documents that support (or refute) claims should be produced by the Bahraini government, showing a new commitment to transparency. Further, since this study has pointed to the social constructions of Shi`a as an internal enemy and criminal class, deliberate attempts to eradicate state-sponsored texts and speech exhibiting anti-Shi`a language will be a cornerstone effort (while not necessarily stifling non-governmental public discourse that may be sectarian—in an effort to support candid dialogue and airing of grievances).

Bahrain would also need to engage in a lustration process, or purification of the previous regime and its personnel through vetting based on the archival record and witness testimony as to abuses of power.[18] This is a starting point for building a more legitimate and human rights-oriented criminal justice system. The lustration model suggested here would not hold anyone criminally responsible for past violence and discrimination, but rather would allow for the disbarment of individuals, whether permanently or for a period of time, from government employment. If the vetting process finds individuals who have used a leadership position in a criminal justice agency to commit serious human rights abuses, or directed others to do so, they can be barred from civil service going forward. To be fair, the lustration process should not hesitate to hold royal family members accountable for their past service to the state.

For example, the lustration process in the Czech Republic as part of the effort to de-communize, prohibited government employment for life for anyone who had been shown to have abused their power in the past regime. A less extreme model is represented by Poland and Hungary, which offered fingered individuals a choice of providing a public statement of their guilt or complicity (judicially verified) or face disbarment.[19] Those who were willing to publicize their role in past abuses were given a second chance. Skeptics of processes of transitional justice feel that the process falls heavy on the victims to participate and relive their traumas, placing a burden on the most vulnerable individuals involved. Critics also point to the lack of punishment as undermining the rule of law as it is codified and should be administered. Closer geographically to Bahrain, the experience of the de-Baathification of Iraq has been considered a less than ideal personnel purge undertaken by the American-led occupying forces in 2003. However, unlike the Eastern European models above, this was a wholesale and collective removal of all Baathists, under a presumption of guilt approach, without individualized determinations of conduct and complicity. The loss of so many, particularly in the Iraqi army, created a situation in which those removed faced few options other than resisting the new government and the policy ultimately fomented the later insurgencies.[20]

Next, new criminal justice system employees must be drawn from historically under-represented groups. For example, police reform would include best practices from state responses to inter-ethnic conflict in post-independent Slovenia.[21] Police human rights training there takes a “joint” approach in which historically marginalized community leaders act as co-instructors with police authorities in frank discussions about cultural differences, police powers, and human rights. Language training is also included and was found to have a profound effect on softening chauvinisms. Having Bahraini officers learn Persian, which some Shi`a in their territories speak, could have a similar effect. This type of co-produced institutional change with difference-yet-unity in mind, in which the historically marginalized are invited in to set the agenda going forward in a formal way, is arguably more sustainable than approaches that are less inclusive, less transparent, and less interactive with the people being protected, policed, adjudicated, or punished, as the case may be.

A similar transitional justice occurred in Northern Ireland, which made police institutions more accountable to and representative of the communities they served after a history of sectarian violence. A key element in that reform effort was the creation of the Independent Commission on Policing (ICP) and the Office of the Police Ombudsman, which together acted as policy-makers, independent investigators, evaluators, and transition-overseers. This allowed conflicts that cropped up within the transition to be heard and addressed by the government, and with civilian oversight, in a way that was independent from the old channels of power. It also allowed for bringing in human rights training,[22] a new recruitment and hiring strategy, and a renewed focus on community policing. As policing scholar Graham Ellison explains:

> Key here was the recognition that policing and justice issues were central to the dynamics of conflict, being both part of the problem and part of the solution. Police reform therefore had an important contribution to make to a broader conflict resolution process within Northern Ireland.[23]

The transition has been moderately successful by most who have analyzed it, turning the tide of sectarian violence and creating increased public safety; however, the pace of change has been slow and the challenge of engaging communities and civil society in the efforts have reportedly been difficult.[24] In addition, reducing efforts to mere box-checking, once the bureaucracy for the transition was created, has reportedly watered down some of the potential gains.[25] Nonetheless, given that transitional justice is almost never a perfect success story whenever implemented, Northern Ireland's approach can be considered a viable and sustainable option for other countries. Despite problems, it now has one of the most "farsighted and robust"[26] police governance structures on the planet.

Overall, the path toward a peaceful and healthier Bahrain can begin with transitional justice focusing on criminal justice institutions. Waking up from a difficult history must start somewhere, and though it is likely to be a long and windy path toward healing, ultimately Bahrainis need to have this conversation publicly, to build a sustainable peace and redress the inequalities that have dogged it since its invention as a modern nation-state. The third historical disruption in the nation's history should be a future one that breaks open the chains of a sectarian past and finds a very Bahraini way, however that might look, of truly providing safety and security for a new society containing sect and other social differences in harmony.

NOTES

1. See appendix C of Strobl 2008: 265–268. In one case, the individual was arrested for running a charity that provided food and clothing for the families of Shi`a political detainees. She described a month-long ordeal of systematic rape and torture as police attempted to extract from her a confession that she was actively conspiring with others to overthrow the government. She explained that her treatment by police had the reverse effect than they may have wanted, turning her into a political activist against state violence and Shi`a discrimination.
2. *Orders-in-Council*, London, August 12, 1913 (India Office Records, R/15/2/7): 6.

3. Handwritten notes from the Indian Assistant's interrogation of witness in criminal case no. 65/399 of 1929 (India Office Records, R/15/3/7004).

4. Marc Owen Jones 2015: 223.

5. The British have returned as a permanent military presence to Bahrain, opening a base with access to Mina Salman harbor. In 2014, human rights activists interpreted the development as a "reward" for British silence on Bahrain's on-going problem with discrimination and violence. [Merrill, Jamie, "British military base in Bahrain is a 'reward' for UK's silence on human rights, say campaigners," *The Independent*. December 6, 2014. https://www.independent.co.uk/news/world/middle-east/british-military-base-in-bahrain-is-a-reward-for-uks-silence-on-human-rights-say-campaigners-9908284.html; The Associated Press, Bahrain hosts first British permanent military base in Gulf, *Al-Arabiya*, April 5, 2018. http://english.alarabiya.net/en/News/gulf/2018/04/05/Bahrain-hosts-first-British-permanent-military-base-in-Gulf.html.]

6. Lawrence G. Potter, "Introduction," *Sectarian Politics in the Persian Gulf*, Lawrence G. Potter (ed.): 7 [1–29].

7. Nicolas Kristof, "Is This Apartheid in Bahrain?" *The New York Times*, February 22, 2011. https://kristof.blogs.nytimes.com/2011/02/22/is-this-apartheid-in-bahrain/; Samir Yousif, "Apartheid Under the Mandate of Islam: The Case of Bahrain," *New English Review*, July 2011. http://www.newenglishreview.org/Samir_Yousif/Apartheid_Under_the_Mandate_of_Islam%3A_The_Case_of_Bahrain; Brian Dooley, "Is Bahrain the New Apartheid State?" *Huffington Post*, undated. https://www.huffingtonpost.com/brian-dooley/is-bahrain-the-new-aparth_b_6895452.html

8. British Broadcasting Corporation (BBC). "Bahrain Unrest: Death Toll from Raid on Cleric's Home Rises to Five," May 24, 2017. http://www.bbc.com/news/world-middle-east-40026813

9. Human Rights Watch, "Bahrain: Activist's Kin Convicted in Flawed Trial," October 30, 2017. https://www.hrw.org/news/2017/10/30/bahrain-activists-kin-convicted-flawed-trial

10. Nabeel Rajab, "Letter from Prison: Trump's Pandering to Bahrain Has Deadly Consequences," *The Washington Post*, December 11, 2017. https://www.washingtonpost.com/news/democracy-post/wp/2017/12/11/letter-from-prison-trumps-pandering-to-bahrain-has-deadly-consequences/?utm_term=.3738ce24a7e9

11. Al Jazeera News, "Bahrain Activist Maryam Al Khawaja Released," *Al Jazeera*. September 18, 2014. http://www.aljazeera.com/news/middleeast/2014/09/bahrain-activist-maryam-al-khawaja-released-2014918131513499744.html

12. Darlene Superville, "Trump Meeting with Bahrain Prince Produces Deals Worth $9 Billion." The Associate Press. November 30, 2017. https://www.pressherald.com/2017/11/30/trump-meeting-with-bahrain-prince-produces-deals-worth-9–billion/

13. Al Jazeera News, "Britain to Open Naval Base in Bahrain." *Al Jazeera*, December 6, 2014. http://www.aljazeera.com/news/middleeast/2014/12/britain-open-naval-base-bahrain-2014126222429935936.html

14. Although distracted throughout 2017–18 by internal cleavages related to member state Qatar, the GCC as a military strategic alliance of Arabian Gulf countries has often cited its mission as quelling unrest in member countries that it perceives as being fomented by Iran. The GCC has used anti-Iran and anti-terror missions as a broad net to define Shi`a as internal enemies in member countries, an example of the alliance's palpable "sectarian threat narrative" operating since at least the time of the Iranian Revolution [Matthiesen 2013: 20]. There is "zero tolerance" for internal unrest that would destabilize any ruling party in the alliance and "foreign agents" were often blamed for the protests of the Arab Spring despite their grassroots participation [Matthiesen 2013: 118]. Furthermore, the threat narrative likely has more to do with Bahraini internal sectarian political culture than Iranian foreign policy. Iran's sectarian narratives are secondary to other types of discourse such as pan-Islamism and anti-Americanism, and when sect-based it represents a divergent social and political meaning. [Afshon Ostovar, "Sectarianism and Iranian Foreign Policy," In F. Wehrey (ed.), *Beyond Sunni and Shia: The Roots of Sectarianism in a Changing Middle East* (pp. 87–114). Oxford: Oxford University Press, 2017.]

15. According to the United Nations, transitional justice is "…an approach to systematic or massive violations of human rights that both provides redress to victims and creates or enhances opportunities for the transformation of the political systems, conflicts, and other conditions that may have been at the root of the abuses." United Nations, "Transitional Justice: A Backgrounder," February 2008. http://www.un.org/en/peacebuilding/pdf/doc_wgll/justice_times_transition/26_02_2008_background_note.pdf

16. Priscilla B. Hayner, *Unspeakable Truths: Transitional Justice and the Challenge of Truth Commissions* (2nd edition, New York: Routledge, 2011): 42–44.

17. Hayner, 2011: 44–45.

18. Roman David, *Lustration and Transitional Justice: Personnel Systems in the Czech Republic, Poland and Hungary*, Philadelphia, PA: University of Pennsylvania Press, 2011: x.

19. David 2011: 6–7.

20. David 2011: 4–5; International Center for Transitional Justice (ICTJ). "Lessons of De-Baathification in Iraq." March 5, 2013. https://www.ictj.org/news/lessons-de-baathification-iraq; James P. Pfiffner, "US Blunders in Iraq: De-Baathification and Disbanding the Army" *Intelligence and National Security* 25 (2010): 76–85.

21. See: Staci Strobl, Emanuel Banutai, Susanne Duque, and Maria (Maki) Haberfeld, "Nothing to Do About Them Without Them: The Slovenian National Police and Roma Joint-Training Program." *International Journal of Comparative and Applied Criminal Justice*, 38 (2014): 211–233.

22. It should be noted here that the Bahraini police already send their upper-ranking officers to human rights courses in the United Kingdom; however, anecdotally, after informal conversations with several Bahraini and Gulf police at Bramshill Police College several years ago, I got the impression that they were influenced by a police subculture of putting up with such training, but not necessarily authentically buying into it. Based on conversations about the Arab Spring, they did not appear to apply the curriculum to the specific police-community conflicts in their national contexts, but rather essentialized Shi`a people as inherently criminal and seditious.

23. Graham Ellison, "A Blueprint for Democratic Policing Anywhere in the World Police Reform, Political Transition, and Conflict Resolution in Northern Ireland," *Police Quarterly* 10, September 2007: 244.

24. Aogán Mulcahy, "The Police Service of Northern Ireland," edited by Tim Newburn, *Handbook of Policing* (204–223). (New York: Routledge, 2012): 219; Ellison 2007: 265.

25. Mary O'Rawe, "Transitional Policing Arrangements in Northern Ireland: The Can't and the Won't of the Change Dialectic." *Fordham International Law Journal*, 26, 2003: 1–55.

26. Ellison 2007: 265.

Appendix A

Cache of Criminal Cases, 1924–1940

IOR file	Charges	Charge description	Serious crime: Yes or No	Final disposition, sentence	Citizenship	Deportatio
R/15/3/ 6995	None listed	Rape; Assault or criminal force to outrage the modesty of a woman; abetment of rape; Enticing, or taking away or detaining with criminal intent, a married woman	Yes	The Persian men received the following sentences: one was given five years imprisonment; and the rest received two years imprisonment and 100 rupees or two months imprisonment, Somali woman receives four years imprisonment and 100 rupees or two months imprisonment	5 Persian; 2 Somalis	1 Somalia

/3/	None listed	Related to Case #1 above, describes citizenship claim of deported Somalian				
/3/	None listed	Attempted murder	Yes	Transportation for life	British India (Kunari) and Persian (Dil Pul)	No
/3/	IPC 506, 507	Criminal intimidation by anonymous communications	No	On appeal: 3 years transportation (reduced by PR from 9 years)	Yemeni	[No]
/3/	IPC 448	House trespass	No	6 months imprisonment	Persian	No
/3/	IPC 189	Threatening a government servant	No	2 months imprisonment	Persian	No
/3/	IPS 460	Housebreaking resulting in death (460)	Yes	2 people received 10 years imprisonment Muhasin and Musaid) and the third got transportation for life (Mulla)	Hasawi/ Saudi	No

R/15/3/7002	IPC 457	Housebreaking by night [with violent assault, murder]	Yes	No sentence in file [related to cases #6, 7, 9, 10, and 11]	Hasawi/ Saudi	No
R/15/3/7003	IPC 460	Dacoity and housebreaking [with violent assault, murder]	Yes	Transportation for life	Hasawi/ Saudi	No
R/15/3/7004	IPC 396, 460,	Murder and grievous hurt	Yes	Two received 10 year imprisonment (Mulla and Muhasin); One was acquitted (Mubarak) [related to cases #6, 7, 8, 9, and 11]	Hasawi/ Saudi	No
R/15/3/7005	IPC 307	Attempted murder	Yes	One defendant (Ali) received ten years imprisonment and the other two (Mulla and Muhasin) received 5 years [related	Hasawi/ Saudi	No

				to cases #6, 7, 8, 9, and 10]		
5/3/6	None listed	Infringement of passport regulations	No	Discharged	Persian	No
5/3/7	IPC 421	Cheating	No	6 months imprisonment	British India	No
5/3/8	None listed	Criminal misappropriation	No	Discharged	Persian	No
5/3/9	IPC 153 and 143	Assault	No	20 defendants; 6 were acquitted; 7 received one month's imprisonment; 4 received 3 weeks imprisonment; 1 received 25 rupees fine; 2 prosecuted further under sec. 153 and 143, but no further information on those proceedings	12 Persian; 6 Somalian	No

R/15/3/ 7010	None listed	Possessing stolen property	No	Dismissed	Qatifi/ Saudi	No
R/15/3/ 7011	IPC 302; was tried by a district magistrate under King's Reg. No. 2 of 1930	Murder	Yes	Convicted, but sentence not recorded in file	Nejdi/ Saudi	No
R/15/3/ 7012	IPC 415, 417; OiC 27, 71(2)	Cheating, importing, selling, and being in possession of stolen pearls	No	Cheating: 6 months, 1,000 rupees or 2 months; Importing: 6 months, 1,000 rupees or 2 months; Selling:3 months, 1,000 rupees or 2 months; Possession: 3 months, 1,000 or 1 month	Qatari	No
R/15/3/ 7013	IPC 307	Attempted murder	Yes	2 years' removal from the limits of Bahrain under section 21(1)	Iraqi	No

				of the OiC (in lieu of a prison term)		
5/3/4	IPC 304A	Causing death by negligence	Yes	1 year imprisonment	Hejazi/ Saudi	No
5/3/5	King's Regulation 2 of 1937	Begging; Breach of Passport regulations	No	Out of 43 original defendants, 21 are deported; references 4 additional Persian defendants from another case also receiving deportation	Persian	Yes
5/3/6	IPC 354, 451	Criminal force to a woman with intent to outrage her modesty; House trespass in order to commit offense punishable with imprisonment	Yes	"Acquitted by order"	Unrecorded; probably British India	No

R/15/3/ 7017	King's Regulation 2 of 1937	Breach of passport regulations	No	17 defendants total; 9 "Irani" Persian; 2 Omani; Nejdi, Hasawi and Najrani Saudis; 1 Baluchi; 1 Zanzibarian; 1 unrecorded	Persian; Omani; Saudi; Zanzibari; unrecorded	Yes
R/15/3/ 7018	Breach of local custom; offering a bribe to a public servant	Breach of local custom; offering a bribe to a public servant	No	British defendant: fine (reduced on appeal) of 150 rupees; 2 co-defendants of unknown citizenship, one sentenced to 400 and 150 rupees or 4 months imprisonment for bribery; the other sentenced in being an accomplice to a bribe and given 200	British	No

				rupee fine or 4 months imprisonment		
3/	302	Murder	Yes	Death	Saudi	No
3/	409	Criminal breach of trust by a public servant	No	1,000 rupees or 1 year imprisonment; dismissal from public service	Persian	No
3/	307	Attempted murder	Yes	7 years Imprisonment	Iraqi	No
3/	408	Criminal break of trust by servant	No	Appeal dismissed; case originally dismissed, so that dismissal is upheld	British India	No
/8907	None listed	Assault	No	6 months imprisonment [for assaulting a watchman] upheld on appeal	Persian	No
3/ 4	IPC 302	Murder	Yes	Related to case # 17; sessions case	Saudi	No

with
conviction,
sentence not
recorded

Appendix B

Total Criminal Cases Adjudicated

tal criminal cases adjudicated, administrative reports (R/15/1/305)

g in on	Cases in which parties were bound to keep good behavior	Cases referred to the sharia court	Cases resulting in discharge or acquittal	Cases in which complainant withdrew charges	Unheard cases because the complainant was absent or the accused could not be apprehended	Total number of c during the year (a including session joint cases)
	6	7	17	13	15	**123**
	23	22	21	26	26	**191**
	42	55	58	23	29	**391**
	5	43	81	43	32	**412**
	53	42	20	9	13	**378**
	21	54	24	28	33	**315**
	20	29	47	8	33	**302**
	30	35	34	7	36	**309**
	14	13	104	48	16	**350**
	27	26	70	56	23	**359**
	29	41	64	42	18	**445**
	32	32	164	25	27	**472**
	17	39	171	14	11	**443**
	8	5	117	25	35	**403**
	3	0	69	19	4	**224**
	37	0	68	6	2	**291**
	25	13	58	0	0	**207**

25	13	109	0	0	**339**
1	2	86	12	0	**294**
				TOTAL	**6,248**

Appendix C

Files Consulted from the India Office Records

The India Office Records are located in the British Library in London.

R/15 = Gulf States; Records of the Bushire, Bahrain, Kuwait, Muscat, and Trucial state agencies
L/PS = external series; relations with non-Indian states

Administrative reports, R/15/1/750, and L/PS/18/B463
Agency administrative reports, R/15/2/296
Agency confidential office files, R/15/2/139
Agitation in Bahrain, R/15/1/343
Ahmad bin Lahej and Abdul Wahab Zaiyani, R/15/2/107
Al-Murra murders, R/15/2/28
Ali bin Khalid, R/15/2/108
Annual reports, L/PS/12/3890, and R/15/2/306 through R/15/2/308
Bahrain OiC, R/15/2/7
Bahrain reforms, R/15/2/131
Bahrain State Police, R/15/2/1202
Chirawi on blacklist: R/15/2/104
Complaint of Sheikh Hamad against Sheikh Isa, R/15/1/316
Correspondence from the Adviser, R/15/2/1824
Criminal cases, 1924–1940, R/15/3/6995 through R/15/3/7021
Criminal appeals, 1939–40, R/15/3/8905 and R/15/3/8907
Dates quota, R/15/2/785
Deportations, L/PS/3327
Deportations and expulsion orders, L/PS/12/3327

Deportations of indigent Persians, R/15/2/494
Dowasir [*sic*] tribe, R/15/1/346
Internal affairs, Bahrain, L/PS/10/1042
Judicial, 1910-1948, R/15/1/295 through R/15/3/313
Joint criminal, 1941, R/15/3/11460
Judicial, R/15/2/573
King's Regulations under the Bahrain OiC, R/15/2/307, and L/PS/12/3329
Levy corp, R/15/2/135, and R/15/1/347
Manumission of slaves, R/15/1/206
Order-in-Council reports, R/15/1/305
Persian affairs, R/15/2/492
Persians subject in Bahrain, R/15/2/150
Police recruitment and training, R/15/2/1203
Police, sepoy run amok, R/15/2/137
Police state shield, R/15/2/1278
Relation of Chiefs with Foreign Powers, R/15/2/319
Reforms, R/15/2/127 through R/15/2/138, and R/15/1/339
Repatriation, R/15/2/1394
Retirement of Sheikh Isa, R/15/2/86
Sessions case, 1933, R/15/3/11574
Sheikh Isa intrigues, R/15/2/100
Sheikh Khalaf, R/15/2/112, 239
Status of converts, R/15/2/8
Sunni-Shi`a relations, R/15/2/88

Appendix D

Files Consulted from the Archive of Charles Belgrave's Personal Papers

The archive is located at the University of Exeter, United Kingdom.

Charles Belgrave's personal diaries, 1926–1957, 148/1
Robert Belgrave's working papers, 148/2/1
Robert Belgrave's layout and synopsis, 148/2/2
Belgrave family papers, 148/2/4

Bibliography

Abu-Lughod, Lila, Veiled Sentiments: Honor and Poetry in a Bedouin Society. Berkeley: University of California Press, 1986.

Abu-Lughod, Lila. "Feminist Longings and Post-Colonial Conditions." in *Remaking Women in the Middle East*, edited by Lila Abu-Lughod, 3-13. Princeton, NJ: Princeton University Press, 1998.

Abu-Lughod, Lila. *Do Muslim Women Need Saving?* Cambridge: Harvard University Press, 2013.

Abu-Nimer, Mohammed. "Conflict Resolution Approaches." *American Journal of Economics and Sociology* 55 (1996): 35-52.

Agius, Dionysius. *Seafaring in the Arabian Gulf and Oman: People of the Dhow*. London: Routledge, 2005.

Ahmadi, Koroush. *Islands and International Politics in the Persian Gulf: The Abu Musa and Tunbs in Strategic Context*. London: Routledge, 2008.

Albarazi, Zahra and Jason E. Tucker. "Citizenship as Political Tool: The Recent Turmoil in the MENA and the Creation and Resolution of Statelessness" SSRN, last posted January 10, 2014 at https://ssrn.com/abstract=2376426 or http://dx.doi.org/10.2139/ssrn.2376426

Alexander, Michelle. *The New Jim Crow: Mass Incarceration in the Age of Colorblindness.* New York: The New Press, 2012.

Al Jazeera News, "Bahrain Activist Maryam Al Khawaja Released," *Al Jazeera*. September 18, 2014. http://www.aljazeera.com/news/middleeast/2014/09/bahrain-activist-maryam-al-khawaja-released-201491813151349974 4.html

Al Jazeera News, "Britain to Open Naval Base in Bahrain." *Al Jazeera*, December 6, 2014. http://www.aljazeera.com/news/middleeast/2014/12/britain-open-naval-base-bahrain-2014126222429935936.html

Altheide, David L. "Reflections: Ethnographic content analysis." *Qualitative Sociology* 10 (1987): 65-77.

Al-Khalifa, Abulaziz Mohamed Hasan Ali. "Relentless Warrior and Shrewd Tactician: Shaikh Abdullah bin Ahmad of Bahrain 1795-1849 A Case Study of Shaikhly Statecraft in the Nineteenth Centuray Gulf." PhD diss., University of Exeter, 2015.

Al-Khawaja, Zainab. "Bahrain, a Brutal Ally." *The New York Times*, December 25, 2012. https://www.questia.com/newspaper/1P2-36296158/bahrain-a-brutal-ally

Al-Radhi, Hassan Ali. *Judiciary and Arbitration in Bahrain*. London: Kluwer Law International, 2003.

Al-Rumaihi, Mohammed Ghanim. "Social and Political Change in Bahrain Since the First World War." PhD diss., University of Durham, 1973.

Al-Tajir, Mahdi Abdalla. *Bahrain 1920-1945: Britain, the Shaikh and the Administration*. London: Croom Helm, 1987.
Amanat, Abbas. *Iran: A Modern History*. New Haven, CT: Yale University Press, 2017.
Amin, Sayed Hassan. *Middle East Legal Systems*. Glasgow: Royston Publishers, 1985.
Anderson, Benedict. *Imagined Communities*. New York: Verso, 2006.
Anderson, David M., and David Killingray. *Policing the Empire: Government, Authority, and Control, 1830-1940*. Manchester: Manchester University Press, 1991.
Anscombe, Frederick, "The Ottoman Role in the Gulf" in *The Persian Gulf in History*, edited by Lawrence G. Potter, 277-294. New York: Palgrave Macmillan, 2009.
Awwad, Amani M. "Gossip, Scandal, Shame and Honor Killing: A Case for Social Constructionism and Hegemonic Discourse." *Social Thought & Research* (2001): 39-52.
Bahrain Center for Human Rights, "Bahrain Revokes Citizenship of 71 People," February 2, 2015, http://www.bahrainrights.org/en/node/7264http://www.genocidewatch.org/images/Bahrain_12_11_07_in_crackdown_bahrain_revokes_the_citizenship_of_31_people.pdf
Bahrain Independent Commission of Inquiry, *Report of the Bahrain Independent Commission of Inquiry*, 2011. http://www.bici.org.bh/BICIreportEN.pdf
Balfour-Paul, Glen. *The End of Empire in the Middle East: Britain's Relinquishment of Power in its Last Three Arab Dependencies*. Cambridge: Cambridge University Press, 1991.
Beeman, William O. "Gulf Society: An Anthropological View of the *Khalijis*—Their Evolution and Way of Life." in *The Persian Gulf in History*, edited by Lawrence G. Potter, 147-162. New York: Palgrave Macmillan, 2009.
Beeman, William O. "The Zar in the Persian Gulf: Performative Dimensions," *Anthropology of the Contemporary Middle East and Central Eurasia* 3, no. 1 (2015): 1-12.
Belgrave, Charles Dalrymple. personal diary, 1926-1957. From the Papers of Charles Dalrymple Belgrave, University of Exeter archives, Exeter, United Kingdom; and https://issuu.com/bahrainlibrary/docs/54167454-alkhalifa-scandals-from-be
Belgrave, Charles Dalrymple. *Personal Column*. Beirut: Librairie du Liban, 1960/1972.
Benton, Lauren. *Law and Colonial Culture: Legal Regimes in World History, 1400-1900*. Cambridge: Cambridge University Press, 2002.
Bhabha, Homi. *The Location of Culture*. New York: Routledge, 1994.
Bhaker, M. Rheda. "The Cultural Unity of the Gulf and the Indian Ocean: A *Longue Durée* Historical Perspective." in *The Persian Gulf in History*, edited by Lawrence G. Potter, 163-172. New York: Palgrave Macmillan, 2009.
Bin Dana, Muhammad, "Our Belief in Dialogue Remains Firm," *Al-Amn* 42 (March 2013): 38.
Bittner, Egon. *The Functions of the Police in Modern Society*. Cambridge: Oelgeschlager, Gunn & Hain, 1970/1979.
Bourdieu, Pierre. *The Sense of Honour in Algeria*. Cambridge: Cambridge University Press, 1979.
Bracey, Dorothy. *Exploring Law and Culture*. Long Grove, IL: Waveland Press Inc., 2006.
Braudel, Fernand, and Immanuel Wallerstein, "History and the Social Sciences: The *Longue Durée*," *Review (Fernand Braudel Center)* 32 (2009): 171-203, http://www.jstor.org/stable/40647704.
British Broadcasting Corporation (BBC), "Arab Uprising—Country by Country: Bahrain." http://www.bbc.com/news/world-12482295
British Broadcasting Corporation (BBC). "Bahrain Unrest: Death Toll from Raid on Cleric's Home Rises to Five," May 24, 2017. http://www.bbc.com/news/world-middle-east-40026813
Brodeur, Jean-Paul. *The Policing Web*. Oxford: Oxford University Press, 2010.
Butler, Judith. *Gender Trouble: Feminism and the Subversion of Identity, 2nd Edition*. New York: Routledge, 1999.
Cannadine, David. *Ornamentalism*. Oxford: Oxford University Press, 2001.
Carrington, Kerry and Ashleigh Larkin. "The Politics of Doing Imaginative Criminological Research." in *Liquid Criminology: Doing Imaginative Criminological Research*, edited by Michael Hviid Jacobsen and Sandra Walklate, Abigdon: Routhledge, 2016.
Carrington, Kerry, Russell Hogg, and Máximo Sozzo. "Southern Criminology," *British Journal of Criminology*, 56 (2016): 1-20.

Chambliss, William J. *Power, Politics and Crime.* Boulder, CO: Westview Press, 2001.
Chatterjee, Partha. *Nationalist Thought and the Colonial World: A Derivative Discourse.* London: Zed Books, 1986.
Cole, B.A. "Post-colonial systems." in *Policing Across the World: Issues for the 21st Century*, edited by R. Mawby, 88-108. London: UCL Press, 2013.
Collins, Randall. "Three Faces of Cruelty: Towards a Comparative Sociology of Violence." *Theory and Society* 1 (1974): 415-440.
Cordesman, Anthony H. *Bahrain, Oman, Qatar, and the United Arab Emirates: Challenges of Security.* Boulder, CO: Westview Press, 1997.
Crystal, Jill. "Criminal Justice in the Middle East," *Journal of Criminal Justice*, 29, 6 (2001): 469-483.
David, Roman. *Lustration and Transitional Justice: Personnel Systems in the Czech Republic, Poland and Hungary*, Philadelphia, PA: University of Pennsylvania Press, 2011.
Dickson, H. R. P. *The Arab of the Desert: A Glimpse into Badawin Life in Kuwait and Saudi Arabia.* London: George Allen & Unwin Ltd., 1949.
Diwan, Kristin Smith. "Royal Factions, Ruling Strategies and Sectarianism in Bahrain," in *Sectarian Politics in the Persian Gulf*, edited by Lawrence G. Potter, 143-177. Oxford: Oxford University Press, 2014.
Donnermeyer, Joseph. "The Place of Rural in a Southern Criminology," *International Journal for Crime, Justice and Social Democracy* 6 (2017): 128.
Dooley, Brian and Staci Strobl. "Four Years On, U.S Should Push Bahrain to Reform Security Forces," *Huffington Post*, February 13, 2015. http://www.huffingtonpost.com/brian-dooley/four-years-on-us-should-p_b_6680326.html.
Dooley, Brian. "Is Bahrain the New Apartheid State?" *Huffington Post*, undated. https://www.huffingtonpost.com/brian-dooley/is-bahrain-the-new-aparth_b_6895452.html
Douglas, Mary. *Purity and Danger: An Analysis of Concept of Pollution and Taboo.* London: Routledge, 1966.
Elias, Norbert. *The Civilizing Process, Vol 2.* Malden, MA: Blackwell Publishing, 1939/1982.
Ellison, Graham. "A Blueprint for Democratic Policing Anywhere in the World? Police Reform, Political Transition, and Conflict Resolution in Northern Ireland," *Police Quarterly* 10, September 2007: 243-269.
Esposito, John L. (Editor), *The Oxford Dictionary of Islam*, Oxford: Oxford University Press, 2004.
Fahim, Kareem. "In crackdown, Bahrain revokes the citizenship of 31 people." *The New York Times*, November 7, 2012, http://www.genocidewatch.org/images/Bahrain_12_11_07_in_crackdown_bahrain_revokes_the_citizenship_of_31_people.pdf
Fibiger, Thomas. "Ashura in Bahrain," *Social Analytics* 54, 3 (2010): 29-46.
Foucault, Michel. *The Archaeology of Knowledge.* New York: Harper and Row, 1972.
Fuccaro, Nelida. *Histories of city and state in the Persian Gulf: Manama since 1800.* Cambridge: Cambridge University Press, 2009.
Geertz, Clifford. *The Interpretation of Cultures: Selected* Essays. New York: Basic Books, 1973.
Gengler, Justin. "Understanding sectarianism in the Persian Gulf." in *Sectarian Politics in the Persian Gulf*, edited by Lawrence G. Potter, 31-66. Oxford: Oxford University Press, 2014.
Gengler, Justin. *Group Conflict and Political Mobilization in Bahrain and the Arab Gulf: Rethinking the Rentier State*. Bloomington: Indiana University Press, 2015.
Goodale, Mark. *Anthropology and Law: A Critical Introduction.* New York: New York University Press, 2017.
Government of Bahrain. *Annual Reports, Volume II.* London: Archive Editions Limited, 1987.
Hayner, Priscilla B. *Unspeakable Truths: Transitional Justice and the Challenge of Truth Commissions* (2nd edition, New York: Routledge, 2011): 42-44.
Hills, Alice, Gary N. Siperstein, Norman Anthony Wieseler, and Ronald Halton Hanson. *Policing Africa: Internal Security and the Limits of Liberalization.* London: Lynne Rienner Publishers, 2000.
Hitti, Philip K. *The Near East in History.* Princeton, NJ: D. Van Norstrand Company, Inc., 1967.

Holman, Zoe. "On the Side of Decency and Democracy: The History of British-Baharani Relations and Transnational Contestation." in *Bahrain's Uprising: Resistance and Repression in the Gulf*, edited by Ala'a Shehabi and Marc Owen Jones, 175-206. London: Zed Books, 2015.

Human Rights Watch, "Bahrain: Activist's Kin Convicted in Flawed Trial," October 30, 2017. https://www.hrw.org/news/2017/10/30/bahrain-activists-kin-convicted-flawed-trial

Human Rights Watch, "Saudi Arabia: 5-Year Sentence for Rights Defender: Increasing Crackdowns on Activists," June 23, 2013, https://www.hrw.org/news/2013/06/22/saudi-arabia-5-year-sentence-rights-defender.

Husayn, Nebil. "Mechanisms of Authoritarian Rule in Bahrain," *Arab Studies Quarterly* 37 (1): (2015): 32-53.

International Crisis Group, "Bahrain's Sectarian Challenge," *Middle East Report* 40 (2005): 1-20.

International Observatory of Statelessnes. "Bahrain." [undated: accessed on January 13, 2018]. http://www.nationalityforall.org/bahrain.

International Center for Transitional Justice (ICTJ). "Lessons of De-Baathification in Iraq." March 5, 2013. https://www.ictj.org/news/lessons-de-baathification-iraq

Jafar, Afshan. "Woman, Islam and State in Pakistan." *Gender Issues* 22 (1995): 35-55.

Jeffries, Charles Joseph. *The Colonial Police.* London: Max Parrish, 1952.

Jones, Marc Owen. "Rotten Apples or Rotten Orchards: Police Deviance, Brutality and Unaccountability in Bahrain." in *Bahrain's Uprising: Resistance and Repression in the Gulf*, edited by Ala'a Shehabi and Marc Owen Jones, 207-238. London: Zed Books, 2015.

Jones, Marc Owen. "Who Really Tried to Assassinate Sheikh Hamad?" Marcowenjones.wordpress.com (blog), April 1, 2013, https://marcowenjones.wordpress.com/tag/shaikh-hamad/

Karolak, Magdalena. "Religion in a Political Context: The Case of the Kingdom of Bahrain." *Asia Journal of Global Studies* 4 (2010): 4-20.

Kelly, J.R.B. *Arabia, the Gulf and the West.* London: Basic Books, 1980.

Khalaf, Sulayman. "Settlement of Violence in Bedouin Society." *Ethnology* 29 (1990).

Khuri, Fuad I. *Tribe and State in Bahrain: The Transformation of Social and Political Authority in an Arab State.* Chicago: The University of Chicago Press, 1980.

Kingdom of Bahrain. *Memorial submitted by the state of Bahrain (Merits) Volume 1, Qatar v. Bahrain.* The Hague: International Court of Justice, 1996.

Knepper, Paul. *The Invention of International Crime: A Global Issue in the Making, 1881-1914.* New York: Palgrave MacMillan, 2010.

Kristof, Nicolas. "Is This Apartheid in Bahrain?" *The New York Times*, February 22, 2011. https://kristof.blogs.nytimes.com/2011/02/22/is-this-apartheid-in-bahrain/

Kwarteng, Kwami. *Ghosts of Empire: British Legacies in the Modern World.* New York: Public Affairs, 2011.

Lienhardt, Peter. *Shaikhdoms of Easter Arabia.* New York: Palgrave, 1950/2001.

Lopez, Ian. *White by Law: The Legal Construction of Race.* New York: New York University Press: 2006.

Louër, Laurence. *Transnational Shia Politics: Religious and Political Networks in the Gulf.* London: Hurst, 2008.

Mangabeira, Roberto. *Knowledge and Politics.* New York: Simon and Schuster, 1976.

Mattheisen, Toby. *Sectarian Gulf: Bahrain, Saudi Arabia, and the Arab Spring that Wasn't.* Stanford: Stanford Briefs/Stanford University Press, 2013.

Merry, Sally Engle. "Foreword," in *Anthropology and Law: A Critical Introduction*, edited by Mark Goodale, New York: New York University Press, 2017.

Messerschmidt, James. *Crime as Structured Action: Gender, Race, Class, and Crime in the Making.* Thousand Oaks, CA: Sage Publications, 1997.

Mitchell, Timothy. *Colonising Egypt.* Berkeley: University of California Press, 1988/1991.

Mohanty, Chandra Talpade. *Feminism without Borders: Decolonializing Theory, Practicing Solidarity.* Durham, NC: Duke University Press, 2003.

Mulcahy, Aogán. "The Police Service of Northern Ireland," edited by Tim Newburn, *Handbook of Policing.* New York: Routledge, 2012: 204-223.

Nadjmabadi, Shahnaz Razieh, "The Arab Presence on the Iranian Coast of the Persian Gulf," In Lawrence G. Potter's (editor), *The Persian Gulf in History* (Palgrave Macmillan, 2009): 129-145.

Nakhleh, Emile. *Bahrain: Political Development in a Modernizing Society*. Lanham, MD: Lexington Books, 2011.

Nasr, Vali. *The Shia Revival: How Conflicts Within Islam Will Shape the Future*. New York: W.W. Norton & Co., 2006.

Onley, James. "Britain's Informal Empire." in *Protection and Politics in Bahrain, 1869-1915*, edited by Talal Toufic Farah, 29-45. Syracuse: Syracuse University Press, 1985.

Onley, James. *The Arabian Frontier of the British Raj: Merchants, Rulers, and the British in the Nineteenth-Century Gulf.* Oxford: Oxford University Press, 2007.

Onley, James and Sulayman Khalef. "Shaikhly Authority in the Pre-Oil Gulf: An Historical-Anthropological Study," *History and Anthropology* 17 (2006): 189-208.

O'Rawe, Mary. "Transitional Policing Arrangements in Northern Ireland: The Can't and the Won't of the Change Dialectic." *Fordham International Law Journal*, 26 (2003): 1-55.

Osella, Filippo and Caroline Osella. "Muslim Entrepreneurs in Public Life Between India and the Gulf: Making Good and Doing Good," *Journal of the Royal Anthropological Society* 15, 1 (2009): S202-S221.

Ostovar, Afshon, "Sectarianism and Iranian Foreign Policy," In F. Wehrey (ed*.), Beyond Sunni and Shia: The Roots of Sectarianism in a Changing Middle East* (pp. 87-114). Oxford: Oxford University Press, 2017.

Pospisil, Leopold J. *Anthropology of Law: A Comparative Theory*. New York: Harper Row, 1971.

Peterson, J.E. "Bahrain First Steps Toward Reform Under Amir Hamad," *Asian Affairs* 33 (2014): 216-227.

Pfiffner, James P. "US Blunders in Iraq: De-Baathification and Disbanding the Army," *Intelligence and National Security* 25 (2010): 76–85.

Potter, Lawrence G. "Introduction" in *Sectarian Politics in the Persian Gulf*, edited by Lawrence G. Potter, 1-29. Oxford: Oxford University Press, 2014.

Qubain, Fahim I. "Social Classes and Tensions in Bahrain." *Middle East Journal* 9 (1955): 269-280.

Radford, Kristopher. "Curzon's Cruise: The Pomp and Circumstance of Indian Indirect Rule of the Persian Gulf." *The International History Review* 4 (2013): 884-904.

Rajab, Nabeel. "Letter from Prison: Trump's Pandering to Bahrain Has Deadly Consequences," *The Washington Post*, December 11, 2017. https://www.washingtonpost.com/news/democracy-post/wp/2017/12/11/letter-from-prison-trumps-pandering-to-bahrain-has-deadly-consequences/?utm_term=.3738ce24a7e9

Reiner, Robert. *The Politics of the Police*. Brighton: Wheatsheaf, 1985.

Rich, Paul J. *Creating the Arabian Gulf: The British Raj and the Invasions of the Gulf.* Lanham, MD: Lexington Books, 2009.

Sahlins, Marshall. *Mythical Realities and Historical Metaphors*. Ann Arbor, MI: University of Michigan Press, 1981.

Said, Edward. *Culture and Imperialism*. London: Vintage Books, 1993.

Salamey, Imad and Zanoubia Othman. "Shia revival and *welayat al-faqih* in the Making of Iranian Foreign Policy," *Politics, Religion, and Ideology*, 12 (2011): 197-212.

Schneider, Irene. "The Concept of Honor and Its Reflection in the Iranian Penal Code." *Journal of Persianate Studies* 5 (2012): 43-57.

Sellin, Thorsten. "Culture Conflict and Crime," *American Journal of Sociology* 44 (1938): 97-103.

Sewell, William. *Logics of History: Social Theory and Social Transformation*. Chicago: University of Chicago Press, 2005.

Shaery-Eisenlohr, Roschanack. "Imagining Shi'ite Iran: Transnationalism and Religious Authenticity in the Muslim World." *Iranian Studies* 40 (2007).

Sharif, Ibrahim. "A trial of thoughts and ideas," in *Bahrain's Uprising: Resistance and Repression in the Gulf*, edited by Ala'a Shehabi and Marc Owen Jones, 43-60. London: Zed Books, 2015.

Shehabi, Ala'a and Marc Owen Jones, eds. *Bahrain's Uprising: Resistance and Repression in the Gulf*. London: Zed Books, 2015.
Sheriff, Abdul. "The Persian Gulf and the Swahili Coast: A History of Acculturation over the *Longue Durée*," in *The Persian Gulf in History*, edited by Lawrence G. Potter, 173-188. New York: Palgrave Macmillan, 2009.
Sinclair, Georgina, and Chris A. Williams., "'Home and away': The Cross-Fertilisation between 'Colonial 'and 'British' Policing, 1921–85." *Journal of Imperial and Commonwealth History* 35 (2007): 221-238.
Singer, Amy. "Soup and *Sadaqa*: Charity in Islamic Societies," *Historical Research* 79, 205 (2006): 306-324.
Spivak, Gayatri Chakravorty. "World Systems and the Creole," *Narrative* 14 (2006): 102-112.
Spivak, Gayatri Chakravorty. "Can the subaltern speak?" *Can the Subaltern Speak? Reflections on the History of an Idea* (1988): 21-78.
Spivak, Gayatri Chakravorty. *A Critique of Postcolonial Reason: Toward a History of the Vanishing Present*. Cambridge: Harvard University Press, 1999.
Steinmetz, George. *The Devil's Handwriting: Precoloniality and the German Colonial State in Qingdao, Samoa, and Southwest Africa*. Chicago: University of Chicago Press, 2007.
Steinmetz, G. (2008). "The colonial state as a social field: Ethnographic capital and native policy in the German Overseas Empire before 1914." *American Sociological Review*, 589-612.
Strobl, Staci, and Hung-En Sung, "Attitudes about Gender Integration among Bahraini Policewomen." *Policing & Society* 19 (2009): 425-441.
Strobl, Staci, Emanuel Banutai, Susanne Duque, and Maria (Maki) Haberfeld, "Nothing To Do About Them Without Them: The Slovenian National Police and Roma Joint-Training Program." *International Journal of Comparative and Applied Criminal Justice*, 38 no. 2 (2014): 211-233.
Strobl, Staci. "From Colonial Policing to Community Policing in Bahrain: The Historical Persistence of Sectarianism," *International Journal of Comparative and Applied Criminal Justice* 35 (2011):19-37.
Strobl, Staci. "Not so Notorious: Crimes Committed by Bahraini Women in the Kingdom of Bahrain." *Al-Raida Journal* (2006): 18-24.
Strobl, Staci. "Progressive or Neo-Traditional? Policewomen in Gulf Cooperation Council (GCC) Countries." *Feminist Formations* 22 (2010): 51-74.
Strobl, Staci. "Postcolonial Policing and the 'Woman' Question: A History of the Women's Police Directorate in Bahrain," in *Policing and Prisons in the Middle East: Formations of Coercion*, edited by Laleh Khalili and Jillian Schwedler, 119-135. London: Hurst, 2010.
Strobl, Staci. "'The Dream Recently Came True': Globalization and Media Discourse about Kuwaiti Policewomen." *Nidaba* 1 (2016): 6-18.
Strobl, Staci. "The Roots of Sectarian Law and Order in the Gulf," In Frederic Wehrey (Ed.), *Beyond Sunni and Shia: The Roots of Sectarianism in a Changing Middle East*. (London: Hurst & Co.: 2017): 205-235.
Strobl, Staci. "The Women's Police Directorate in Bahrain: An Ethnographic Exploration of Gender Segregation and the Likelihood of Future Integration." *International Criminal Justice Review* 18 (2008): 39-58.
Strobl, Staci. "Women and Policing in Bahrain." PhD diss., City University of New York, 2007.
Sulaibeeck, Khalifa. *Tales from Al-Hoora, Bahrain, 2nd Edition*. N.p.: al-Sayah Public Relations, 2004.
Superville, Darlene. "Trump Meeting with Bahrain Prince Produces Deals Worth $9 Billion." The Associate Press. November 30, 2017. https://www.pressherald.com/2017/11/30/trump-meeting-with-bahrain-prince-produces-deals-worth-9-billion/
Sweet, Louise. "Pirates or Polities? Arab Societies of the Persian or Arabian Gulf," *Ethnohistory*, 11 (1964): 262-280.
Teles e Cunha, Jaou. "The Portuguese Presence in the Persian Gulf," in *The Persian Gulf in History*, edited by Lawrence G. Potter, 207-234. New York: Palgrave Macmillan, 2009.

Thacher, David. "Order maintenance policing," in *The Oxford Handbook of Police and Policing*, edited by Michael D. Reisig and Robert J. Kane, 122-124. Oxford: Oxford University Press, 2014.

Tilly, Charles. "War Making and State Making as Organized Crime," in *Bringing the State Back In*, edited by Peter B. Evancs, Dietrich Rueschemeyer, and Theda Skocpol, 169-187. Cambridge: Cambridge University Press, 1985.

Torpey, John. *The Invention of the Passport: Surveillance, Citizenship and the State*. Cambridge: Cambridge University Press, 2000.

Tuson, Penelope. *A Brief Guide to Sources for Middle East Studies in the India Office Records*. London: India Office Library and Records, 1982.

Tuson, Penelope. *The Records of the British Residence and Agencies in the Persian Gulf* (London: India Office Records [IOR R/15], British Library, 1979).

Unger, Roberto Mangabeira. *Knowledge and Politics*. New York: Simon and Schuster, 1976.

United Nations, "Transitional Justice: A Backgrounder," February 2008. http://www.un.org/en/peacebuilding/pdf/doc_wgll/justice_times_transition/26_02_2008_background_note.pdf

Visser, Reider. "Britain in Basra: Past Experiences and Current Challenges," last modified July 11, 2006, http://www.hisotriae.org/cosmopolitanism.asp.

Wacquant, Loïc. *Punishing the Poor*. Durham, NC: Duke University Press, 2009.

Wacquant, Loïc. "The New 'Peculiar Institution': On the Prison as Surrogate Ghetto." *Theoretical Criminology* 4 (2000): 377-389.

Wehrey, Frederic M. *Sectarian Politics in the Gulf: From the Iraq War to the Arab Uprisings*. New York: Columbia University Press, 2014.

Wheatcroft, Andrew. *The Life and Times of Shaikh Salman bin Hamad Al-Khalifah, Ruler of Bahrain 1941-1961*. London: Kegan Paul International, 1995.

Wilson, James Q. "Dilemmas of Police Administration." *Public Administration Review* 28 (1968): 407-417.

Yassine, Nahla. "Arab Political Dispute Resolution." PhD diss., Wayne State University, 1999.

Young, Jock, J. Ferrell, and Keith Hayward. *Cultural Criminology: An Invitation*. Thousand Oaks, CA: Sage, 2008.

Young, Jock. "Radical Criminology in Britain: The Emergence of a Competing Paradigm." *British Journal of Criminology* 28 (1988): 159.

Yousif, Samir. "Apartheid Under the Mandate of Islam: The Case of Bahrain," *New English Review*, July 2011. http://www.newenglishreview.org/Samir_Yousif/Apartheid_Under_the_Mandate_of_Islam%3A_The_Case_of_Bahrain

Index

About the Author

Dr. **Staci Strobl** is a department chair and associate professor of criminal justice at the University of Wisconsin-Platteville. Her research focuses on comparative criminal justice in the Middle East and Eastern Europe with particular attention paid to issues of gender, ethnicity, and religious identity. In 2009, she won the Radzinowicz Memorial Prize for her article in the *British Journal of Criminology* about the criminalization of female domestic workers in Bahrain.

www.ingramcontent.com/pod-product-compliance
Ingram Content Group UK Ltd.
Pitfield, Milton Keynes, MK11 3LW, UK
UKHW041628031026
15587UKWH00001B/136

9 781498 541602